Samuel

Samuel

The Man of God

SHAUL BAR

WIPF & STOCK · Eugene, Oregon

SAMUEL
The Man of God

Copyright © 2022 Shaul Bar. All rights reserved. Except for brief quotations in critical publications or reviews, no part of this book may be reproduced in any manner without prior written permission from the publisher. Write: Permissions, Wipf and Stock Publishers, 199 W. 8th Ave., Suite 3, Eugene, OR 97401.

Wipf & Stock
An Imprint of Wipf and Stock Publishers
199 W. 8th Ave., Suite 3
Eugene, OR 97401

www.wipfandstock.com

PAPERBACK ISBN: 978-1-6667-1664-1
HARDCOVER ISBN: 978-1-6667-1665-8
EBOOK ISBN: 978-1-6667-1666-5

FEBRUARY 3, 2022

Jewish Publication Society Bible (1917) (public domain)

[*Scripture quotations are*] from the Revised Standard Version of the Bible, copyright © 1946, 1952, and 1971 the Division of Christian Education of the National Council of the Churches of Christ in the United States of America. Used by permission. All rights reserved.

*With loving memories of Einat Makover Bobrov,
a daughter, sister, wife and mother
a life taken too soon, forever in our hearts*

Contents

Acknowledgments | ix

Abbreviations | x

Introduction | 1

1   SAMUEL'S CHILDHOOD | 7
      Samuel's Family | 9
      Visit to Shiloh | 11
      Samuel's Birth | 14
      The Song of Hannah | 16
      Service in Shiloh | 18

2   GOD'S APPEARANCE TO SAMUEL | 23
      God's Call to Samuel | 24
      God's Message to Samuel | 28
      The Message of the Man of God | 31
      Samuel's Prophecy VersUs the Man of God's Prophecy | 34
      The Nature of the Theophany | 35

3   THE ASSEMBLY AT MIZPAH | 40
      Samuel Calls Israel to Serve Yhwh | 41
      The Gathering at Mizpah | 43
      The Defeat of the Philistines | 45
      The Purpose of the Story | 49

4   SAMUEL AND THE KINGSHIP | 52
      Appoint a King for Us | 53
      Moral and Economic Changes | 56
      Samuel's Denunciation of Kingship | 58

5   SAMUEL THE KING MAKER | 63
    The Lost Donkeys of Kish | 64
    The Meetings | 66
    Saul's Anointing | 68
    The Coronation at Mizpah | 70
    Saul Proclaimed King at Gilgal | 72
    The Anointing of David | 74

6   SAMUEL'S FAREWELL SPEECH | 80
    Samuel Establishes his Integrity | 81
    The Witness of History | 83
    The People Acknowledge their Error | 86
    Samuel Encourages the People | 88
    The Purpose of Chapter 12 | 90

7   SAMUEL, SAUL, AND DAVID | 95
    Saul and Samuel's First Clash | 96
    Saul and Samuel's Second Clash | 99
    Tearing the Robe | 101
    God and Kingship | 103
    Samuel and David | 104

8   WHO WAS SAMUEL? | 110
    Priest | 111
    Judge | 114
    Prophet | 117
    Seer | 121
    The Man of God | 123

9   RETURNING FROM THE DEAD | 127
    The Death of Samuel | 128
    Posthumous Meeting of Samuel with Saul | 130
    Life After Death | 136
    Conclusion | 140

Bibliography | 143

Index | 153

Acknowledgments

To start with, I would like to thank my readers who read the early drafts of my manuscript and offered many perceptives and insightful comments: Anna S. Chernak, who read the initial manuscript and offered valuable advice and continuous encouragement; and Vivian and Dena Arendall, who made many suggestions and offered their wisdom.

I want to express appreciation to the staff of the Harding School of Theology in Memphis: library director Bob Turner, who led me to many resources; associate librarian Sheila Owen and circulation assistant Tina Rogers, who both helped with research; and graduate student Cana Moore, who helped with the bibliography.

Special thanks to Hebrew Union College Library in New York City, where head librarian Yoram Bitton provided me with help, wisdom, and friendship.

Finally, a special thanks to the people of Wipf & Stock for their devotion and expertise in transforming my manuscript into this book.

Shaul Bar
Memphis, TN
May 2021

Abbreviations

ABD	*The Anchor Bible Dictionary.* Edited by D. N. Freedman. 6 vols. New York: Doubleday, 1992. AnBib Analecta biblica
AJBA	*Australian Journal of Biblical Archeology*
ANET	*Ancient Near Eastern Texts Relating to the Old Testament.* Edited by J. B. Pritchard. Princeton: Princeton University Press, 1969.
ARM	*Archives Royales de Mari: 18.* Paris: Impr. Nationale, 1977.
B. Bat.	*Baba Batra*
B. Ḳam.	*Baba Ḳamma*
B. Meṣ	*Baba Meṣiʿa*
BA	*Biblical Archaeologist*
BASOR	*Bulletin of the Americans Schools of Oriental Research*
BDB	Brown, F., S. R. Driver, and C. A. Briggs, *A Hebrew and English Lexicon of the Old Testament.* Oxford: Clarendon, 1907.
Ber.	*Berakot*
BethM	*Beth Miqra: Journal for the Study of the Bible and Its World*
BHH	*Biblisch-historisches Handwörterbuch: Landeskunde, Geschichte, Religion, Kultur.* 4 vols. Edited by B. Reicke and L. Rost. Göttingen: Vandenhoeck & Ruprecht, 1962–66.
Bib	*Biblica*
BibOr	*Biblica et orientalia*
BibRev	*Biblical Review*
BN	*Biblische Notizen*

BTB	*Biblical Theology Bulletin*
BZAW	*Beihefte zur Zeitschrift für die alttestamentliche Wissenschaft*
CAD	*The Assyrian Dictionary of the Oriental Institute of the University of Chicago*. 21 vols. Edited by I. J. Gelb et al. Chicago: Oriental Institute, 1956–2010.
CBC	Cambridge Bible Commentary
CBQ	*Catholic Biblical Quarterly*
CQR	*Church Quarterly Review*
CS	*The Context of Scripture*. 3 vols. Edited by W. W. Hallo. Leiden: Brill, 1997.
Eccl. R.	*Ecclesiastes Rabbah*
EM	*Encyclopedia Miqrait*
EncJud	*Encyclopedia Judaica*. 22 vols. 2nd ed. Jerusalem: Keter, 2007.
ErIsr	*Eretz-Israel*
Exod. R.	*Exodus Rabbah*
FAT	Froschungen zum Alten Testament
FRLANT	Forschungen zur Religion und Literatur des Alten und Neuen Testaments
Gen. R.	*Genesis Rabbah*
Ḥag.	*Ḥagigah*
HALOT	Koehler, L., W. Baumgartner, and J. J. Stamm. *The Hebrew and Aramaic Lexicon of the Old Testament*. 4 vols. Translated and edited by M. E. J. Richardson. Leiden, 1994–99
HSM	Harvard Semitic Monographs
HUCA	*Hebrew Union College Annual*
ICC	International Critical Commentary
IEJ	*Israel Exploration Journal*
JAOS	*Journal of the American Oriental Society*
JBL	*Journal of Biblical Literature*
JCS	*Journal of Cuneiform Studies*
JJS	*Journal of Jewish Studies*
JNES	*Journal of Near Eastern Studies*

ABBREVIATIONS

JSOT	*Journal for the Study of the Old Testament*
JSOTSup	Journal for the Study of the Old Testament: Supplement Series
JSS	*Journal of Semitic Studies*
JTS	*Journal of Theological Studies*
Ket.	Ketubbot
Lev. R.	Leviticus Rabbah
LXX	Septuagint
Mak.	Makkot
Meg.	Megillah
Midr. Sam.	Midrash Samuel
Midr. Ps.	Midrash Psalms
Mish.	Mishnah
NEAEHL	*The New Encyclopedia of Archeological Excavations in the Holy Land*. 4 vols. Edited by E. Stern. Jerusalem: Israel Exploration Society, 1993.
Ned.	Nedarim
Num. R.	Numbers Rabbah
OTL	Old Testament Library
OTWSA	Die Ou-Testamentiese Werkgemeenskap in Suid-Afrika
PEQ	*Palestine Exploration Quaterly*
Pes.	Pesaḥim
PRU	*Le Palais royal d'Uagrit*
Roš Haš	Roš Haššanah
RSP	*Ras Shamra Parallels*. Edited by Loren R. Fisher et al. Rome: Pontifical Biblical Institute, 1975.
Sanh	Sanhedrin
SBLDS	Society of Biblical Literature Dissertation Series
SHCANE	Studies in the History and the Culture of the Ancient Near East
Soṭah	Soṭah
SSN	Studia Semitica Neerlandica
ST	*Studia Theologica*
Taʿan.	Taʿanit

Tanḥ Lev.	*Tanḥumah Leviticus*
Tarbiz	*Tarbiz*
Tg.	*Targum*
Tg. Jon.	*Targum Jonathan*
TDOT	*Theological Dictionary of the Old Testament.* 15 vols. Edited by G. J. Botterweck and H. Ringgren. Translated by J. T. Willis, G. W. Bromiley, and D. E. Green. Grand Rapids: Eerdmans, 1974–2004
TZ	*Theologische Zeitschrift*
UF	*Ugaritic-Forschungen*
VAB	*Vorderasiatische Bibliothek.* 7 vols. Leipzig: J. C. Hinrichs, 1907–16.
VT	*Vetus Testamentum*
VTSup	*Vetus Testamentum, Supplements*
WBC	World Bible Commentary
WHJP	Mazar, Benjamin, et al. *World History of the Jewish People.* New York: Jewish History Publications, 1964
WMANT	*Wissenschaftliche Monograph zum Alten und Neuen Testament*
WTJ	*Westminster Theological Journal*
WVDOG	Wissenschaftliche Veröffentlichungen der deutschen Orientgesellschaft
Yoma	*Yoma*
ZAW	*Zeitschrift für die alttestamentliche Wissenschaf*

Introduction

SAMUEL THE PROPHET LIVED in the eleventh century BCE; he was instrumental in the transition of a loose confederacy of Hebrew tribes to a centralized monarchy. According to the Talmud, Samuel wrote the book that bears his name, as well as Judges and Ruth.[1] It is believed that he wrote his biography up to his death (chapters 1–24), and the prophets Gad and Nathan completed the work.[2] This tradition is probably based on the book of Chronicles: "The acts of King David, early and late, are recorded in the history of Samuel the seer, the history of Nathan the prophet, and the history of Gad the seer " (1 Chr 29:29). It has also been suggested that some parts of the book were written by high official(s) in the court of David or Solomon such as Abiathar the priest, Jehoshaphat the *mazkir*, or Ahimaaz son of Zadok the priest. The royal officials were responsible for the archival material; thus, it is possible that they wrote part of the narrative.[3]

In the Jewish tradition 1 Samuel and 2 Samuel were considered one book. It is only in the LXX that we start to find the division into two books. This division was accepted by the Masoretic text. However, in the LXX it is referred to as "the books of Kings," because it was attached to the book of Kings; thus, we have 1 Kings, 2 Kings, 3 Kings, and 4 Kings. In the Vulgate it is called the four books of Kings. The division into two books was probably due to the length of the book. The death of Saul is a logical ending to First Samuel. Second Samuel continues with the David story, but David's story extends into the first two chapters of 1 Kings.

---

1. B. Bat. 14b.
2. B. Bat. 15a.
3. Gottwald, "Samuel," 17:758.

Samuel

Modern scholarship rejects the theory that the book is written by one man or the joint authorship of Samuel, Gad, and Nathan. The question of authorship has been long studied. We don't know who wrote the book of Samuel since there is no objective evidence of the author. What is clear is that the book was not written by an eyewitness to the events narrated. There are phrases which appear in the book of Samuel which show that it was written at a later date. This includes: "to this day" (1 Sam 5:5); "Formerly in Israel" (9:9); there is also a reference to "all Israel and Judah (1 Sam 18:16), which suggests that this was written sometime after the division of the nation. There are also phrases which suggest that it was not Samuel who wrote the book. In several instances, Samuel praises himself, which is unlikely: "Young Samuel, meanwhile, grew in esteem and favor both with God and with men" (2:26); "Samuel grew up and the Lord was with him" (3:19).

In modern scholarship, 1 Samuel is part of the so-called Deuteronomistic History.[4] This includes the books of Deuteronomy, Joshua, Judges, 1–2 Samuel, and 1–2 Kings. These books tell the history of Israel from the time of Moses to the destruction of the kingdom of Judah in 586 BCE. They are believed to comprise a single work because they share the elements of structure, writing style, and theological outlook. The books examine the history of Israel according to the laws set forth in Deuteronomy. The main doctrines of Deuteronomy are centralized worship in Jerusalem, obedience to the Deuteronomistic law, and abstinence from apostasy. Victory and defeat accordingly result from obedience or disobedience to the law. Hence it is more theological history than pure history. However, examination of the book of Samuel reveals limited influence of the Deuteronomistic redaction. According to McCarter, the most striking aspect of the Deuteronomistic redaction of the books of Samuel is its sparseness.[5] The strict Deuteronomistic structure that is found in the books of Judges and Kings is not evident in Samuel.

Reading the book of Samuel reveals that it contains various duplicate and conflicting traditions which the compiler made no effort to harmonize. Twice we read about the prophecy on the house of Eli (2:27–36; 3:11–14); three times Saul is anointed as the king of Israel (10:1, 20–24; 11:15). The story of Saul's anointment parallels David's anointment. According to 7:13,

---

4. For the study of Samuel and the Deuteronomist see Polzin, *Samuel and the Deuteronomist*.

5. McCarter, *1 Samuel*, 15; For a similar conclusion see Weiser, *The Old Testament*, 168.

God defeated the Philistines, and they did not invade the territory of Israel again for as long as Samuel lived. However, in the following chapters we read of continued battles with the Philistines. Twice Saul is rejected by Samuel (1 Sam 13:13–14; 15:26). David is called to Saul's court to dispel the king's evil spirit by playing the harp (1 Sam 16:23). Later, when David fights against Goliath it appears that he was unknown to Saul (17:55). In chapter 17, David kills Goliath, but according to 2 Samuel 21:19, it was Elhanan, son of Jaare-oregim. Twice Saul tries to kill David by throwing his spear at him (1 Sam 18:11; 19:10). Two times David escapes from Saul's courtyard (1 Sam 19, 20); and two times he run away to King Achish of Gath (1 Sam 21:11–16; 27). Saul's pursuit of David is described in chapters 24 and 26; in these two chapters, David could have killed Saul, but instead he spared his life.

This leads us to believe that the book of Samuel in the present form is a collection of different written and oral sources. The similar stories were not thought of as a description of the same event, but as a description of different events that took place at different times. The inconsistencies evidently did not bother the authors of the book. Their aim was to preserve different traditions and to shed light on the stories regardless of the discrepancies between them. These oddities in the stories point to the diverse sources in oral and written material that were at the disposal of the authors. The differences in style and the use of different literary devices exhibit proof that several authors added and omitted material to create the book until the author or its last editor gave it its final shape.[6]

The book serves as a bridge between the period of the judges and the monarchic period. It describes how the tribal league became a monarchy and defeated its enemies, in particular the Philistines, and the subjection of other nations. This was a long process that began in the judges' period and ended with the establishment of David's kingship. The important events that took place are indirectly recorded through the important personalities of this period, such as Eli, Samuel, and David. This method of writing the history of the Israelite nation is according to the belief that it is God who directs human events. He punishes the wicked and rewards the righteous. The faith of the nation is dependent on the actions of its leaders; hence, the stories are limited to them. Daily life of the people of Israel, the economic situation, relationships within the family, and the relations between the tribes, the life in the villages and the cities: all of these are described

---

6. Bar-Efrat, *I Samuel*, 15–16.

laconically. Still, sometimes when the narrator describes the life of its leaders, he gives us a glimpse into the life of the people during that era.[7]

Samuel played a major role in the transition between the judges' period and the monarchic period. Therefore, not surprisingly, he is compared as an equal to Moses and Aaron (Jer 15:1; Ps 99:6); also, the sages compared some of his acts to Moses' acts.[8] There are no chronological dates to the events that are narrated. The details and length of Samuel's activities and his lifespan are missing. We are told that he was born when Eli served as a priest in Shiloh, and he died when Saul was already the king of Israel. But the narrator did not specify in what years these events took place. The sages claimed that he died at a young age, when he was fifty.[9] The years that Saul reigned as the king of Israel are also not clear according to 1 Samuel 13:1: "Saul was one year old when he became king, and he reigned over Israel two years." Both statements are impossible: the first one is obvious and the second one, as Ralbag (Levi ben Gershon, also known as Gersonides, 1288-1344) noted, "It is difficult to believe that all the events of Saul's reign could have been crowded into two years." According to Josephus, based on the biblical details on the reigns of king David and Solomon, which he cited from Hellenistic authors, it is possible that Samuel was active during the eleventh century BCE.[10]

The book of Samuel is a blend of historiography, literary poetics, and ethical and theological perceptions. Examination of it reveals that the stories about Samuel are found in:

1. 1 Samuel 1–3: A story of Samuel's boyhood, which describes his birth and service in Shiloh, where he became a prophet of the Lord.
2. 1 Samuel 7: Samuel the intercessor and a judge.
3. 1 Samuel 8: The rise of the monarchy; the request for kingship.
4. 1 Samuel 9–10; 11:12–14: Samuel anoints Saul as a king.
5. 1 Samuel 12: Samuel's farewell address.
6. 1 Samuel 13:8–15; 15: Samuel condemns Saul and announces his rejection as king.
7. 1 Samuel 16:1–13: Samuel anoints David as a king.

---

7. Segal, *Books of Samuel*, 28.
8. *Ned.* 38a; *Ta'an.* 27a; *Exod R.* 16.4; *Num R.* 18.8.
9. *Midr. Sam.* 3.3.
10. Josephus, *Against Apion* 1.106–27.

INTRODUCTION

8. 1 Samuel 19:18–24: Samuel, David, and Saul at Naioth.

9. 1 Samuel 25:1; 28:3–20: The death of Samuel and the witch of Endor.

In other words, only thirty percent of the book is devoted to Samuel. The rest of the remaining chapters deal mainly with the stories about Saul and David and describe the feuds between the two rivals.

The character of Samuel serves as a link between the stories. The book starts with the birth of Samuel and ends with Saul's death on Mount Gilboa. It was Samuel who told Saul about his upcoming death on Mount Gilboa. Samuel is the last judge who was leading the nation, like Moses and Deborah (Exod 18:13; Judg 4:4–5). He is the first prophet that is followed by prophets, such as Gad and Nathan, who served as advisers to the king. Samuel inaugurated a new period, the monarchic era. He anointed Saul as a king, which led to the anointment of David and his kingship forever. Samuel made the rounds and judged Israel with righteousness throughout his life (3:19–20; 12:2, 3–5; 7:15–17). Not many details are given about this period. The book mainly concentrates on two phases in Samuel's life, Samuel's younger years and then his older years. His young age is linked to Eli, who represents the older generation, while in his older age he is connected to Saul and David, who signify the future. Samuel is associated with Saul from his arrival (chapter 9) until his tragic death on mount Gilboa (28). He met David and anointed him, but David's rise to kingship would take place after the death of Samuel and Saul.

In the current book, our main goal is to try to bring Samuel to life, to rediscover him, and to have a better understanding of his personality, ambitions, achievements, and failures. To achieve this goal, we will use the synchronic method, analyzing the chapters that pertain to Samuel as they stand and comparing them to the other biblical texts. This in turn will shed more light on the persona of Samuel. Contemporary views and commentaries on Samuel will be considered. Additionally, to have a better read of the Samuel stories, material found in the Talmud, the Midrashim, and the Jewish medieval commentators will be reviewed. The Talmud contains a vast amount of *aggadot*—stories. The Midrash includes anthologies and compilations of homilies, including biblical exegeses and public sermons. The various sects and currents in Judaism left their marks on the Samuel stories, and almost everything that Jews thought during a period of more than one thousand years can be found there. Though the interpretative methods of medieval commentators vary, we still can find that they compromise between the literal and Midrashic interpretation of the biblical text. In addition, they

SAMUEL

pursue philological contextual interpretation with a logical and scientific perspective. We trust this study will afford a provocative and useful insight into the character of Samuel and to his tumultuous period.

1

Samuel's Childhood

SAMUEL'S BIRTH IS LIKE many other stories in the Hebrew Bible. A barren woman, yearning for a child, is comparable to stories about Sarah, Rachel, and Samson's mother. Also common to these stories is the existence of a rival wife who has borne children and then looks down on the barren women, such as Hagar and Sarah, Leah and Rachel–and in our story, Peninnah and Hannah. The birth of a son brings great joy as it is a reversal of fates, a common folktale motif. Just as with Moses, Samuel's life is described in detail in the Bible. He is the only prophet whose story includes his birth, upbringing, and burial. The story is built step by step. The first years of Samuel's youth are described in 1 Samuel 1–3, which includes his birth and dedication (1:1–28), Hannah's Song (2:1–10), the behavior of Eli's sons (2:12–17, 22–26) versus Samuel (2:11, 18–21), the message of doom by the man of God (2:27–36) and Samuel receiving a message from God (3:1–21).

Scholars debate the nature of the traditions which are found in the first three chapters; that is, whether they should be viewed as a coherent unit, or units of tradition which were gathered over time. Noth suggests that three traditions were combined. First, Samuel's birth and dedication at Shiloh (1:1–3a, 4–28; 2:11, 18–21), which is favorable toward Shiloh and the Elide priesthood and has its roots in the premonarchic times.[1] The second tradition is critical of the Elides and announces the divine punishment on them (2:12–17, 22–36). It is polemic by the Jerusalem priesthood

---

1. Noth, "Samuel and Silo," 391, 393, 395–97.

against the Elide priesthood and Shiloh and dates after the death of Solomon.[2] A third tradition considers Samuel's message of the Elides' punishment which displays Samuel's role as a prophet (3:1–20). This tradition dates to the time after the destruction of Shiloh and the death of Samuel; it was created by the editor who had at his disposal the first two traditions. Hertzberg's analysis of 1 Samuel 1–3 is significantly different from Noth's. He speaks of the rise of Samuel (1:1–28; 2:11, 18–21, 26; 3:1–10, 15–21) and the traditions about the Elides (2:12–17, 22–25, 27–34). He points to the transitions from Samuel's accounts to the accounts of the deeds of Eli and his sons. At first these traditions were separated but were then woven by the compiler. Later the compiler added the hymn (2:1–10) and created 2:35–36 and 3:11–14. Samuel is portrayed as a great figure who is possessed with priestly, prophetic, and political powers of leadership: "The story of his youth is of extreme importance for theological appreciation of the rise of Samuel and of the period of the kings, which was to be inaugurated by him."[3] In contrast, there are scholars who suggest that the different parts should be viewed as a coherent unity. Bourke omits 2:1–10 and 27–36 and refers to the rest of the material as a unified Ephraimite source.[4] Willis suggests that the three chapters should be viewed as a literary unit. He points to the contrast between Samuel and the Elides. Specifically, he stresses the repetition of theme and words which are prevalent in the three chapters.[5] Similarly, Garsiel points to comparative literary structures, to the contrast between the greatness of Samuel's parents versus Eli, and the sons of Eli versus Samuel's. According to him, the usage of similar themes and phrases indicates the author's intention to bind these sections together.[6]

In the current chapter and in chapter 2, we will examine the context of 1 Samuel 1–3. The different units of Samuel's birth and childhood will be analyzed to see if they are isolated stories or linked to each other and to the later stories in the book of Samuel. Their content, meaning, relationships, and theological outlook will be scrutinized. This will help us to see the meaning of 1 Samuel 1–3, the reason for its creation, and the purpose behind it.

---

2. Noth, "Samuel and Silo," 391–94.
3. Hertzberg, *I & II Samuel*, 44.
4. Bourke, "Samuel and the Ark," 73.
5. Willis, "Cultic Elements," 38–39; Willis, "An Anti-Elide," 293–94.
6. Garsiel, *First Book of Samuel*, 33–57.

SAMUEL'S FAMILY

The story begins by introducing Samuel's father Elkanah and his two wives, Hannah and Peninnah. The statement about Elkanah, "there was a man," is a typical formula in the books of Judges and Samuel. The same phrase appears later in the story of Saul (1 Sam 9:1) and twice in the book of Judges in the Samson story (Judg 13:2), as well as in Micah (17:1). Therefore, according to Schultz, the story should be read in light of the previous stories in the book of Judges.[7] Elkanah is from Ramathaim, a place that is located in the hill country of Ephraim.[8] Ramathaim is only mentioned here, and is later called Ramah (1:19; 2:11; 8:4; 25:1; 28:3), which is the name of Samuel's hometown.[9] It appears sixteen times in 1 Samuel and is reserved for the character of Samuel from his birth to his death.[10] Ramah was Samuel's base, and the end of chapter 7 reports that he kept returning to it. The last time the name of the city is mentioned is at Samuel's burial, in 25:1, "and they buried him in Ramah, his home," and in 28:3, "he was buried in his own town of Ramah."

Elkanah, Samuel's father's name, means "God created"; the name appears only in the first two chapters of the book of Samuel and is mentioned later in 1 Chronicles 6:12, 19.[11] In addition, Elkanah's genealogy is given; he is the son of Jeroham, son of Elihu, son of Tohu, son of Zuph an Ephrathite. According to Driver, the land of Zuph received its name from Zuph, the ancestor of Elkanah who settled in that part of the land.[12] The next time that the land of Zuph would be mentioned is after introduction of another father, Saul's. Saul, in his attempt to find his father's asses, went to the land of Zuph. There he met Samuel; whose task it was to find the future king.

In 1 Chronicles 6:11, 19, the genealogy of Elkanah is given with a slight variation; his ancestry is traced back to Kohath, a son of Levi.[13]

---

7. Schultz, *Die Bücher Samuel*, 2

8. Eusebius identified the site with Arimathea of New Testament times (Matt 27:57; John 19:38) and places the village at Remphis (M. R. 151159), 14 km northeast of Lod (NHI, 378–80). Another suggestion is the site of Beit Rima (M. R. 159160), 21 km northeast of Lod.

9. Ramathaim is dual of Ramah, literally "two hills." According to the Talmud, Ramathaim refers to "two heights facing (tsophoth) each other. See *Meg.* 14a.

10. Fokkelman, *Narrative Art and Poetry*, 4:7.

11. *HALOT*, 1:60.

12. Driver, *Notes on the Hebrew*, 1.

13. His father's name Jeroham is spelled in LXX "Jerahmeel." Elkanah's grandfather,

However, the texts in 1 Samuel 1:1 say that he was an Ephraimite. In other words, according to the book of Chronicles, Elkanah's family belonged to the Levitical Kohathite settlement in the territory of Ephraim (Josh 21:20). It appears that in the book of Chronicles there is an effort to present Samuel as a Levite, a descendent of Kohath.[14] This coincides with 1 Samuel 3:1, where it says that Samuel was "ministering to the Lord under Eli," a role that was carried by the Levites. The genealogical list in Chronicles was created in order to answer questions about Samuel's legitimacy to serve in the temple in Shiloh. According to the biblical law only Levites could serve in the temple (Num 1:50–51; 3:5–9; 18:2–4, 22–23). Any outsider or unauthorized person who encroached upon the sanctuary would be put to death (1:51). Samuel merited the death penalty, and the author of the book of Chronicles tries to settle the contradiction between the book of Samuel and the biblical legislation. According to Kalimi, the author created an artificial genealogical list which presents Samuel as a Levite, in contrast to the book of Samuel where he is from the tribe of Ephraim.[15] Klein similarly says that the Chronicler's information is non-historical. It was necessary for the Chronicle to create this link.[16] However, Albright suggests that "Samuel was not a member of the tribe of Levi by birth, but he became attached as a lay Nazirite to the Tabernacle."[17] Similarly, Leuchter says that the Levites were not a "tribe" but a caste that was composed from different groups of the population connected to the priestly institution. "The institution of the Levites and priests was always permeable, with commoners becoming Levites and Levites becoming priests, as Samuel's own track exemplifies."[18] However, there is no basis for this assertion in the texts.

Elkanah was from a family of means, as suggested by his pedigree and his two wives, Hannah and Peninnah.[19] Polygamy was acceptable by ancient Israelite law but there is no proof that it was widely exercised; economic means dictated the situation. Hannah is mentioned first because of her role in the ensuing events. She was Elkanah's first wife and, due to her barrenness, Elkanah married a second wife, Peninnah, in order to produce

---

Elihu, is spelled "Eliel" in 1 Chr 6:19 and "Eliab" in 1 Chr 6:12.

14. Japhet, *I & II Chronicles*, 155–56.
15. Kalimi, *Book of Chronicles*, 150n80.
16. Klein, *1 Samuel*, 6.
17. Albright, *Samuel and the Beginning*, 12.
18. Leuchter, *Samuel and the Shaping*, 24, 40.
19. Gordon, *1 & 2 Samuel*, 72.

an heir. Lipínski has suggested that the names of the women testify to their function in the story. Therefore, Hannah means "charming," which alludes to the fact that she was the loved one. Peninnah means "prolific" or "fecund," pointing to her role as the one who bore children.[20] Elkanah's love for Hannah is specified clearly; there is no reference to his feelings for Peninnah, who is a secondary character and appears in contrast to Hannah. Hannah's barrenness is the focal point, and it is mentioned three times in chapter 1 that God closed her womb (1 Sam 1:5, 6, 11). The motif of barrenness is repeated in chapter 2, but it is reversed. Hannah praises God and says, "While the barren woman bears seven" (2:5). God blessed Hannah and she conceived and bore three sons and two daughters (2:21). This is a natural outcome and development of the story of Hannah's vow and Eli's promise to her from chapter 1.

VISIT TO SHILOH

Elkanah went annually to Shiloh "*miyyamim yamimah*." This phrase appears with reference to observance of pilgrimage or sacred seasons (Exod 13:10; Judg 11:40; 21:19). It is mentioned three times in chapter 1 (1 Sam 1:3, 21, 24), and once in chapter 2 (2:19), cementing the link between the two chapters. The Targum translates "from one festival to another." The three annual festivals are the Feast of Unleavened Bread, the Feast of Weeks, and the Feast of Booths. However, these festivals are not mentioned in our text. Elkanah's visit to Shiloh was made only once a year (1 Sam 1:7; 21). Haran suggested that it was an annual sacrifice: "a family or clan feast, confined to the family and celebrated by all its members, women and children included."[21]

Shiloh was the amphictyony capital of Israel in the time of the judges, where the Tabernacle was hosted; it was the center of Israelite worship. The ark remained in this site until it was taken to Eben-Ezer, where it was captured by the Philistines. Excavations reveal that the place was destroyed in that period, a fact that is mentioned in later times (Jer 7:12, 14; 26:6, 9; Ps 78:60).[22] The fall of the city marked the peak of the Philistines' power over Israel. When the ark was returned it remained in Kiriath-Jearim. The priestly family retained its importance and moved to Nob (1 Sam 21:1–9).

20. Lipínski, "Peninna," 68–75.
21. Haran, *Temples and Temple-Service*, 306.
22. Kempinski, "Shiloh," 1364–70.

Samuel

In Solomon's era the priestly family of the city was ousted (1 Kgs 2:27). Later Rabbinic tradition views Shiloh as the precursor to Jerusalem. It was the central shrine for 369 years, in contrast to fourteen years for Gilgal and fifty-seven years for Nob and Gibeon.[23]

In Shiloh, two sons of the priest Eli, Hopni and Phinehas, served. Their names are Egyptian, a reminder of Israel's history. They were the active priests of the Lord. The statement that they were priests of the Lord is ironic. Later their wickedness and deaths will be described and will play a significant role in the development of the narrative. Eli their father is also mentioned. The mention of Eli and his sons with the description of Elkanah's piety is the first occurrence of a series of contrasts between Samuel and the Elides throughout chapters 1–3.[24] Elkanah is described as worshiping and making sacrifice to the Lord, while the sons of Eli are just mentioned without any reference to their priestly functions.

On his visit to Shiloh, Elkanah made a sacrifice. The sacrificial meal was accompanied by eating and drinking. The portions of the sacrifice were divided by the head of the family. He gave a sacrificial portion to Peninnah and each of her children. It is believed that these portions were eaten by the worshipers (1 Sam 9:23). Hannah, Elkanah's favorite wife, received special attention, such as a double portion, because he loved her.[25] The double portion that Elkanah gives to Hannah was to compensate for the lack of children. It shows Elkanah's love for her; despite not having sons with her, he cares for her. But this was little help as Peninnah torments Hannah because she is childless, just as Hagar despised Sarah after Ishmael was born. Hannah broke into tears and refused to eat.

Hannah wept greatly, asking God for a son. In her prayer she poured out her heart before the Lord. The expression "praying before" appears here for the first time in the Hebrew Bible. It has the sense of direct communication between man and God.[26] Samuel's parents are "depicted in their moral nobility and delicacy towards others; by contrast, Eli is shown as

---

23. Brinker, *Influence of Sanctuaries*, 168–69.

24. Bourke, "Samuel and the Ark," 82.

25. The Hebrew phrase "double portion" is difficult. The Hebrew word ʾ*appāyim* can mean "nose" and sometimes "wrath" and also often means "face," especially when it refers to of bowing down before man or man of high position. Hence, "portion of the face," implies a large piece, a portion of honor. The Targum has "choice;" Radak, "to appease her anger (aph)." See Hertzberg, *I & II Samuel*, 24

26. For the different interpretation for "praying before the Lord" see Fowler, "Meaning of lipne," 384–90.

hard and obtuse."²⁷ Hannah pledged to consecrate the boy to the service of the sanctuary. Interestingly, Hannah made a vow to give her son to YHWH without consulting her husband. According to Numbers 30:6–15, a wife's vow could be approved or negated by her husband. But it is possible that this law was originated later than 1 Samuel. The structure and the style of the vow was similar in pattern to the story about Jacob (Gen 28:20–22), of Jephthah (Judg 11:30–31), and of Absalom (2 Sam 15:8). In each case the person pledged himself to a certain course of action upon the fulfilment of the desired conditions.

As a Levite, Samuel would have had to serve in the sanctuary, but Hannah's vow makes Samuel's consecration lifelong, where other Levites served only from the age 25–50 (Num 8:24). Like Samson, he was placed under Nazarite vow. This element of Samuel as a Nazirite was probably taken from the Samson story. The significance of Hannah's prayer was noticed in the Talmud, where we read: "How many important rules can be deduced from Hannah's prayer! That she spoke from her heart teaches that prayer requires devotion; that her lips moved tells us that it is necessary to articulate the words of prayer with one's lips; that her voice could not be heard gives the rule that it is forbidden to raise one's voice loudly in prayer."²⁸

The scene which describes Hannah's prayer in the sanctuary contrasts Samuel's parents and Eli.²⁹ While Hannah prayed and wept greatly, she was watched by Eli the priest. It was a silent prayer and only her lips moved, which led Eli to believe that she was drunk. Eli's old age and deficient eyesight (1 Sam 3:2; 4:15) probably contributed to this belief as well. It is possible that drunken frenzy was common at the shrine and the authorities failed to curtail it.³⁰ Indeed, Biblical texts suggest that drunkenness and depravity were common at Israelite religious centers (1 Sam 2:22; Judg 9:27; 21:21–23; Isa 28:7). Since Eli thought that Hannah was drunk, he rebuked her: "Put aside your wine away from you!" (1 Sam 1:14). This description comes to attest the difference between Hannah and Eli: Hannah, who prays to God in the temple, and Eli, who sees but does not comprehend the situation and therefore rebukes her. In the Septuagint the rebuke comes from the priest's lad and not Eli. This is to soften the image of Eli and to portray him in a more favorable light. Hannah responded to Eli courteously, saying

27. Garsiel, *First Book of Samuel*, 36
28. *Ber.* 31a
29. Alter, *Art*, 81–86.
30. John Wills, "Cultic Elements," 55.

that she is not drunk but hard of spirit. She asked him not to consider her as "daughter of Belial" (1 Sam 1:16). The term "Belial" will be used in the next chapter to describe the wickedness and immorality of Eli's sons (1 Sam 2:12). By using the same term to describe Hannah and Eli's sons, the author guides the reader to compare Eli's attitude towards Hannah and his sons.[31] He hurries to criticize Hannah and refers to her as a daughter of Belial, but on the other hand, he does not see his own sons as sons of Belial. This comparison diminishes his image. He accepted her explanation but did not apologize for his misjudgment. The final exchange between the two ends with Eli sending Hannah and telling her that God will grant her petition. Ironically, the fulfilment of her request meant that Samuel would replace Eli as Israel's leader. The Jewish commentators suggest that Eli gave Hannah a prophetic assurance that her prayer would be fulfilled. Although his sons are the active priests, Eli could still invoke a blessing as the priest of the Lord (Num 6:22–27; Deut 10:8); interestingly this is the only passage where a priest blesses an individual worshipper.[32]

SAMUEL'S BIRTH

Hannah's prayer was heard, and a year later she conceived and bore a son. Samuel's birth narrative is similar to Samson's birth narrative. In both stories there is a promise of a son (Judg 12:3–4, 7; 1 Sam 1:17), the dedication of a son (Judg 13:5, 7, 25; 1 Sam 1:24–28), and the mothers are initially barren (Judg 13:2; 1 Sam 1:15). The phrase "no razor shall touch his head" is mentioned in these stories (Judg 13:5; 1 Sam 1:11). Samson and Samuel fought against the Philistines. Samuel succeeded in his battle against the Philistines, while Samson failed. Samuel is pious while Samson is ill-behaved.

God remembered Hannah and fulfilled his promises. According to McCarter, "Remembering in the religious terminology of Israel and other Northwest Semitic societies referred to the benevolent treatment of an individual or group by a god, often, as in this case, in response to a specific plea."[33] Hannah named her son Samuel because "I *asked* the Lord for him" (1 Sam 1:20). There is no indication that Elkanah played any part in this name-giving. The root š' l, שאל, appears nine times in the story of Samuel's birth and consecration (1 Sam 1:17, 20, 27–28; 2:20). Based on

31. Garsiel, *First Book of Samuel*, 37.
32. Gordon, *1 & 2 Samuel*, 75.
33. McCarter, *I Samuel*, 62.

the recurrence of the root *š'l*, שאל, it was suggested that the name Samuel is derived from it. However, since it is impossible to accept this explanation, the meaning of the name Samuel is by way of assonance rather than etymology; in other words, *Sha'ul me'el*, "Asked-of-God." This interpretation was suggested by Radak (Rabbi David ben Joseph Kimḥi, 1160–1235). Among modern scholars various explanation were proposed, such as: "Heard of God," "He Who Is from God," "His Name Is El,"[34] and "Name of God,"[35] which is followed by Gordon's translation, "Name of El" or "El is exalted."[36] Other possible interpretations include: "The Name Is God," like royal names which are found in the first dynasty of Babylon, *Sumu-la-ilu*; "The Name Is Verily God"; and Sumu-Abu, "The Name Is Father."[37] In other words, Hannah requested a son, so God fulfilled her wish and gave her a son who bears the name of God.

There are scholars who suggest that the story of naming Samuel is not original, that it is a tradition that is taken from Saul's stories that was transferred to Samuel.[38] According to 1 Samuel 1:28: "For as long as he lives, he is lent, *ša'ul* שאול, to the Lord"; this relates to Saul and not to Samuel. Moreover, the root *š'l* etymologically better fits the name Saul than Samuel; therefore, the story was originally about Saul. It is noteworthy that the root *š'l* appears four times when the people ask God for a king (8:10; 12:13, 17, 19), creating an analogy between Hannah's request for a son and the people's request for a king. On the other hand, there are scholars who do not accept the idea of transfer material from the story of Saul to Samuel; they have treated it with suspicion and rejected it.[39] More than likely, the narrator is delivering a subtle message here that leads from Samuel to Saul, foreshadowing the future. Samuel is the true leader who leads the nations and not a king who became disobedient to God.[40]

When the time of nursing ended, Hannah took Samuel to Shiloh. The age at which infants were weaned varied in different societies. In Egypt and

---

34. Tsumura, *First Book of Samuel*, 127.
35. Driver, *Notes on the Hebrew Text*, 16–19.
36. Gordon, *1 & 2 Samuel*, 76.
37. Gordon, "Eblaitica," 25–26; Tsumura, *First Book of Samuel*, 127.
38. Lods, *Israel-From Its Beginning*, 354–55; McCarter, *I Samuel*, 62, 65–66; Zakovitch, "A Study of Precise," 41n45.
39. Willis, "Cultic Elements," 34; Uffenheimer, *Ancient Prophecy*, 143; Zalevski, "Hannah's Vow," 305–08; Hertzberg, *I & II Samuel*, 26; Noth, "Samuel und Silo," 395. Amit, "He Is Lent to God," 238.
40. Willis, "Cultic Elements," 53–54; Gnuse, *Dream Theophany of Samuel*, 182.

Assyria, it was at about three years, similar to Israel in the Second Temple period (2 Macc 7:27). In the Talmud we read of twenty-four months, while another reference speaks of age four to five years.[41] It is hard to believe that Hannah committed her son to Eli at an early age. It is more than likely that she committed him when he was independent of his mother. Stressing again the pious nature of Samuel's family, the text mentions for the third time that the family went to Shiloh. Hannah, who did not join the family on the previous journey, brought Samuel to Shiloh together with three bullocks and one *ephah* of meal and a bottle of wine. Although the whole family went to Shiloh, it was Hannah who played an active role here. She is the one who took Samuel with her and brought the sacrifices. She delivered Samuel to the house of the Lord and spoke to Eli. Hannah fulfils here the vow she made to lend her son to the Lord as long as he lives. She reminded Eli of who she is and told him, "And the Lord granted me what I asked of Him" (1 Sam 1:27); she also repeats Eli's blessing of 1 Samuel 1:17, "And may the God of Israel grant you what you have asked of Him." Hannah is the leading character of 1 Samuel 1 and is described as the mother of Samuel. Her portrayal is similar to that of Samson's mother (Judg 13) and the mother of Abimelech (9:1–4, 18). These three women were mothers of Judges in Israel. They had the respect of those who served under their sons.[42]

THE SONG OF HANNAH

Scholars maintained that Hannah's song of praise is secondary in its present context and was added to the birth story of Samuel (1 Sam 2:1–10).[43] This song cannot be earlier than the monarchic period, since verse 10 speaks of "His king" and "His anointed one," which points to a monarchic setting. In addition, there is no link between Hannah's situation, which is described in chapter 1 and this song, except for verse 5, which speaks of the barren woman who bears seven. The sages of the Talmud and medieval commentators solve the difficulties in the text by maintaining that these were a series of prophecies regarding future miracles of salvation.

---

41. *Ket.* 60a.

42. Wills, "Cultic Elements," 60.

43. Wellhausen, *Der Text der Bücher Samuelis*, 42; Smith, *Critical and Exegetical Commentary*, 14; Hertzberg, *I & II Samuel*, 29; Mauchline, *1 and 2 Samuel*, 50; McCarter, *I Samuel*, 75.

"Hannah was a prophetess, as it is written: "And Hannah prayed and said, my heart rejoices in the Lord, my horn is exalted in the Lord (1 Sam 2:1), and her words were prophecy, in that she said: 'My horn is exalted,' and not, 'My pitcher is exalted.' With regard to David and Solomon, who were anointed with oil from a horn, their kingship continued; whereas with regard to Saul and Jehu, who were anointed with oil from a pitcher, their kingship did not continue. This demonstrates that Hannah was a prophetess, as she prophesied that only those anointed with oil from a horn will merit that their kingships continue.[44]

"The antiquity of Hannah's song is also suggested by the type of the song, the poetic style and language and thought. Many expressions and views of the song of Hannah are found in earlier Hebrew poems.[45] It was proposed that this song belonged to the same category as the Song of the Sea (Exod 15:1–18), Oracles of Balaam (Num 23:7–10, 18–24; 24:3–9, 15–19, 20–24), Song of Deborah (Judg 5), Royal Psalm in 2 Samuel 22, Psalm 18, the Psalm of Habakkuk (Hab 3), and Psalms 29 and 68.[46] There is also similarity between the poetic style of this song and the style of Ugaritic epics and poems, including repetitive parallelism.

Hannah's song expresses faith in God's rule and providence; it is a prayer of thanksgiving and celebration of God giving a child to the barren Hannah. It was customary among the Israelites to thank and glorify God for a miracle that happened to them. As Moses and the Israelites sang a song and praised God for deliverance (Exod 15:2, 6–7, 9) so too did Hannah. Her prayer is part of the Israelite literary epic, like the Song of the Sea (Exod 15:1–18) and the Song of Deborah (Judg 5:2–31). What these songs have in common is that they refer to the present and to future events.[47] However, the person who sang the song was not an eyewitness to the

---

44. *Meg.* 14a.

45. Willis, "Song of Hannah," 140–50.

46. On Exod 15:1–18: Cross and Freedman, "Song of Miriam," 237–50; Coats, "Song of the Sea," 1–17. On Num 23:7–10: Albright, "Oracles of Balaam," 207–33. On Deut 32:1–43: Albright, "Some Remarks," 339–46. On Judg 5: Albright, "Song of Deborah," 26–31; Gerleman, "Song of Deborah," 168–80. On Hab 3: Albright, "Psalm of Habakkuk," 1–18. On 2 Sam 22, Ps 18: Cross and Freedman, "Royal Song," 15–34. On Ps 68: Albright, " Catalogue," 1–39. On Ps 29: Cross, "Notes on a Canaanite Psalm," 19–21; Freedman, "Archaic Forms," 101–07.

47. The building of the temple is already mentioned in the Song on the Sea (Exod 15:17).

narrated events.[48] The first two verses of Hannah's prayer refer to Hannah's current situation and allude to her previous situation (1 Sam 1:6–7). Important events in Samuel's life, such as victory against the Philistines (2:4–5), are mentioned and later described in detail in 7:13. She started to praise God by saying: "There is no holy one like the Lord, Truly, there is none beside You; There is no rock like our God" (2:2). And she ended the poem declaring that God would vanquish foes and that "He will give power to His king" (2:10); this alludes to the coronation of David by Samuel.

Based on the last verse, "And he will give strength unto his king and exalt the horn of his anointed" (verse 10), there are scholars who suggest that Hannah's song is late and was composed during the first generation of the monarchic period; perhaps as early as the tenth or as late as the ninth century.[49] On the other hand, there are critics who maintain that the prayer was composed during the eleventh century BCE and that it is a promonarchic addition.[50] It's alluding to the future conflict about who shall rule in Israel, God or man, and gives us an answer: that it is God who will raise the anointed king. More than likely the song was originated in Ramah, Samuel's hometown. It was Samuel's disciples who composed the Song of Hannah and the stories about Samuel. The song comes to portray the pious nature of Samuel's mother and alludes to Samuel's victory against the Philistines (2:4–5), which is mentioned again later (7:13). By mentioning "his king" and "his anointed one" the aim was to prepare the reader for Samuel's roles in the next chapters as a leader and his part as a kingmaker of the Davidic dynasty.

SERVICE IN SHILOH

Samuel's service in Shiloh starts with the declaration, "And the child did minster unto the Lord before Eli the priest" (1 Sam 2:11b). In other words, he was under the care and guidance of Eli. The verse serves as a transition between the story of Elkanah's family and the story of Eli's family. Verses 12–17 describe the behavior and activities of Hophni and Phinehas, contrasting them to Samuel. They were wicked and did not know or obey

---

48. Deborah was not present at the killing of Sisera (Judg 5:24–27), and to the conversation between Sisera's mother and the wisest of her ladies.

49. Wright, "Lawsuit of God," 57–58; McCarter, *I Samuel*, 74–76.

50. Willis, "Song of Hannah," 139–54; Freedman, "Psalm 113," 56–69; Lewis, "Textual History," 18–46.

YHWH (verse 12) and were disrespectful to people. Their bad-mannered behavior was exemplified by their neglect of the Deuteronomistic law concerning sacrifice (Deut 18:3).[51] They were taking the priestly share of the fellowship offerings "before the fat was burned," in other words, before the Lord had been given his portion (Lev 3:3–5; 7:30). They treated the sacrifices and offerings to the Lord impiously, a theme that repeats itself in the description of their deeds (1 Sam 2:13, 17), and in the message of doom by the man of God to Eli (verse 29), and later in God's revelation to Samuel in chapter 3:14. Worshipers protested their practice and offered them to select any portion of the meat after the fat had been burned. However, they refused and threatened to use force to get their way. The narrator ends this description by stating that this behavior was a great sin in the eyes of the Lord. It is notable that their names are not mentioned in verses 12–17, the sons of Eli are called נערים, young men; this evidently came to show the difference between them and Samuel, who is called נער, na'ar, young man (1 Sam 2:11, 18, 26).

The contrast between Eli's sons and Samuel (verses 18–21) is a central theme in the development of the story. The house of Eli is in decline, while Samuel grows in stature. The narrator switches from Samuel to the house of Eli, back and forth, and by that stresses the differences between them (verses 11–19). The description of the sons of Eli and Samuel ministering at the temple in Shiloh further accentuates the difference between them. There is an idyllic description of Samuel's service in the temple, which is in sharp contrast to the previous description of the sons of Eli. At first, we read about Samuel: "and the boy entered the service of the Lord under priest Eli" (verse 11b), while in verse 18 we read that "Samuel was engaged in the service of the Lord as an attendant." Here he is ministering before the Lord without the aid of Eli, and the narrator stresses the fact that Samuel had a direct relationship with God. This would be manifested clearly in chapter 3, where Samuel would receive direct revelation from God. Samuel's name is mentioned for the first time as he is serving the Lord (verse 18). This probably came to avoid misunderstanding and confusion with the priest's

---

51. According to the priestly legislation the clergy were to receive the breast and the right thigh of sacrificial animals (Lev 7:28–36) only after God's share of the offering, that is, the fatty parts had been burned on the altar. The fat was offered as a burnt offering to God (Exod 23:18; 29:13; Lev 3:3–5). It was burned as "an aroma pleasing to the Lord" (Lev 3:5). At the same time, the book of Deuteronomy specifies that the priests were to receive the shoulder, the two cheeks, and inner parts of the bull or sheep (Deut 18:3).

servant in verse 11 (Samuel) and with the priest's servant of verses 13–17 (Sons of Eli).

Following the description of the corruption of the Elides, Samuel's family is back for its annual visit to Shiloh for the fourth time (1 Sam 1:3, 21, 24; 2:19). Samuel's service in Shiloh is illustrated by wearing a linen ephod. This was a short garment with linen secured around the waist by a girdle.[52] In addition, Hannah, Samuel's mother, made him a little robe, מְעִיל, *meʿîl*, a new outer garment. This kind was worn by people of rank or special status. It has been suggested that it was a special garment for a priest, like the Akkadian *tēlītu* garment.[53] The coat is one of the recognizable signs of Samuel as a prophet and of his dramatic encounters with Saul; it foreshadows future events. First, Saul will tear Samuel's robe (1 Sam 15:27), and then the witch of Endor will raise Samuel from his grave, describing him as wrapped in a robe (28:14). It is significant to note that this coat is a symbolic act that is also found in the stories of Ahijah (1 Kgs 11:29–31) and Elijah (2 Kgs 2:8, 12–14).[54]

On their annual visit to Shiloh to see Samuel and to offer yearly sacrifice, Eli blessed Elkanah and his wife. The family was blessed, and Hannah conceived and bore three sons and two daughters, a reversal of her barrenness which was mentioned in chapter 1 (verses 2, 5, 6; 2:5). The narrator uses here the idiom *pkd* "took note," which is also used in the Isaac story (Gen 21:1). In both cases, the infant born is a child of destiny. This blessing comes to show how important Samuel's service at the sanctuary was; it was his service which merited such a blessing. The passage ends with the statement that "Young Samuel meanwhile grew up in the service of the Lord" (1 Sam 2:21). The same verb *grew* was used with Moses (Exod 2:10). This probably refers to spiritual and moral development as well as physical growth. We should point out that verses 18–21 are a continuation of Hannah's story and seal it. As in chapter 1, there is mention of a blessing by Eli (1 Sam 1:17; 2:20); pregnancy and birth by Hannah (1:20; 2:21); and returning home (1:19; 2:11). There is also similarity in the usage of phrases such as "every year" (1:3; 2:19); "the annual sacrifice" (1:21; 2:19); and "grant you what you have asked for" (1:17, 27).[55]

---

52. Tidwell, "Linen Ephod," 505–07.
53. Hurowitz, "'Sun Disk,'" 367.
54. Fokkelman, *Narrative and Poetry*, 4:124n16.
55. Bar-Efrat, *I Samuel*, 69.

The chapter starts with Hannah's prayer (verses 1–10) at Shiloh and ends with Elkanah returning home and Samuel serving the Lord (verse 11). Samuel, Hannah, and Elkanah reappear again in verses 18–21 at the end of Hannah's story. Between these two sections there is a description of the ill-mannered behavior of Eli's sons (verses 12–17). By inserting the story of Eli's son's behavior at this juncture the narrator highlights the differences between Eli's sons, who failed to serve the Lord, and Samuel's deepening relationship with YHWH; Samuel serves the Lord faithfully.

To further highlight the contrast between Eli's sons and Samuel, the narrator inserted a passage which includes a rebuke by Eli of his sons' behavior (1 Sam 2:23–25). The passage is a continuous description of their sins (verses 12–17) and adds to it. Eli is very old; according to 1 Samuel 4:15, he was ninety-eight. This probably prevented him from serving at the sanctuary and led to the sinful acts of his sons. The sins of Eli's sons and his old age are alluded to in the prophecy by the man of God: "A time is coming when I will break your power and that of your father's house, and there shall be no elder in your house" (verse 31). Later it also appears in the description of Eli's death: "He broke his neck and died; for he was an old man and heavy" (4:18).

According to the text the sons of Eli were sleeping with the women who were serving at the entrance of the Tent of Meetings. Sleeping with the women may indicate the Canaanite practice of sacred prostitution at this shrine,[56] or it is possible that the sons were taking sexual advantage of the women who came to sacrifice.[57] In his rebuke Eli did not mention their actual acts nor did the man of God. Instead, Eli said: "Why do you do such things? as I get evil reports about you ... It is no favorable report I hear" (2:22–24). But they ignored their father's plea and continued to sin (verse 25). It appears that Eli was hesitant to rebuke his sons; he did not mention the nature of their sins and referred to it as evil rumors that were spread by other people.

Showing further the difference between the sons of Eli and Samuel's growth in stature, the text repeatedly says: "Samuel was engaged in the service of the Lord" (2:18) "Young Samuel meanwhile grew up in the service of the Lord" (2:21); "Young Samuel, meanwhile, grew in esteem and favor both with God and with men" (1 Sam 2:26). Samuel's service to the Lord is also repeated in chapter 3, pointing to the links between the chapters.

56. Ackroyd, *First Book of Samuel*, 36
57. Josephus, *Ant.* 5.10.1.

Chapter 3 starts with the announcement: "Young Samuel was in the service of the Lord under Eli," and at the end of the theophany "Samuel grew up and the Lord was with him" (verse 19). This recurrence has one purpose: to show that it is Samuel who would be Eli's successor. Samuel received divine approval, while the sons of Eli were condemned to death.

In conclusion, the stories of Samuel's birth and youth in Shiloh, Eli the priest versus Hannah, the behavior of Eli's sons versus that of Samuel, and Hannah's prayer, which appear in the first two chapters of the book of Samuel, were combined into one story. Their aim was to describe the decline of the Shilonite priesthood and the rise of Samuel to prominence. Samuel is a person who serves the Lord righteously, in contrast to the sons of Eli, who are sinners. There is an idyllic description of Samuel's service in the temple; the Lord was with him. In contrast, the sons of Eli were wicked and did not obey YHWH and were disrespectful to people. Their behavior was a grievous sin in the eyes of the Lord. To further diminish the image of the Elide priesthood the narrator contrasts Samuel's pious parents with Eli. Hannah prays to God in the temple, and Eli, who sees but does not comprehend the situation, rebukes her. He hurries to criticize Hannah and refers to her as a daughter of Belial; on the other hand, does not see his own sons like sons of Belial. This comparison diminishes his image. The contrast between the priestly family and Samuel is the central theme to the development of the story. It serves as a background to the ensuing events, which culminate with God's revelation to Samuel in chapter 3. In addition, it also foreshadows future events, which include the death of Hopni and Phinehas, the death of Eli, and the loss of the sacred ark in the war against the Philistines (1 Sam 4). All these events led to the growth of Samuel as a loyal servant to the Lord. This growth in Samuel's stature will be the subject of our next chapter, which examines the nature of the message that Samuel received at Shiloh from God; a theophany where Samuel became a trustworthy prophet of the Lord.

2

God's Appearance to Samuel
(1 Samuel 3)

THE THEME OF SAMUEL serving the Lord (1 Sam 2:11, 18) continues in chapter 3. The chapter begins with, "Young Samuel was in the service of the Lord under Eli" (3:1) and ends with, "Samuel grew up and the Lord was with him: He did not leave any of Samuel's prediction unfulfilled" (verse 21). This declaration points to the growth and development of the relationship between Samuel and God which manifested itself in a special divine revelation to Samuel. It is the first direct encounter between Samuel and God which shows Samuel's exclusive relationship with God and highlights his rise as a prophet. Samuel was laying down to sleep in the temple when God called him. This call to Samuel was repeated three times, and each time Samuel ran to Eli, because he thought that it was Eli who called him. Only after three times did Eli realize that it was God who called Samuel. The priest instructed Samuel how to respond to the next call. The call to Samuel was repeated for the fourth time, and this time, Samuel replied by saying: "Speak, for Your servant is listening" (verse 10). Scholars are divided as to the nature of this theophany and compare it with "call" narratives of other Old Testament prophets. Newman, for example, refers to Samuel's experience as "a prophetic call narrative."[1] Gnuse, on the other hand, says that it is an "auditory message dream theophany."[2] In the current chapter the nature of God's theophany to Samuel will be examined. Was Samuel

---

1. Newman, "Prophetic Call," 86–97; Habel, "Form and Significance," 297–323; Long, "Prophetic Call Tradition," 494–500.

2. Gnuse, *Dream Theophany*, 119–57.

awake when God spoke to him, or was he asleep, and the message that he received was in the form of a dream? What was the content of God's message to Samuel? Was it a message which gave him the authority to speak for YHWH? We compare this message to the previous message of the man of God to Eli (2:27–36). The old priest received a message of doom first by the man of God and then a second one from Samuel; how close or different are these messages? Or was it Samuel who twice delivered the message to Eli (2:27–36; 3:11–14). In addition, we will examine the context of 1 Samuel 3 within the first three chapters of the book of Samuel to determine its place, origin, purpose, and theology.

GOD'S CALL TO SAMUEL

The story of God's appearance to Samuel in chapter 3 is the direct sequel to the first two chapters of the book. Samuel's birth, in the wake of his mother's prayer and vow at Shiloh (chapter 1), leads to his vocation as a spiritual leader in Israel, as do his growth and education in the sanctuary in chapter 2. Just as his mother consecrated him to the Lord, now the Lord consecrates him to his mission. Both consecrations take place in the sanctuary, with the theophany of chapter 3 elevating Samuel to the status of a prophet and announcing the disasters that will befall the house of Eli.

Although Samuel hears God's voice, he is different from other prophets, as many scholars have noted: the Lord does not impose a mission on him, nor instruct him as to what he must do in the future—details prominent in the consecrations of Isaiah, Jeremiah, and Ezekiel.[3] Accordingly, on the basis of a comparison with dreams from Mesopotamia, some have assigned chapter 3 to the genre in which a deity appears to an individual in a dream and only tells him what is going to happen without telling him what to do.[4]

The story has a clear setting; it starts with the declaration that "the word of the Lord was rare" (verse 1). But at the end of the theophany this is changed, when the Lord has revealed himself to Samuel "by the word of the Lord (verse 21). When the prophet Amos spoke about the coming

---

3. Isa 6; Jer 1:4–10; Ezek 1–3. Compare also the commissions to Moses (Exod 3), Gideon (Judg 6:11–17); and Jehu (2 Kgs 9:5–10). Some scholars, however, believe that the story is nevertheless a consecration to prophecy. See Elat, *Samuel*, 30, N. 76.

4. Elat, *Samuel*, 30; Gnuse, "Reconsideration," 379–90; Gnuse, *Dream Theophany*, 133–52.

God's Appearance to Samuel

judgment on Israel, he mentioned the lack of God's words: "Men shall wander from sea to sea and from north to east to seek the word of the Lord, but they shall not find it" (8:12). It is suggested that the scarcity of the word of the Lord is a sign of divine disfavor (Ps 74:9; Lam 2:9; Mic 3:6).[5] According to Josephus, Samuel completed his twelfth year when the word of the Lord came to him; he reached his religious maturity.[6] The main characters and their functions are mentioned in verse 1, with Samuel, Eli, and the Lord. Samuel is described as ministering Eli before God. This was mentioned already in the previous chapter (1 Sam 2:11, 18), and is repeated here to point to continual growth in the relationship between God and Samuel.

The account of the Lord's appearance to Samuel begins by marking the day of its occurrence, "one day" (verse 2). It was interpreted by Ralbag that it was when the prophet appeared to Eli. In other words, the message of destruction was repeated twice on the same day. In the Hebrew Bible repetition comes to stress a point: "As for Pharaoh having had the same dream twice; it means that the matter has been determined by God and that God will soon carry it out" (Gen 41:32). Another interpretation for "one day" suggests that it was "the memorable day which left such a deep mark upon Samuel's life."[7] On that day "Eli was asleep in his usual place; and his eyes had begun to fail, and he could barely see" (verse 2). This detail comes to explain why Samuel was sleeping close to the priest. He slept there to help the priest whose health had deteriorated, and he could not see. It also explains why Samuel thought that it was Eli who called him; he thought that the old priest needed his help. A similar description is mentioned with Isaac: "When Isaac was old, and his eyes were too dim to see" (Gen 27:1). The Hebrew Bible and other ancient Near Eastern texts describe the eyesight and other faculties as an indication of whether the person remained healthy or became feeble.[8] In contrast to Eli, we read of Moses that "his eyes were undimmed and his vigor unbated" (Deut 34:7). Through the description of Eli and Samuel the narrator highlights the differences between them. The old priest Eli has difficulties carrying out his duties; on the other hand, Samuel stays in the temple, ready to fulfill any assignment.

---

5. Tsumura, *First Book of Samuel*, 174.
6. Josephus, *Ant.* 5.10.4.
7. Kirkpatrick, *First Book of Samuel*, 64.
8. Willis, "Instruction," 412, line 10; Oppenheim, "Mother of Nabonisus," 561c.

In addition to the day and the hour, the setting is mentioned: "The lamp of God had not yet gone out" (1 Sam 3:3),[9] suggesting that the voice called to Samuel around daybreak (cf. verse 15, "Samuel lay there until morning."). The lamp is mentioned in order to explain why Samuel ran to Eli's couch: the voice that called came from inside the sanctuary of the Lord, which was lit up—but Samuel saw no one there. Thus, the narrator presents the background for the revelation, which is to take place next to the ark of the Lord, the very core of the priestly ritual.[10]

The ancients were gravely perplexed by the fact that Samuel was "lying down in the temple of the Lord (בהיכל) where the ark of God was."[11] How could a non-priest lie down in a holy place where only priests serve, and then only in an upright posture (see Deut 18:5)? Accordingly, some have taken the prepositional *bet* to mean not "in" but "next to" or "near" the sanctuary—a common usage.[12] Evidently Samuel was lying down in a chamber adjoining the sanctuary, from which it was possible to see the ark, the focus of divine revelation.[13] In Samuel 3, the word היכל, "sanctuary," refers to a structure that contains a number of rooms.[14] Samuel and Eli were not sleeping in the same room; later we also read that Samuel opened the doors of "the House of the Lord," as the sanctuary is called both here and in 1:7. In both Ugaritic literature and the Bible, the terms house (בית) and

---

9. The lamp here is evidently the candlestand on which the oil lamps were placed. In the Pentateuch, the candelabrum is also referred to as a "lamp" (Exod 27:20 and Lev 20:2). The lamp burned before the ark and was accordingly called the "lamp of God." In the Pentateuch, we find that the Israelites were commanded to keep a lamp burning before the Lord from evening to morning (Exod 27:11). The lighting of the lamp was considered to be a sacred ritual.

10. Amit, "Story of Samuel's Consecration," 31.

11. Batten, "Sanctuary at Shilo," 29–33. Batten believes that Samuel was sleeping where the ark was located and that he was a watchman, as Joshua had been. It should be remembered, however, that the verse notes that Samuel was lying down in the sanctuary. Within the sanctuary there were a number of rooms, since Samuel and Eli did not sleep in the same room, and, what is more, the text notes that it was a building with doors (3:15).

12 For example, "Abimelech ... encamped at [i.e., outside or near] Thebez (בתבץ)" (Judg 9:50); "Israel was encamping at [i.e., adjacent to] the spring (בעין) in Jezreel" (1 Sam 29:1).

13 Driver, *Notes on the Hebrew*, 42.

14. היכל is derived from the Akkadian *ekallu*, "palace," which is in turn a borrowing from the Sumerian *égal*, "large house." With this sense it is also found in Northwest Semitic, including both Ugaritic and Hebrew.

sanctuary (היכל) are frequently used interchangeably.[15] The fact that the ark of God stood in the Holy of Holies suggests that the voice that called to Samuel originated from the Holy of Holies.

The mention of the ark at this juncture has a special significance considering the following events, which are described in chapters 4–6.[16] It links the ark here to YHWH's message of doom. Samuel receives a message in the presence of a cultic object that will be part of the destructions of the Elides.[17]

The revelation itself builds up step by step. Three times the Lord calls Samuel. Three times Samuel thinks that it is Eli who is summoning him, goes to him, and states his willingness to do his bidding.[18] After the third time, Eli understands that it is the Lord who is speaking and tells Samuel how to reply. The text makes it clear that Samuel did not expect the Lord to appear to him, but some see the repeated summons as an artistic device meant to heighten the suspense. Be that as it may, here we have a contrast between the naiveté of the young Samuel and the slowness of Eli, who should have known that it was a divine revelation and should himself have been the object of the theophany.[19] Samuel finally responds to the Lord's summons by saying, "Here I am," the normal response in dreams (Gen 31:11 and 46:2), though it also is found in waking revelations (Gen 22:11).

The fourth time that the Lord calls Samuel, the author, unlike in the previous times, describes the appearance of the Lord: "The Lord came, and stood there" (1 Sam 3:10). In other words, the Lord came to the place where Samuel was lying down and appeared to him there,[20] calling to mind the Lord's appearance to Jacob in a dream at Bethel: "And the Lord was standing" (Gen 28:13). The image that God is standing alongside the dreamer is also found in extrabiblical sources.[21]

---

15. Cassuto, "Biblical Literature," 6.
16. Eslinger, *Kingship of God*, 149.
17. Eslinger, *Kingship of God*, 150.
18. Gnuse, *Dream Theophany*, 156, says that the threefold summons is a literary motif found in other cultures and offers a number of examples thereof.
19. There are many contrasts in this story: Eli, the blind priest, ultimately understands but does not see, while Samuel does not understand, but will eventually hear and see. Eli lies in his place and Samuel lies in the sanctuary. Samuel has not previously known the Lord, while the sons of Eli are described as not knowing the Lord (1 Sam 2:12).
20. So too with Moses: "The Lord came down in a cloud; He stood with him there and proclaimed the name Lord" (Exod 34:5).
21. Bar, *Letter*, 16n38–40.

For both Jacob and Samuel, the revelations come in holy places, Bethel and Shiloh. But in Samuel's case, "came" indicates that the Lord journeyed, as it were, from his sanctuary to the place where Samuel was lying. The verb "come" is also associated with dreams (Gen 20:3 and 31:24).²² "The Lord came, and stood there" may indicate that this time Samuel beheld an image in a prophetic vision; this is why the text reads "stood there (וַיִּתְיַצַּב)" as in the story of Balaam, when "an angel of the Lord placed himself (וַיִּתְיַצֵּב) in his way as an adversary" (Num 22:22) (thus Radak: cf. "The Lord came down in a cloud; He stood [וַיִּתְיַצֵּב] with him there" [Exod 34:5]). This time, Samuel does answer the Lord, but not in the terms Eli had told him to use: "If you are called again, say, Speak, Lord, for your servant is listening." (1 Sam 3:9). Samuel does not refer to the Lord by name. Radak comments that this was "because he was still afraid to mention the name in a prophetic vision." Rashi (Rabbi Solomon ben Isaac, 1040–1105), however, says that "[Samuel] said, 'Perhaps it is a different voice.'" Evidently Samuel found it difficult to digest the fact that the Lord was addressing him.

In Malamet's opinion, the fact that the Lord summoned Samuel four times on the same night is of great importance.²³ He refers to a dream from Mari (ARM XIII, no. 112), in which a deity appears to a lad in a dream and warns him against building a house. The lad does not tell anyone about the dream, and the next night the god appears in another dream with the same message. Malamat believes it was only after the dream was repeated that the lad became convinced of the divine origin of the message. In Samuel's theophany, the divine summons occurs three times during the same night before Samuel discloses the message to Eli. In both cases the repetition of the dream is intended, according to Malamat, to persuade the dreamer that it was authentic, given that both dreamers were young, had no prior experience of divine revelation, and were thus unable to evaluate it.

GOD'S MESSAGE TO SAMUEL

The Lord's message to Samuel relates to the future and to the fate of the house of Eli (verses 11–14).²⁴ The body of the prophecy begins with the

---

22. It should, however, be emphasized that both "come" and "stand" are associated with waking revelations; see, for example, Amos 7:7 and 9:1 and Exod 19:9.

23. Malamat, *Mari and the Bible*, 78–79.

24. This prophecy has already been delivered in 2:27–36. Here, however, the Lord reveals to Samuel the actual catastrophe that will befall the house of Eli.

God's Appearance to Samuel

announcement, "I am going to do in Israel..." (1 Sam 3:11). What he is going to do, however, is not made explicit until the next episode in chapter 4, which recounts the capture of the ark, the destruction of Shiloh, and the rout of the Israelites. The unfinished prophecy creates a sense of impending doom, but we are merely told that the doom is so intense that "both ears of anyone who hears (שמע) about it will tingle"—a picturesque image for the gravity of the catastrophe. Later prophets employ the same verb about the destruction of the First Temple (2 Kgs 21:12, Jer 19:3).[25]

The usage of the verb "to hear" (שמע) connects the punishment with the sin in chapters 2–4. In 1 Sam 2:22–24 the verb appears five times: "And Eli was very old, and he *heard* everything his sons did... and he said to them, 'Why do you do such thing as I *hear* of... no, my sons, for it is not a good rumor [lit. "hearing"] which I *hear*...'" In the following verse we are told that the sons "they ignored [lit. "hear"] their father's plea." The divine punishment which was revealed to Samuel uses the same language: "I am going to do in Israel such a thing that both ears of anyone who *hears* about it will tingle" (3:11). The verb is also found in chapter 4 in the description of the punishment: "And when Eli *heard* the sound of outcry" (4:14); and "His daughter-in-law, the wife of Phinehas, was with child about to give birth. When she heard the report [lit. "hear"] that the ark of God was captured, and her father-in-law and her husband were dead..." (verse 19).

Eli's sin was that, despite his knowledge of his sons' misdeeds, he did not deter or hinder them.[26] As Radak wrote, "Even though he [admonished] his sons, this was when he was old, and they were not afraid of him. But when they began their misdeeds and he could have prevented them and argued with them forcefully, he did not do so." According to verse 13 Eli did not rebuke (כָּהָה) them. This term appears as a preface to the revelation: "One day, Eli was asleep in his usual place; his eyes had begun to fail (כֵּהוֹת)

---

25. It has been pointed out that the message has typical Deuteronomistic elements. McCarter pointed out that language such as "all they hear, their ears will ring" is parallel to verses in 2 Kings 21:12 and Jeramiah 19:3. The language "I will fulfill all that I have said" is found in 1 Kings 2:4. There are words such as *bēt* and *'ôlām* which are distinctly Deuteronomistic. McCarter, *1 Samuel*, 98.

26. The misdeeds of Eli's sons are described as "his sons cursed themselves" (1 Sam 3:13). The classical exegetes understood "themselves" to be a scribal emendation introduced out of respect for the Lord, instead of the original "cursed Him." According to Rashi, "what should have been written is 'they curse Me'; but the text was amended out of respect for the Almighty." Another possibility is מקללים, "curse," should be understood in the sense of מקילים, "make light of"; in other words, they did not actually curse God, but treated him with disdain. As Rashi wrote, "Every curse signifies disrespect and disdain."

and he could barely see" (verse 2). Although there is a change of meaning, the use of the homonym creates a link between the Eli's sin and his physical situation.[27] This further stresses the sins of Eli and gives justification for Samuel receiving a prophecy of doom against the house of Eli. The prophecy concludes with an oath phrased in the negative. Even the sacrifices and meal-offerings that normally atone for sins against God will be of no avail; they cannot atone for the iniquity of the house of Eli. Some view this as measure for measure, since Hophni and Phineas were priests who offered sacrifices and meal-offerings.[28]

This prophecy, although brief, is crucial, because it is addressed by the Lord to Samuel and highlights his rise as a prophet. The prophecy also serves as the introduction to the next chapter, which recounts the Philistines' capture of the ark of the Lord, as well as the deaths of the sons of Eli—and of Eli himself. In contrast to other prophets, Samuel did not receive a mission. Samuel received a revelation: he heard God's voice, which made him a prophet. There is no description of what Samuel saw, only what he heard.

Following the revelation, Samuel laid down until the morning and then opened the doors of YHWH's house. He was not instructed by God to deliver the message to Eli; actually he was afraid to tell him the vision. It was Eli who encouraged Samuel to tell all. Eli refers to Samuel fondly as "my son," and the latter replies, quickly and modestly, "Here I am." Eli asked Samuel: "Keep nothing from me. Thus, and more may God do to you" (verse 17). The words "Thus and more may God do to you," are an adjuration, in which "thus" stands for some evil that is stated explicitly elsewhere. Over time, oath-takers tended to omit the curse and retain only this formula. The idiom appears only in the books of Samuel, Kings, and Ruth.[29] Samuel does tell Eli everything the Lord had said to him. Eli responds, "He is the Lord; He will do what He deems right" (verse 18)—that is, Eli accepts the divine decree against himself and his house and does not question the Lord's justice.[30] Hence the section begins with *do*—"I am going to *do* in

27. Garsiel, *First Book of Samuel*, 60.

28. Radak: "He said this because they were priests who offered sacrifices and meal-offerings; that is, their priesthood will avail them nothing before Me. This punishment is measure for measure: they sinned by dishonoring the offerings, and their punishment is to have no atonement through offerings."

29. 1 Sam 14:44; 20:13; 25:22; 2 Sam 3:9, 35; 19:14; 1 Kgs 2:23; 19:2; 20:10; 2 Kgs 6:31; Ruth 1:17.

30. David says something similar: "I am ready; let Him do with me as He pleases" (2

Israel such a thing" (verse 11)—and ends with *do*: "He will *do* what He deems right." The conclusion indicates Eli's faith in the Lord and Samuel's devotion and loyalty to Eli.

THE MESSAGE OF THE MAN OF GOD

The message of doom on the house of Eli appears in the previous chapter (1 Sam 2:27–36). It is not announced directly to Eli by God; it is delivered through an unnamed man of God that foretells judgment on the Shilonite priesthood. The prophecy serves as theological explanation for the rejection of the Elide priesthood, and it contains three parts. The first part of the prophecy refers to the past; it mentions God's revelation to Eli's ancestors and their election to serve as priests (verses 27–28). The second part deals with the present; it speaks of the abuse of cultic responsibility by the Elides (verse 29). The third part discusses the future; it is a declaration of doom. God would revoke his promise to the Elide for perpetual priesthood, and instead he would establish a new priesthood (verses 30–36).

Westermann has pointed out that 1 Samuel 2:27–36 is an early and simple form of a prophetic judgment speech to an individual person. He identified several components that are typical to this form of speech, which includes 1. Commission of the messenger, 2. Summons to hear (verse 27), 3. Accusation (verse 29), 4. Messenger formula (verse 30), 5. Announcement (30–36).[31] All elements that Westermann pointed out are found in our text, except the commissioning of the messenger.

The person who delivered the prophecy to Eli is referred to as the man of God. He reports the message from God by the opening formula: "Thus says YHWH." In the book of Samuel this formula appears several times (1 Sam 2:27; 10:18; 15:2; 2 Sam 7:5, 8; 12:7, 11; 24:12) and is typical of later prophetic speeches. It was customary for the messenger to repeat the message that he received verbatim. The message recounts the history of Eli's ancestry, stressing its unique status of priesthood. It links the start of the priesthood leadership to the time of the enslavement in Egypt without mentioning Moses and Aaron. This is the earliest reference of the Israelites' sojourn in Egypt in the Prophets and Writings excluding the Torah.

As a branch of Aaron's priesthood, Eli's house was supposed to serve as priests to God forever (Exod 39:9). But because they did not honor God,

---

Sam 15:26). See also 2 Kgs 20:19 and Isa 39:8.

31. Westermann, *Basic Forms*, 129–68.

they were going to lose this privilege. Eli is criticized for not preventing his sons from abusing the sacrificial worship. The sons of Eli took more than their share of God's sacrifice and offerings. According to Radak, Eli is also rebuked because, unavoidably, he himself ate with his sons. In addition, Eli is also blamed because "You have *honored* [*tekabed*-תכבד] your sons more than Me" (1 Sam 2:29). The root *kbd* (כבד) which appears here is repeated at the announcement of the punishment: "For I *honor* those who *honor* Me, but those who spurn Me shall be *dishonored*" (verse 30). Garsiel pointed out that the root *kbd* also means "weighty, heavy," which creates a link between Eli's sin and punishment.[32] Upon receiving the news from the battlefield, "[Eli] fell backward off the seat beside the gate, broke his neck and died; for he was an old man and heavy [*kbd*-כבד] (4:18). When his daughter-in-law, the wife of Phinehas, heard about the capture of the ark and that her father-in-law and husband were dead, she named her born son Ichabod (אי-כבוד) literally meaning "no honor." "The glory departed from Israel," which is repeated in verses 21–22.

The house of Eli would be destroyed; none of its members would attain an *old age* (verse 31). This is repeated in the following verse: "But there shall never be an *elder* in your house" (verse 32). Tsevat viewed this punishment as *karet,* which is premature death at the hand of God.[33] Eli's old age, which was mentioned already, "Now Eli was *very old*" (verse 22), is one of the reasons that prevented him from harshly criticizing his sons. By mentioning it, the narrator creates a linkage between Eli's old age and the punishment which is described in chapter 4: "[Eli] fell backward off the seat beside the gate, broke his neck and died; for he was *an old man* and heavy" (verse 18), thus fulfilling part of the prophecy.

The fulfillment of the other part of this oracle would take place with the massacre of the priests of Nob by King Saul (1 Sam 22:11–23) and the expulsion of Abiathar, who was one of David's two high priests. Later he was removed from his priestly office by Solomon for supporting Adonijah's quest for the throne (1 Kgs 2:27). Eli would not see these calamities but would live to hear about the death of his two sons, Hophni and Phinehas, as a sign of things to come. There is no mention of the loss of the ark, which was a major shock to Eli, nor to the death of Eli himself, although it is alluded to. The message of the man of God still contains a positive note with the announcement of the establishment of faithful priest. At first, we might

---

32. Garsiel, *First Book of Samuel*, 61.
33. Tsevat, "Studies," 191–216.

think that it refers to Samuel who seems to be the successor to the house of Eli and is described as a *faithful* prophet (1 Sam 3:20).[34] But the text mentions *faithful* priests which implies the Zadokite priesthood. The Zadokite family held the High Priesthood from the time of King Solomon until the destruction of the temple. The prophecy ends with a negative description of the survivors of Eli's house as performing lowly chores for the Zadokites. They are portrayed in the text as beggars who ask for favors from those who displaced them. According to Ralbag, this is a fitting punishment because before they were greedy, taking more than their rightful share of sacrificial meat.

There are scholars who suggest that the message of the man of God is a later insertion into the text by the Deuteronomist which represents theological explanations to the events which have been described.[35] Others maintain that there are several additions (verses 35–36) which are an attempt of a later author to explain certain circumstances of their times.[36] Examination of the prophecy points to the existence of early elements in the message. Therefore, it does not mention the capture of the ark and the defeat at Aphek; it is only referring to the death of Hophni and Phinehas. Also missing is the killing of the priests of Nob by Saul. There is a glorification of the house of Eli when they were subject to the house of Pharaoh. This kind of glorification would not appear in a later period. On the other hand, the description of the survivors of the house of Eli who would seek favors from those who displaced them suits the time of the united monarchy. In other words, what we have here is a prophecy that contains ancient elements from the time of Eli that was transmitted and edited during the time of united monarchy no later than Solomon's era after the expulsion of Abiathar the priest from Jerusalem.[37]

---

34. For a different view see Leuchter, "Something Old."

35. Smith, *Critical and Exigetical Commentary*, 21; Hertzberg, *I & II Samuel*, 37; de Ward, "Eli's Rhetorical Question," 117; McCarter, *I Samuel*, 92; Brettler, "Composition," 601–12.

36. Press, "Der Prophet Samuel," 187; Tsevat, "Studies," 195; Mauchline, *1 and 2 Samuel*, 54; Miller and Roberts, *Hand*, 21, 30.

37. Rendsburg maintains that 1 Samuel 1–2 is a composition of a single author, as there is no evidence of an exilic editor. It is a northern composition; it was the tribe of Ephraim that told and preserved the story of Samuel and Eli, centered on the cultic site of Shiloh. SeeRendsburg, "Some False Leads," 43, 45.

Samuel

SAMUEL'S PROPHECY VERSUS THE MAN OF GOD'S PROPHECY

The repetition of God's message to Samuel is part of the narrator's gradual revelation of Gods rejections of the house of Eli.[38] Samuel received a direct message from God, while Eli received a message of doom through an unnamed man of God. The message to Samuel appears in abbreviated form. God repeats the verdict on the house of Eli. God confirmed what he had said already, which is judgment on the house of Eli "from the beginning to end" (1 Sam 3:12). According to Rashi, the prophecy is fulfilled completely beginning with the death of Eli's sons and continuing with the whole prophecy of doom is fulfilled. The judgment is forever, and there is no anticipation of repentance; it is final. Typically the sins of priests could be expiated by special offering, but this is not the case here.[39] Eli is admonished for not rebuking his sons but reading the text shows otherwise; he did rebuke them (2:23–25). Eli's house would suffer endless punishment (עַד עוֹלָם) which is repeated twice (1 Sam 3:13–14). This statement is linked to the previous message by the man of God (2:30); however, in that prophecy the descendants of Eli were supposed to remain in Gods' service forever (עַד עוֹלָם). Eli did not react to the devastating oracle by the man of God. In contrast, after hearing Samuel's message Eli responded by saying, "He is the Lord; He will do what He deems right" (verse 18). Eli accepts the divine decree against himself and his house and does not question the Lord's justice.

The prophecy is shorter in length; nevertheless it adds some detail to the previous prophecy by the man of God. The prophecy stresses the fact that the calamity is near. It serves as introduction to the battle of Eben-Ezer where the sons of Eli died and after which Eli himself died upon hearing of the loss of the ark on the battlefield. There is also a hint that the catastrophe will hit Israel, and its fulfillment is found in the next chapter. The prophecy serves as a link between chapters 1–3 to 4–6. But above all the repetition of the message of doom to Samuel by God came to establish him as a trustworthy prophet of the Lord (1 Sam 3:20).

There are scholars who suggest that the prophecy by the man of God in 2:27–36 is a prophecy that was delivered by Samuel and is a doublet for

---

38. Polzin, *Samuel*, 51.

39. In the Talmud however, we find a contrary view that their sins can be expiated by Torah and charitable deeds. See *Roš Haš* 18a.

all chapter 3.⁴⁰ Leuchter maintains that the anonymous man of God serves as a rhetorical substitute for Samuel that was created by DtrH. The text of 1 Samuel 2:27–36 points to two key stages: first Ephraimite composition that established Samuel as the primary religious figure at Shiloh, and a later Dtr stratum that changed the earlier material to relate to the rise of the Zadokites (as per 1 Kgs 2:26–27). 1 Sam 3:11–18 contains a prophetic revelation which is similar in purpose to that of 2:27–36 in its pre-Dtr form. Therefore, "The placement of Samuel's oracle into the mouth of a rhetorical literary figure, cast in the image of the person who first spoke it, allowed for both early tradition and later meaning to find an equal voice in the text."[41]

Examination of the prophecies reveals that although there are similarities between them there are also major differences. The first prophecy's main subject is the priestly house of Eli, its history, and its future. The second prophecy comes to establish Samuel as a loyal prophet to the Lord, which is not the case in chapter 2. Indeed, most of the material in chapters 1–3 deals with Samuel's growth as a loyal servant to the Lord, which culminates with him becoming a trustworthy prophet of the Lord. Therefore, the call to Samuel was placed after the prophecy on the house of Eli to show that the events of chapter 3 are the fulfilment of chapter 2 which are linked to it, the decline of the Elides and the rise of Samuel.

THE NATURE OF THE THEOPHANY

Some compare the Lord's appearance to Samuel with the inscription of Sargon recounting his biography before he became the king of Akkad, when he served Uzrababa, the king of Kish.[42] That inscription describes Sargon's dream, which is similar in many ways to Samuel's theophany.[43] The deity

---

40. Press, "Der Prophet Samuel," 187–89.
41. Leuchter "Something Old."
42. Elat, *Samuel*, 30–31.
43. 12 *At that time, the cupbearer, in the temple of Ezinu,*
    13 *Sargon, lay down not to sleep, buy lay down to dream.*
    14 *Holy Inana, in the dream, was drowning him [Urzababa] in a river of blood.*
    15 *Sargon, screaming, gnawed the ground.*
    16 *When King Urzababa heard those screams,*
    17 *He had them bring him [Sargon] into the king's presence.*
    18 *Sargon, come into the presence of Urzababa, (who said):*
    19 *"O cupbearer, was a dream revealed to you in the night?"*
    20 *Sargon replied to his king:*

informs Sargon of the impending doom of his master. Both Sargon and Samuel serve in a temple and experience their dreams there. Both react with fear, and as a result both masters become aware of the theophanies. Although both revelations announce the end of the reigns of the ruler whom they serve—and the rulers press the servitors to learn the content of the revelations—a major difference between the two is that Eli submits to the decree while Uzrababa endeavors to get rid of Sargon, who threatens his position.

Whatever the literary analysis of Samuel's theophany, the question remains whether this revelation in a vision is the same as a revelation in a dream. Did Samuel dream while he was sleeping? Or was this a waking epiphany? Those who hold the second option maintain that he must have been awake, since each time he heard the voice calling him he ran to Eli. Furthermore, he engages in a dialogue with the Lord and the word *dream* does not appear in the text.[44] On the other hand, the latter omission is irrelevant if all the indications of dreams are present. In addition, a colloquy between the dreamer and the deity is found in both Abimelech's and Solomon's dreams. As for Samuel's running to Eli, it can be argued that he kept waking up to do so and then fell asleep again.

Some scholars do believe that Samuel's was a dream theophany.[45] Hertzberg, for example, notes the verb שכב, "lie down," which he believes connotes sleep.[46] The text says that Samuel was lying down each time the Lord called him (verses 3, 5, and 9)–and the root ש.כ.ב. appears seven times in the story. Even after he receives the oracle, we read that Samuel lay there until the morning (verse 15). Hence it may be that he fell asleep after the Lord called him by name and that the revelation took place while

---

21 "O my king, this is my dream which I will have told you about:
22 There was a single young woman, she was high as the heavens, she was broad as the earth,
23 She was firmly set as the [bas]e of a wall.
24 For me, she drowned you in a great [river], a river of blood."
25 [. . .] U[rzab]aba chewed his lips, became seriously afraid.
See translation: Cooper and Heimpel, "Sumerian," 77.

44. Smith, *Critical and Exegetical Commentary*, 27; Mauchline, *1 and 2 Samuel*, 59; Resch, *Der Traum*, 111–12; Amit, "Samuel's Consecration," 342.

45. Ehrlich, *Traum*, 47; Brockington, "Audition in the OT," 5n2; Gnuse, *Dream*, 140–52; Oppenheim, *Interpretation*, 188–90.

46. There is ample evidence of this. See 1 Sam 26:5, 7; 2 Sam 4:5, 7; 11:9, 13.

God's Appearance to Samuel

he was asleep.⁴⁷ It should be noted that שכב occurs twice in the account of Jacob's dream at Bethel: before the revelation—"He lay down in that place" (Gen 28:11)—and then in the Lord's promise to Jacob—"the ground on which you are lying" (Gen 28:13). On the other hand, one can argue that שכב does not necessarily indicate sleep, and that Samuel was recumbent but fully awake during the revelation. Similarly, Samuel's repetition of the response that Eli had dictated to him calls into question the idea that this is a dream. It is implausible for a person who receives instruction when awake to repeat them precisely when asleep.⁴⁸ On the other hand, as noted previously, Samuel does modify what Eli told him to say.

Some say that the fact that Samuel was lying down in the sanctuary of the Lord indicates that this was an incubation dream.⁴⁹ In the ancient Near East, one way to try to receive a divine message in a dream involved going to a place deemed sacred and sleeping there. Here, though, Samuel did not go to the sanctuary; he lived there,⁵⁰ by virtue of his assigned task, which was to guard the sacred place. Moreover, the text does not describe any preparations for an incubation. Indeed, Samuel is quite astonished each time God calls him and thinks that it is Eli who is summoning him.⁵¹ At the same time, Eli does not originally comprehend that it is the Lord who is calling the lad. Hence, we must reject the opinion that this is an intentional incubation.⁵²

Another element found here that some associate with dreams is the divine summons to the dreamer. In our text, Samuel is called three times: Jacob, too is called in his dream (Gen 31:11), and again when God appears to him in a vision by night (46:2). In extrabiblical sources, too, the deity calls the dreamer by name. Oppenheim cites a text in which the priest of the goddess Ishtar of Arbela was sleeping, only to be awakened, like Samuel: "He woke up with a start and Ishtar made him see a nocturnal

---

47. Hertzberg, *I & II Samuel*, 42.

48. McAlpine, *Sleep*, 61–62; Resch, *Traum*, 112.

49. Eichrodt, *Theology*, 1:105; Jirku, "Ein Fall," 153; Gaster, *Thespis*, 271; Kraus, *Worship in Israel*, 110, 175.

50. Smith, *Critical and Exegetical Commentar*, 27–28, says that this is not an incubation but something quite similar.

51. Klein, *1 Samuel*, 32.

52. Ehrlich, *Traum*, 45–48. According to him, only 1 Kings 3:4 contains legitimate references to incubation rites; Gaster, "Dreams," 6:208, rejected the idea of incubation; Smith, *Critical and Exegetical Commentar*, 27–28; Klein, *1 Samuel*, 32.

vision."[53] According to Oppenheim, the summons by name had a single objective, which was to prepare Samuel for God's appearance to him in a dream.[54] He understands the experience of the priest of Ishtar in the same fashion.[55] Oppenheim also refers to the motif of wakefulness, also found in the Greek world, where gods would address the sleeper and ask him, "Are you asleep?"[56]

Accordingly, Oppenheim believed that the dream is "a *sui generis* state of consciousness, a hovering between the eclipse of sleep and the stark but dull reality of the day."[57] To buttress his view, he cites the Egyptian word *rśwt*, "dream," which is not only etymologically connected with a root meaning "to be awake," but is also written with the determinative representing an opened eye. Oppenheim thus believes that there was an element of wakefulness in dreams. Gnuse, who follows Oppenheim, asks: "Is the dreamer awake, semi-conscious, or asleep and yet dreaming that he is conscious? This is unanswerable, but we cannot exclude these experiences from the category of dream because the recipients seem awake, as some commentators do with the Samuel experience."[58]

To summarize, the description of the revelation is linguistically identical to the description of God's appearance in dreams, and the message relates to the future. It is a personal message in addition to a judgment message of the Shilonite priesthood. Samuel's reaction to the theophany is like other reactions to dreams in the Bible. The message of doom that Samuel received from God is an abbreviated form of the message that the man of God delivered to Eli. The messages serve different purposes. The first one by the man of God; its main subject is the priestly house of Eli, its history, and its future. The second one that is delivered to Samuel comes to establish Samuel as a trustworthy prophet of the Lord. Both predicted the calamity that the house of Eli would suffer. The narrator placed Samuel's call after the prophecy on the house of Eli, to show that the events of chapter 3 are the fulfilment of chapter 2 and are linked to it. The repetition of the message

53. Pfeifer, "Akkadian Oracles," 451; Oppenheim, *Interpretation*, 249.

54. Oppenheim, *Interpretation*, 190.

55. In Akkadian, the revelation is called *tabrīt mūši* and is translated as "nocturnal vision." Oppenheim says that one must be careful when translating this phrase and that it may be a poetic idiom for "dream." The precise meaning, however, remains unclear. See Oppenheim, *Interpretation*, 201, 205.

56. Oppenheim, *Interpretation*, 189.

57. Oppenheim, *Interpretation*, 190.

58. Gnuse, *Dream Theophany*, 145.

of doom to Samuel came to stress that the catastrophe was near. Samuel started the chapter in the service of the Lord under Eli (verse 1) and ends as a prophet (verses 20–21). From now on he would deliver God's words and lead the Israelites. Since Samuel is described as a trustworthy prophet of the Lord in the next chapter, we will examine the roll that Samuel played in gathering all Israel at Mizpah, leading them in a fight against the Philistines and judging Israel all his life.

3

The Assembly at Mizpah

FOR THE FIRST TIME after God's revelation to Samuel in Shiloh, Samuel is back and takes a role in leading all the house of Israel (1 Sam 7:3).[1] Samuel disappeared from the public eye; he is last mentioned in chapter 4, "And the word of Samuel came to all Israel"(4:1). In the following chapters (4:1b–7) the ark was lost and so too the religious leadership. So where was Samuel during this period of national crisis? It is suggested that chapters 4:1b–7 are an independent ark story, a distinct unit within the larger Deuteronomistic history. It celebrates the power of YHWH's ark. Now, when Samuel returns, he leads the Israelites to repent and to decisive victory against the Philistines. Scholars are divided as to how to view verses 7:2–17 within the Samuel story. McCarter says about the story: "It gazes backward with satisfaction to Samuel's boyhood, giving new significance to his prophetic commission, and at the same time looks suspiciously ahead to the rise of kingship."[2] In other words, it is the climax of Samuel's boyhood and prophetic commission. There is no need for kingship: it shows how Israel functioned through the intervention of YHWH's prophet. R. P. Gordon points out that in chapter 7, God is directing everything through his chosen judge; "to ask for a king in these circumstances would, it is implied, be an

---

1. The words that are used to reintroduce Samuel in verse 3 offer a link to 4:1, which is the last place that Samuel was mentioned. See Schulz, *Die Bücher Samuel*, 114.

2. McCarter, *1 Samuel*, 148.

impertinence."³ Samuel is described here at the height of his powers as prophet, priest, and judge.⁴ Hertzberg characterized chapter 7 as a theological introduction to chapters 7–15. It defines Samuel and shows how God works through the man he has chosen. Samuel appears as a judge; he is the last judge in whom all the characteristics of the previous judges are infused.⁵ Tsumura sees chapter 7 as "a terminal literary unit." The chapter closes the narrative of Samuel's life and prepares us for the next episode. Chapter 8 is an independent chapter and serves as a transition to the story of Saul.⁶ In this segment our work examines the structure and setting of chapter 7, to find its purpose and place within the book of Samuel. In addition, we explore what we can learn about Samuel's persona as it is depicted in chapter 7.

SAMUEL CALLS ISRAEL TO SERVE YHWH

Israel turning to God is a repeated motif in the book of Judges. The Israelites are unfaithful, disaster is taking place, and they repent then appeal to God. A deliverer is sent by God who defeats their enemy, which leads to a peaceful period. The same pattern appears in our chapter. The Israelites are oppressed by the Philistines, so God sent Samuel to rescue the Israelites. A battle against the Philistines takes place and the Israelites are victorious. In contrast to the book of Judges, no human warrior is needed; it is God who fights for Israel. The battle is described in a theological manner rather than military. Probably one of the traditions about the fights against the Philistines was used here to give it a theological meaning. This part of our chapter is later than the book of Judges as well as the first chapters of the book of Samuel.

Samuel reappears at an important juncture: the ark is at Qiryath Yarim, the Israelites are dominated by the Philistines, and they are looking to renew their ties with God. They turn to Samuel to mediate between them and God. The fact that they turn to Samuel to listen to his advice and guidance shows that he was widely known as a trustworthy prophet of the Lord (1 Sam 3:20). More than likely, the long period that Samuel seemingly was missing from the public eye is not the case; all along he was teaching and

---

3. Gordon, *1 & 2 Samuel*, 106.
4. Gordon, *1 & 2 Samuel*, 105–06.
5. Hertzberg, *I & II Samuel*, 66.
6. Tsumura, *First Book of Samuel*, 230.

instructing the laws. It was a period of despair, without leadership, which gave Samuel the opportunity to set himself as mediator between the people and God. The Israelites were worshiping other gods and had forgotten the laws of Moses. Now the Israelites were yearning for God. It is described in the text by the verb נָהָה, "*nāhâ*," which means to mourn or lament for the dead (Mic 2:4; Ezra 32:18). This is odd, since returning to YHWH could not be a time for such mourning. In Aramaic the verb וַיִּנָּהוּ, "*vayinahu*," is an expression of drawing in, and according to Targum Jonathan ben Uziel, they were drawn after the worship of God. Based on this interpretation Barr suggested "follow after, be devoted."[7]

To renew their ties with God, Samuel urges the Israelites to renounce idolatry, to remove the foreign gods and worship YHWH. By doing so God would deliver them from the hand of the Philistines. The foreign gods that are mentioned are the Baalim and Ashtaroth (1 Sam 7:3–4). "Baalim" is the plural form of "Baal"; he was the Canaanite storm god and an important god in most of Ugaritic myth. He brought rain and was the source of fertility. "Ashtharoth" is also in the plural form, in the singular form it represents the Canaanite goddess Ashtart and relates to the Babylonian Ishtar, a goddess of fertility and war. The fact that Israelites obeyed Samuel's call to remove the foreign gods and served the Lord shows how much power and influence Samuel had over the nation.

It has been suggested that Samuel's call to remove the foreign gods was interpolated by the Deuteronomistic editor who lived during the sixth century BCE and was influenced by themes, motifs, and style of the book of Deuteronomy. Forsaking other gods, showing loyalty to God, and renewing the covenant with him are central themes in the book of Deuteronomy. By complying with Samuel's demand, the Israelites showed that they were worthy of God's deliverance from the Philistines. According to Gordon, by their repentance the Israelites fulfill "the third element in that scheme of apostasy-oppression-repentance-deliverance which is outlined for the period of the judges (Judg 2:11–23)."[8] Samuel's call to remove the foreign gods and to worship God is very similar to Joshua 24:23. "Then put away alien gods that you have among you and direct your hearts to the Lord, the God of Israel," and Judges 10:6, 16: "They removed the alien gods from among them and served the Lord." Also, "They served the Baalim and the Ashtaroth" (verse 6). We believe that Samuel's call is very similar to Jacob's

---

7. Barr, *Comparative Philology*, 264–65.
8. Gordon, *I & II Samuel*, 106.

call to the members of his household, "Rid yourself of the alien gods in your midst, purify yourselves, and change your clothes" (Gen 35:2). When the sons of Jacob complied with the order, God sent terror and the enemies did not pursue the sons of Jacob (verse 5). Likewise, Samuel, after he told the people to remove the foreign gods, ordered them to pour water and fast which are equal to Jacob's demand to "purify yourself." In both episodes God came to the aid of the people. It is noteworthy that in the Jacob story is the first time that the tension between Israel and its neighbors is mentioned.

THE GATHERING AT MIZPAH

The meeting between Samuel and the people of Israel took place at Mizpah, which was an important religious and political center. Muilenburg maintains that none of the Mizpah references in our chapter are original and were inserted later into the text. He claims that Mizpah became a place of worship only after the exile.[9] Examination of the Hebrew Bible shows otherwise; the place is already mentioned in the book of Judges as a place of religious gathering (20:1, 3; 21:1, 5, 8). In our chapter it is a place where a great act of salvation takes place (1 Sam 7:11–12); it is one of the places Samuel made the rounds as a judge (verse 16); later, Mizpah is the place where Saul was chosen as a king (10:17). Many centuries later Judas Maccabees and his men assembled and marched to Mizpah because the people of Israel previously had a place of worship there. There they mourned, fasted all day, put on sackcloth, threw ashes on their heads, and tore their clothes (1 Macc 3:46–48).

In Mizpah, Samuel intercedes on behalf of the people, and a similar intervention appears later in 12:19. The verses from the book of Samuel serve as a background to what we read in the book of Psalms. In Psalms, Samuel acting as intercessor is compared to Moses: "Moses and Aaron among His priests, Samuel among those who call on His name when they called to the Lord, He answered them" (99:6). A similar description appears in the book of Jeremiah: "The Lord said to me, even if Moses and Samuel were to intercede with Me, I would not be won over the people" (15:1). As Kennedy pointed out, Samuel was both the child of prayer and a man of prayer (1 Sam 8:6; 12:19, 23).[10]

---

9. Muilenburg, "Mizpah of Benjamin," 25–42; Muilenburg, "Chapters III and IV," 27–28.

10. Kennedy, *Samuel*, 69.

Samuel, in his capacity as a prophet, assembled all Israel at Mizpah. Under his instruction the Israelites engaged in a public expression of sorrow which included pouring water and fasting. The people recognized his authority. According to McCarter these rituals served as ceremony of purification because Israel worshiped other gods,[11] while Weiser viewed these rites as covenant renewal.[12] Rashi interpreted it as a symbol of humility comparing themselves to poured water. Radak said that the act of pouring water symbolize their prayer, that God should disregard their sins like water poured on the ground, or that they had cleansed themselves of sin. The Targum has: "They poured out their hearts in repentance like water." In Lamentations 2:19 we read: "Pour out your heart like water." This command to pour out the heart serves as an expression of sorrow. There is no exact parallel in the Hebrew Bible for the act that is described in our chapter.[13] As Gordon pointed out "If there is a ritual significance it is not clear what it is."[14]

Fasting is the second ritual that is mentioned. This act expresses mourning, repentance, and prayer (Judg 20:26; 2 Sam 12:16–23; 1 Kgs 21:27). According to the Hebrew Bible (Lev 16:29–31; 23:27–32; Num 29:7) on Yom Kippur the Israelites are supposed to practice self-denial. Ibn Ezra (Abraham ben Meir Ibn Ezra; 1089–1167) observed that this idiom always implies fasting (Isa 58:3, 10; Ps 35:13). Yoma 8:1 interprets self-denial as abstention from food and drink, bathing, use of oil or ointment on the body, wearing leather shoes, and sexual intercourse.[15] It is noteworthy that the word "fasting" is not mentioned in the verses cited from the Hebrew Bible. The word "fast" appears for the first time in the aftermath story of the concubine in Gibeah (Judg 20:26). When King Saul fought against the Philistines, he made the army take an oath to fast (1 Sam 14:24). David pleaded for the life of his son, so he did not eat, drink, or bathe and slept on the floor (2 Sam 12:16). The combined acts of pouring water and fasting were part of the atonement ritual. It was a public display where people came together

---

11. McCarter, *I Samuel*, 144

12. Weiser, *Samuel*, 15n1.

13. There was a ceremony in the Temple of *missuch hammayyim*, but this act of libation was symbolic for inducing rain. Indeed, we read of water pouring with Elijah's contest on Mt. Carmel, which was a rain-inducing rite (1 Kgs 18:33–35); McCarter mentions libation of water with the Feast of Booths which supplemented the customary wine offering. McCarter, *I Samuel*, 144.

14. Gordon, *I & II Samuel*, 107.

15. Levine, *Leviticus*, 109.

to repent and pray and showed their humility. Pouring water, fasting, and confession served as repentance and as a form of purification. These religious rites were necessary to the act of deliverance by God.

THE DEFEAT OF THE PHILISTINES

The Philistines heard about the Israelites gathering at Mizpah, so they assembled their forces and marched against Israel. The meeting of the Israelites at Mizpah was for religious purposes. But from the reaction of the Philistines, it appears that they perceived it as a threat. A large crowd of people was a reason for concern. It is possible that the gathering of the Israelites had a military purpose, to rebel against the Philistines. In the past on several occasions the Israelites came out from their local shrine and went directly to the battlefield (Judg 20:1; 1 Sam 13:4–12). The Philistines were aware of this danger and took military measures. Alternatively, because this was only a religious assembly, the Philistines may have thought to take advantage of the situation. The Israelites came to Mizpah unarmed; they were unprepared militarily.[16] Fear seized the Israelites, so when they saw the Philistines, they appealed to Samuel for intercession. They told Samuel that their courage had gone. According to Josephus, the fear and memory of their former defeat against the Philistines was still lingering.[17] Israel's call to Samuel has some smiliarities to chapter 4:3, where Israel called for the ark;[18] when brough to the battlefield, it was believed that "he will be present among us and will deliver us from the hands of our enemies." In this chapter Israel has faith in Samuel's ability to enlist God to help and deliver them from the Philistines and they accept Samuel's role as intercessor.

Samuel's appeal to the Lord included a blood sacrifice of "suckling lamb" as a whole burnt offering to the Lord (verse 9). This means that the entire sacrifice was burnt, and the worshippers did not share any part of it. There is no mention of sacrifice of a "suckling lamb" in the Hebrew Bible. In addition, according to biblical law, the animal must be one year old, which is not the case here. The sages were puzzled by Samuel's act and tried to explain it by saying that it was shortness of time which compelled Samuel to act in this manner.[19] Lamb as sacrifice was used in Mesopotamia and

16. Josephus, *Ant.* 6.2.2.
17. Josephus, *Ant.* 6.2.2.
18. Willis, "Samuel Versus Eli," 211.
19. *Midr. Ps.* 1, 2; *Midr. Sam.* 13, 2.

among the Hittites. According to Hittite sources lamb was used as sacrifice, burning it completely in ceremonies of purification and atonement.[20] By mentioning sacrifice the narrator again highlights the differences between Samuel and Eli's sons. The later abused the sacrificial system which led to their deaths. Samuel, on the other hand, offered a burnt offering to YHWH and the Israelites became victorious. The ideas of atonement and intercession are merged here.

Samuel cried to the Lord on behalf of the people of Israel and the Lord answered him. Samuel is depicted here as prophetic mediator rather than a hero-judge who led Israel in victory.[21] This is the first time that God answered in a positive manner after answering Hannah's petition (1 Sam 1:19). Samuel was involved in both incidents, and the answer is positive.[22] Crying to the Lord is a common motif in holy war. God answered by a loud voice and thunder (verse 10). Thunder as a weapon in a holy war is also mentioned in 1 Samuel 2:10 and 2 Samuel 22:14. It is God who fought alone against the Philistines, using natural phenomena to defeat the enemies. In the Bible we read many times how God used elements such as hail (Josh 10:14), darkness (24:7), the stars (Judg 5:20), and lightning (2 Sam 22:15; 1 Kgs 18:38). As mentioned above, thunder is referenced in Hannah's prayer: "The foes of the Lord shall be shattered: He will *thunder against them in the heavens*" (1 Sam 2:10). Thus, the victory against the Philistines in chapter 7 is the fulfilment of Hannah's prophecy. In the literature of the ancient Near East as in Israel, the battlefield was also described in terms of a storm, and the storms were described in war language.[23] What was left to the Israelites after God's intervention was to chase the Philistines. This led Hertzberg to suggest that "Samuel's battle against the Philistines is not of a military, but of theological nature." He further states that the victories are not the victories of Israel but of YHWH.[24]

De Vaux pointed out that in the ancient world war was linked with religion.[25] The battle that is described presents Samuel as carrying out holy war rites at the cult center of Mizpah.[26] Samuel is a messenger, a prophetic

---

20. Goetze, "Hittite šipant," esp. 85.
21. Klein, *1 Samuel*, 67.
22. Eslinger, *Kingship of God*, 240.
23. Tsumura, "So-called 'Chaos Tradition,'" 95–96; Tsumura, "Deluge," 351–55.
24. Hertzberg, *I & II Samuel*, 68.
25. de Vaux, *Ancient Israel*, 260.
26. Bach, *Die Aufforderungen zur Flucht*, 112.

The Assembly at Mizpah

agent, of God's victory in a holy war. It is YHWH who fought for Israel: "He called into service the elements of nature" (Josh 10:11; 24:7; Judg 5:20; 1 Sam 7:10) and "threw the enemy into confusion" (Judg 4:15; 7:22; 1 Sam 7:10; 14:20), striking a "divine terror" into them (1 Sam 14:15)."[27] The great and loud thunder confused and discomfited the Philistines; they were on the run and the Israelites chased after them from Mizpah to Beth-car and defeated them.[28] It is possible that the Israelites used the Philistine's weapons which they abandoned in their flight.

To commemorate the great victory against the Philistines Samuel set up a stone between Mizpah and Shen and called it Eben-Ezer. Similarly, Jacob set up a pillar to commemorate YHWH's theophany at Beth El (Gen 28:18, 22). A large stone was used to commemorate the covenant between God and Israel that took place at Shechem: "See, this very stone shall be a witness against us, for it heard all the words that the Lord spoke to us" (Josh 24:27). Evidently, stones were set to serve as mute witness to the events that took place. Samuel named the place Eben-Ezer, "The Stone of Help." Eben-Ezer is already mentioned in chapter 4:1, where the Israelites fought against the Philistines and lost the battle. Twenty years passed between the Israelites' defeat and their victory at Eben-Ezer. Is it possible that Samuel named the place after the place-name Eben-Ezer of chapter 4? We believe that, indeed that is what happened here, and it came to highlight the difference between chapters 4–6 and 7:3–13. Before, the Israelites lost the battle against the Philistines; now, after they repented, they were victorious. Samuel received God's aid, in contrast to the Elides, who did not. The Elides brought the ark of the covenant to the battlefield but, because of their sins, the Israelites lost the battle. They died and the ark was captured by the Philistines. On the other hand, before the battle Samuel urged the Israelites to overturn their idols and to serve the Lord. They confessed and fasted, and Samuel prayed for them. This is completely different from what we read of the days of Eli. Therefore, it is more than likely that the name Eben-Ezer was used in anticipation. It came as a "reminder of God's powerful intervention in the history of Israel, as well as her former failure at the other Eben-Ezer."[29]

---

27. de Vaux, *Ancient Israel*, 260.

28. The place Beth-car is unknown, never mentioned in the Bible. It was probably west of Mizpah on the road back to Philistia.

29. Tsumura, *First Book of Samuel*, 238.

Following their defeat, the Philistines did not enter the territory of Israel again (1 Sam 7:13). This statement is in sharp contradiction to the events that are narrated later about Saul's battles with the Philistines. In 2 Kings 6:23, there is a description of the Syrians ending their attacks, while in the next verse, there is a description of a new phase of invasions by the Syrians. Therefore, it is possible that our verse speaks only to the time of Samuel when the Philistines incursion ceased, and Samuel exercised sole authority before the anointment of Saul as the king of Israel. Radak interpreted this passage similarly, saying that it refers to the years Samuel exercised sole authority before he delegated his responsibilities to his sons. All the cities that the Philistines had taken from Israel were restored to Israel, from Ekron to Gath. These cities were close to the territory of Israel and returned to the Israelites' control in addition to towns in their vicinities. With the passing of time the Philistines reestablished their control over the territories that they had lost.

Among modern scholars we find the view that verses 13–14 were inserted by the Deuteronomist, who was also responsible for verses 3–4. The aim was to fit the tradition of 1 Samuel 5–12 into the same agenda that is found in the book of Judges.[30] The verses present the Deuteronomist's theological interpretation of Samuel's victory and not the actual historical accomplishment.[31] The language that is used to summarize Samuel's military career is similar to that in the book of Judges. Therefore, the subjugation of the enemy is described by the verb "humble" (Judg 4:23; 1 Sam 7:13) or "be humble" (Judg 3:30; 8:28; 11:33b).[32] In addition to the victory against the Philistines, peace existed between Israel and the Amorites. McCarter suggests that such a statement is "a part of careful negative preparation for the people's demand for a king."[33] However, we believe that this summary of verses 13–14 came to convey the impression that under the leadership of Samuel a lengthy period of peace existed; there was no internal or external threat to Israel.[34]

In addition to the summary of Samuel's career (verses 13–14) there is a summary of the Samuel era (verses 15–17) which comes to stress the nature of Samuel's active leadership. He is a leader and a teacher. Samuel

30. Birch, *Rise of Israelite Monarchy*, 20; McCarter, *I Samuel*, 147.
31. Klein, *1 Samuel*, 69.
32. McCarter, *I Samuel*, 147.
33. McCarter, *I Samuel*, 147.
34. Eslinger, *Kingship of God*, 244.

is traveling throughout the land to teach and judge the Israelites (on the subject of Samuel as a judge, see chapter 8). This is a positive outlook on this period. The first part of the chapter is devoted to the acts that were taken by Samuel because of pressure from the Philistines. The second part describes the situation following the victory which ended the threat of the Philistines and Amorites. All of this is attributed to Samuel's leadership.[35] It was the prophetic writer who had the last word and fashioned our story to glorify Samuel's leadership. Despite the summary of Samuel's life, he did not disappear from the story. It was the author's way of alerting the reader that a new stage was reached. From now, on the focus will be on Saul, and later, David.

THE PURPOSE OF THE STORY

The story of Samuel's fight against the Philistines has no links to Samuel's objection to kingship. It continues the story of Samuel's elevation and the decline of the Elide house which is narrated in chapters 1–4. More than likely, it is the same author who wrote both chapters. Samuel's depiction as delivering the Israelites from the Philistines oppression appears to be fictional. While some historical facts are present in these stories describing Samuel's life, the description of Saul's continuing war with the Philistines raises question about the validity of Samuel's victory against them. Wellhausen suggested that the entirety of chapter 7 is unreal, with no links to any historical event. It was part of the antimonarchic agenda, where the author tried to convey that the people's demand for a king was a sin against God and unnecessary. Samuel succeeded, by prayers and sacrifices, in delivering Israel from the Philistines, which would not be the case with the king who followed him.[36]

McCarter notes that chapter 7 gives new meaning to Samuel's prophetic commission but also has its eyes on the future, to the rise of kingship.[37] The chapter describes how the leadership functioned during a time of crisis. Israel is saved through the intervention of YHWH's prophet. Samuel invokes YHWH, who comes to the aid of the Israelites. Samuel is an intercessor, not a YHWH; he makes the battle through prayer. The war was won by divine intervention; credit belongs to YHWH. There is symmetry between chapter

---

35. Bar-Efrat, *I Samuel*, 113–14.
36. Wellhausen, *Prolegomena*, 254–56.
37. McCarter, *I Samuel*, 148.

4, which describes the defeat at Eben-Ezer, and the victory at Eben-Ezer in chapter 7. The situation that existed before the defeat is restored. McCarter believes that it was a prophetic hand that gave the Samuel stories their basic shape. The goal was to increase the reputation of Samuel and the nonroyal leadership. There are Deuteronomistic themes and expressions which are found in certain verses. This expansion was done by a later hand that wanted to incorporate the age of Samuel into Deuteronomistic theology.[38] Samuel's success against the Philistines drew its inspiration from some of the stories about David's earlier career. It is possible that David's achievements were the inspiration for a prophetic writer. Chapter 7 is the climax of the preparation for a demand for a king. Until now, any major crisis was overcome by YHWH, who was ruling through the leadership of his prophet Samuel. Now things would change, and in next chapter the Israelites would ask Samuel to give them a human king.[39]

We believe that the story in chapter 7 did not come to show the advantages of a judge as opposed to a king. It comes to demonstrate that Samuel, who faithfully served and followed God, is better than the prestigious priestly house of the Elides, who committed sins.[40] Samuel appears here as a leader who is communicating with God and who replaced the sinful house of the Elides. The story of Samuel 7 is not to be viewed as the creation of an antimonarchic author who lived during the period of the decline of the Kingdoms of Israel and Judea, as Wellhausen suggested. It was probably written by the prophetic band who stressed the nature of Samuel's active leadership. The story of 1 Samuel 7:5–14, as well as the stories in chapters 1–4, were written when the house of Eli was still fighting for its status and its hegemony and was a threat to the Zadokite priesthood. The stories were written during the time of King David or the beginning of Solomon's reign. Through Samuel the theocratic system of government was maintained; there was no reason to demand a change of leadership. Samuel led the people all the days of his life. Samuel interceded on behalf of the people and served as intermediary between the people and God. He was a leader and a teacher.

In conclusion, chapter 7 comes to glorify Samuel, who is described independently, with no links to the other main characters that are mentioned in the book of Samuel, such as Saul and David. The idealization of Samuel

---

38. McCarter, *I Samuel*, 149–50.
39. McCarter, *I Samuel*, 150.
40. Elat, *Samuel*, 55.

The Assembly at Mizpah

is done through the descriptions of his actions and words. He succeeded in the removal of the foreign gods and led the people to follow God. He appears here as a prophet and a teacher who instructs in the law, like Moses. Samuel directed and led the people instead of the priestly house of the Elides, who committed sins. Therefore, he assembled the people at Mizpah made a sacrifice and cried to the Lord. The Lord answered him and defeated the Philistines. Samuel is portrayed as a moral teacher who delivers God's words and intercedes on behalf of his people. This portrayal foreshadows the image of the future prophets, who also communicated with God and prayed on behalf of the people. This image of Samuel will be more apparent in the rest of the book of Samuel. Samuel is the only one who proclaimed the coming of the institution of kingship, which will be the next subject of discussion. He is the last premonarchic leader.

4

Samuel and the Kingship

IN ANCIENT NEAR EASTERN civilizations, it was believed that kingship came down from heaven. It was a divine institution, and some kings were even considered to be the offspring of gods, or at least semi-divine in nature. Not so in the Hebrew Bible, which records that a human was elected king; this was none other than Saul. The Book of Samuel is the only book from the ancient world that gives us a detailed description of how a monarchy was established. The inauguration of kingship was a significant development in the history of Israel. Its formation brought major changes. The king and kingship influenced the history of the Israelites from both religious and social perspectives. The monarchies of Israel and Judah lasted more than four centuries and left a profound mark on religious traditions. Before the establishment of the monarchy, YHWH was the undisputable king of the Israelites, a theme already mentioned in the Pentateuch and Deuteronomistic History (Exod 15:18; Num 23:21; Judg 8:23; 1 Sam 8:7; 10:19; 12:12). Israel was a theocracy, and their heavenly king endowed earthly judges with charismatic powers to fight and deliver the Israelites from their enemies. Now the elders of Israel demanded a king who would govern and rule them. This is described not as a myth or a legend that existed among other nations, but as an accurate tradition reflecting a historical process. Therefore, we will investigate what prompted the Israelites to reject God and to demand a king, especially a human king. Was it fear of the Philistines? Or were there social and political motives for the request?

In two major speeches, "the rights of the king" (1 Sam 8:1-22) and in his farewell speech to the people of Israel (1 Sam 12), Samuel harshly rejects the idea of kingship. This rejection is puzzling, since God already told Samuel to anoint Saul and he was already the king. In addition, there is no prohibition against human kingship in the law of Deuteronomy. It was suggested that Samuel's antimonarchic views were composed in the Second Temple period. They reflect the disappointment arising from the destruction of the temple and view human kingship as a sin. Alternatively, Samuel's objections to kingship do not reflect a later period; they do describe the reality that existed during Saul's period. Thus, in what era were these antimonarchic views composed, and by whom? What was the main reason for Samuel's objections to kingship? Was there a personal agenda behind his rejection of the institution of kingship?

APPOINT A KING FOR US

Samuel's old age and his sons' corruption led the elders of Israel to implore Samuel to appoint a king to judge them (1 Sam 8:5). Surprisingly, in the Hebrew Bible, old age is not always a sign of grace and wisdom, and sometimes is the reason for failure by the biblical hero. Therefore, Isaac's old age facilitated Rebecca and Jacob's deception, and helped appropriate the birthright from Esau (Gen 27). Eli, in his old age, did not rebuke his sons for their sins (1 Sam 2:22; 3:2, 13). King David, in old age, did not scold Adonijah for his boasting (1 Kgs 1:6); and the aged King Solomon married foreign women and worshiped other gods (11:4).

Another reason was the behavior of Samuel's sons. They are described as bent on gain, accepting bribes, and subverting justice. These transgressions are associated with judges and people with power, personality types the biblical narrators criticize. In Deuteronomy (10:17; 16:19; 27:25) and Exodus (23:6, 8) they appear as transgressions against God's laws. The wicked lives led by Samuel's sons are analogous to those of Hophni and Phinehas, the sons of Eli, who were known for their sinful activities (1 Sam 2:12-17). Evidently, the criticism of Samuel's sons initiated a crisis and caused tension between Samuel and the elders. This tension is noted as: "Samuel was displeased" (1 Sam 8:6).

At first glance, it is not clear whether the appointment of Samuel's sons as judges was to replace him or to relieve him of judicial responsibilities at a remote site.[1] It was not customary for a judge to appoint his own sons as judges, since judgeship was not hereditary. By appointing his sons, Samuel broke the customary practice of God appointing a new judge. Samuel probably tried to create "a hereditary succession" to replace the house of Eli.[2] Therefore, after the destruction of Shiloh he did not ask the people to rebuild it, but built an altar in his hometown of Ramah (1 Sam 7:17).

Moreover, he called the people to fast, pray, and sacrifice at Mizpah. He did not even mention the presence of the ark of the covenant housed in Kiriath-Jearim.[3] It appears that Samuel sought to establish his own dynasty, but the people opposed this attempt. According to P. Gordon, Samuel conducted his own "little dynastic experiment."[4] The people of Israel did not want to confront Samuel directly, so they raised concerns about his age and his sons' behavior. Their opposition was directed against the dynastic idea.

The elders believed that the current system was insufficient to handle the Philistine threat. Therefore, the elders did not request a new righteous judge, but asked instead for a king to judge them like all the other nations.[5] This request is repeated after Samuel describes "the rights of the king" (1 Sam 8:11–17). Samuel attempts to persuade the people to abandon the idea of human kingship. Despite Samuel's harsh criticism of human kingship, the people refuse to listen and repeat their demand for a king (8:19; 10:19; 12:12). In 8:20, the people demand that the king "go out before us and fight our battles." Ackroyd points out that this verse refers to functions of kingships that emphasize "order and security."[6] The people of Israel thought and believed that kingship would bring military advantages; the king would lead them and fight their battles. The Israelites constantly battled with the Philistines, who had oppressed them at the end of the period of the judges and during Eli's tenure as priest. After the defeat at Aphek, the Philistines controlled a large part of the territory of Ephraim, and occupied part of the land of Israel; they set prefects to control those areas. Recent archaeological data show that late in the eleventh century BCE many villages were

---

1. Josephus mentions a tradition that places one son in Bethel and the other in Beer-Sheba, see Josephus, *Ant.* 6.3.2.

2. Hertzberg, *I & II Samuel*, 71.

3. Ne'eman, "המלכת שאול," 97.

4. Gordon, *1 & 2 Samuel*, 109.

5. The verb *špṭ* can mean either "to govern" or "to judge." For a detailed discussion of the word *špṭ* in West semitic languages, see Ishida, *History and Historical Writings*, 41–44.

6. Ackroyd, *First Book of Samuel*, 73.

destroyed and abandoned, and others grew and became regional centers.[7] Inhabitants of these villages moved to larger and more protected sites. The Philistine threat induced this process. The war with the Philistines was long and continued throughout Saul's lifetime. During Samuel's era, the Philistines were repelled from Ekron to Gath in the south (7:11–14). This victory was short-lived. Later, during Saul's monarchy, after the victory over Goliath, the Israelites chased the Philistines from Gath to Ekron (17:52). Evidently, the temporary leadership that existed since the time of the judges could not deal effectively with the Philistine threat. Therefore, strong leadership was necessary, and a drastic change inevitable. But was there more than just a threat from the Philistines?

The threat from the Philistines in the west was not the only problem faced by Israel. At the same time, the Ammonites posed a threat on the east side of the Jordan River. The Ammonites had oppressed the Israelites since the time of Jephthah. The victory against the Ammonites was brief (Judg 11:29–34; 12:1–7). There is probably historical truth to the story of the rise of Nahash, the king of the Ammonites (1 Sam 12:12). Most likely, the Israelite tribes in the Transjordan asked for a king to face the threat from the Ammonites. Their proximity, coupled with the fact that Ammon and Moab were monarchies, contributed to their fears. Additionally, 1 Samuel reads: "But when you saw that Nahash, the king of the Ammonites, had come against you, you said, 'no! A king shall rule over us'" (12:12). This is the first example of a demand for a king to fight the Ammonites.

As mentioned above, the demand for a king for military reasons is a repeated motif in the other parts of the narrative. The desire was to have a planned government leadership in war, which is embodied in kingship. A king would lead the people in battle instead of a temporary charismatic leader. This wish by the people was fulfilled when God chose Saul to deliver the Israelites from the hands of the Philistines (9:16). According to Ralbag, there is merit to the request, since "a king would be able to mobilize the whole people behind him, whereas before only those immediately attacked had resisted and the rest of the tribes had refrained from helping them." By demanding a king, the people of Israel rejected YHWH's leadership in war. They wanted a king to lead them in human war, not YHWH's wars.[8] The demand for a king and the desire to be like other nations is ironic. God calls

---

7. Faust, "Settlement Patterns," 14–38.
8. Klein, *1 Samuel*, 78.

the Israelites his own people; however, they aspire to be like all the other nations. God was their king; nevertheless, they wanted a human king.

MORAL AND ECONOMIC CHANGES

There was also a moral dimension to the request for a king. Starting at the period of the judges, there are repeated statements about a lack of justice that prevailed among the Israelites because there was no king. In Judges 17–21 we find the common refrain: "In those days there was no king in Israel; everyone did as he pleased." This formula unifies diverse stories in Judges by demonstrating the chaos that existed in the absence of a king.[9] The author describes murders, wars, strife among brothers, rapes, and cultic sins. This kind of reality also existed on the eve of the monarchic period. It was the lack of justice and prevailing anarchy that also contributed to the demand for a king. Interestingly, an almost identical formula appears in Egyptian literature from the same period. Papyrus Harris I, most likely dating from the reign of Ramesses IV (ca. 1150 BCE), includes a retrospective history of the interval before the pharaoh Sethnakht's accession, which is described as a time of lawlessness: "The land of Egypt was abandoned, every man a law unto himself. They had no leader (for) many years previously, until other times, when the land of Egypt had officials and city rulers, one (man) slew his fellow, great and humble."[10] After this period, the document describes another time consisting of "empty years" in which the Syrian Irsu set himself up as a prince of Egypt, followed by an account of Sethnakht being chosen by the gods, saying, "He (re)established order (in) the entire land, which had languished: he slew the rebels who had been in Egypt; he cleansed the Great throne of Egypt."[11]

This was not an unusual request, since, according to the biblical narrative, the king was a symbol of social order. Among his main functions were the maintenance of order in his kingdom. In addition, he acted as a warrior (1 Sam 8:20); judge (1 Sam 8:5; 2 Sam 12:1–15; 14:1–24; 15:1–6; 1 Kgs 3; 21:1–20; 2 Chr 19:4–11); and priest (1 Sam 13:10; 14:33–35; 2 Sam 6:13, 17; 24:25; 1 Kgs 3:4, 15; 8:62; 9:25; 12:32; 13:1).[12]

---

9. Greenspahn, "Egyptian Parallel," 129–30.
10. Peden, *Egyptian Historical*, 213.
11. Peden, *Egyptian Historical*, 213.
12. Whitelam, "King and Kingship," 4:44

Another possible explanation for the formation of the monarchy in Israel lies in social and economic changes that occurred in Israelite society. The boost in population and growth in agriculture needed to be accommodated.[13] It was technological advancements, such as agricultural terracing and plastered cisterns for holding rainwater, coupled with new iron technology, that enabled the expansion of settlements and the creation of agricultural surplus. These new independent settlements with their flourishing agriculture attracted Philistine aggression, which led to the formation of kingship. Gottwald mentions the Philistines as the main reason for the establishment of the monarchy; nevertheless he also claims that the use of iron and plastered water cisterns allowed the expansion of agriculture in the hill country, and thus led to population growth. The production of surpluses required complex management beyond the family unit, which led to social changes.[14]

By the end of the eleventh century the population in the central hill country more than doubled, and other regions of the highlands followed this pattern.[15] The growth in population increased the growth in agricultural productivity, which transformed the Israelite social structure. Population growth within the social structure of Israelite society, where the oldest son received double the inheritance, deprived many young men from relying solely on farming for a livelihood. The land in the highlands was very limited, and thus many young, unmarried males looked for other economic opportunities. Yet the establishment of the monarchy created new opportunities; it offered the young people a "safety valve," enabling careers in the military, government, or priesthood.[16] It is believed that David, who was the youngest in his family, was forced to leave home because there wasn't much inheritance left for him when he came of age. David left home because he was looking for a new resource for his livelihood. He found it in military activity in the service of Saul and later as the leader of his own outlaw band of mercenaries.[17]

---

13. Frick, *Formation of State*, 26, 66, 138, 191–204.

14. Gottwald, *Tribes of Yahweh*, 655–58.

15. Finkelstein, "Emergence . . . Socio-Political Aspects," 21; Finkelstein, "Emergence . . . Socio-Economic Aspects," 59.

16. Stager, "Archaeology of the Family," 25–27.

17. McKenzie, *King David*, 22.

SAMUEL

SAMUEL'S DENUNCIATION OF KINGSHIP

In contrast to the elders' demand for a king, Samuel the prophet vehemently rejected the idea of human kingship. Modern scholars disagree strongly concerning the reason behind Samuel's denunciation of kingship, and the timing of its composition. Wellhausen believed that the stories describing Samuel's antimonarchic views were composed in the Second Temple period. Theocratic views were prevalent among the priests and sages who governed during that period. The disappointment arising from the destruction of the temple buttressed this ideology, which viewed human kingship as a sin. The ideal was a religious community, which, through the study of the Torah and the fulfillment of God's commandments, would receive God's mercy and salvation.[18]

Budde held that the antimonarchic stories were composed in the second half of the eighth century BCE, marked by the decline of the northern kingdom and its eventual destruction. To support his view, he pointed to the prophecies of Hosea that describe disappointment with human kingship (Hos 3:4–5; 8:4, 10; 13:10–11).[19] Nevertheless, the same prophet embraced messianic expectations, prophesying that in the end days the Israelites "will seek the Lord their God and David their King" (3:5). The objections to kingship in Samuel describe a reality that existed in Saul's period. These speeches were probably composed at the beginning of Saul's reign, not in any later period.[20]

Opposition to human kingship is an early phenomenon and appears in the book of Judges with the story of Gideon.[21] When the men of Israel said to Gideon, "Rule over us—you, your son, and your grandson as well," Gideon replied, "I will not rule over you myself, nor shall my son rule over you; the Lord alone shall rule over you" (Judg 8:22–23). Rejection of human kingship is also found in the fable of Jotham (Judg 9:8–15). The fable parodies human kingship, with its origin in the "plants legend" found in Sumerian literature.[22] In the fables of Gideon and Jotham, the rejection of

---

18. Wellhausen, *Prolegomena*, 255–56; Wellhausen, *Die Composition*, 240.
19. Budde, *Die Bücher Samuel*, 184.
20. Kaufmann, *Toledot ha-'emunah*, 371–73.
21. In contrast, according to Garsiel, the rejection of the monarchy originated from the opposition to change in the existing rules reflected in 1 Sam 8:7–8; 8:11–18, "the law of the king," and in 1 Sam 10:17–19; 12. He believes that "the law of the king" was written during or after Solomon's reign. See Garsiel, "Dispute," 325–27.
22. Lambert, *Babylonian Wisdom*, 151–59.

human kingship is a theme. The stories possess literary traits of an earlier period and do not have traits of later composition, such as Deuteronomistic terminology. One senses that people did not want to give up their individual freedom and liberties.[23] The people who lived in a tribal society supported direct divine rule.

The objection to kingship in 1 Samuel 8 is also based on social grounds. The future king will enslave his own people and will levy high taxes on them. He will take their sons and daughters, their fields, vineyards, and olive groves and give them to his courtiers. The "ways" of the king described by Samuel depict the king as a feudal tyrant who oppresses his people. Mendelsohn pointed out that the king's ways represent a Canaanite form of feudalistic kingship where the king's subjects were considered his slaves. According to him, the Israelite knowledge of such form of kingship points to an early date. He based his assertion on new material from Alalakh and Ugarit dating from the eighteenth to the thirteenth century BCE. He believes that Samuel's account is an authentic description of the Canaanite society that existed at his time or before. Moreso, Samuel could be its author, or it could have been a spokesman of the antimonarchic period of that time. "The rights of the king" does not represent a rewriting of history from an opponent to kingship from a later period, but represents an authentic call to the people to reject Canaanite institutions which were alien to their way of life.[24]

Samuel prophesied that the people would cry because of the king they had chosen, but God would not answer. This kind of outcry is mentioned later during the Solomon and Rehoboam era. Solomon introduced forced labor in Israel to accomplish his building projects (1 Kgs 4:22–28; 9:15–22); this hardship later led to Jeroboam's rebellion (1 Kgs 11:26). Rehoboam, Solomon's son, refused to listen to the plight of the people to reduce the burden on them which led to the formation of the northern Kingdom of Israel. Indeed, from Rehoboam's exchange with the elders of Israel, hardship was the main reason for the division of the kingdom. The oppression that was listed by Samuel coincides with Solomon's acts: he had a large court and luxurious palace, and to achieve it he introduced harsh measures on the people. Solomon's goal was to establish a monarchy that was similar to that of an oriental tyrant. Samuel's words foreshadow the future: he prophesied what would happen with the establishment of the monarchy. The ways of

---

23 Tsevat, "Emergence," 67.
24. Mendelsohn, "Samuel's Denunciation," 17–22.

the foreign kings, with which he was familiar, served as a model on which he built his antimonarchic views. The whole description of kingship in 1 Samuel 8 has its roots from the early stages of the monarchic period. More than likely the author of Samuel describes a typical Canaanite king.

The historical outcome of kingship is not mentioned or alluded to in the books of Samuel. The books of Samuel do not contain any insinuation to the later historical experience of kingship. Israel would be divided into two nations, the Kingdom of Israel and the Kingdom of Judah. These two nations would be destroyed, but there is not a single word about it. The passages that reject kingship in the books of Judges and Samuel are from an earlier period. What we have in Samuel is the author's view of kingship and not the judgment on kingship from a later period. In other words, these passages were composed during the early stages of Saul's kingship, probably by the person who wrote the book of Samuel.

It was Samuel, not God, who was unhappy with the people's request.[25] Samuel's main objection was the fear that the Israelite king would be like "the other nations," but as noted already, Samuel had a different agenda; he tried to establish his own prophetic dynasty.[26]

To express his objections to human kingship Samuel outlined the rights of the king (1 Sam 8:11–18). The whole section is directed against the demand for a human king. Samuel included the following reasons for his objections: the demand for a human king displays distrust in God and his ability to save his people; the request for a king is similar to worshiping other gods; human kings will appropriate all the people's possessions, control their lives, and revoke their liberties; since humans and not God choose the king, God will not answer their pleas or deliver them of their distress (8:18).[27]

This is one-sided; Samuel avoids mentioning the positive elements of kingship, such as establishing justice, providing leadership, and maintaining security. The people of Israel were aware of Samuel's motives and told him: "Let our king rule over us and go out at our head and fight our battles" (1 Sam 8:20).[28]

The rejection of human kingship is also repeated in Samuel's farewell speech (1 Sam 12). The speech is presented as a dialogue between Samuel

---

25. Givati, "משפט המלך," 220–27.
26. Givati, "משפט המלך," 224.
27. Elat, *Samuel*, 60.
28. Garsiel, "Dispute," 341.

and the people, where Samuel is the protagonist. It has three major sections: (1) the prophet is compared to the king; (2) the power of the prophet is demonstrated; and (3) the future of the prophet is foretold.[29] In the speech, the king is portrayed as a person who acts for his own self-interest, not as a leader, judge, and warrior. Moreover, the king is described as a person who would take (*laqaḥ*) everything from the people and enslave them.[30] Yet Samuel takes nothing from the people. The king in Samuel's speech is antithetical to the judges who previously delivered the Israelites from oppression. The implication is clear: this kind of leader is neither needed nor desirable.

Samuel viewed himself as God's messenger on earth and saw human kingship as a threat to his authority and status. It was a direct threat to establishing his dynasty. The demand was also a threat against the authority of the priests in the holy places like Mizpah, Bethel, and Gilgal. A human king meant a decline in priestly power and influence. Evidently, Samuel's fears were justified, and from the time that Saul was elected, Samuel's stature declined steadily. He had no role in the establishment of the army (1 Sam 13:2), or the recruitment of people in the war against the Philistines. Moreover, Saul assumed the cultic leadership of making sacrifice, a function formerly held by Samuel. Another blow to his status was the return of the priests of the house of Eli, who became priests in the service of the king. Not surprisingly, Samuel opposed the idea of kingship, realizing that kingship meant a diminution in his power. Samuel's speeches reflect the early monarchic period, foreshadowing the future of constant battles over power and influence between the prophets and kings of Israel.

In conclusion, the main reason for the elders of Israel's demand for a king was the Philistine threat. The temporary leadership that existed since the judges' period could not deal effectively with it. In addition, the Ammonites posed a threat on the east side of the Jordan River, having oppressed the Israelites since the time of Jephthah. There were other reasons which required a change: a moral decline as well as social and economic development in Israelite society. Starting at the period of the judges, there are repeated statements about a lack of justice that prevailed among the Israelites because there was no king. Murders, wars, strife among brothers,

---

29. McCarter, *I Samuel*, 218.

30. Weiser, *Samuel*, 40. There are some similarities here to Moses's speech. Korah, Dathan, and Abiram challenged Moses' leadership. In his response, Moses said: "I have not taken the ass of any one of them, nor have I wronged any one of them" (Num 16:15). For Hittite parallels see Hoffner, "Crossing," 18.

rapes, and cultic sins were common on the eve of the monarchic period. This lack of justice and prevailing anarchy contributed to the demand for a king. Another factor included social and economic changes. Increased population and expanded agrarian productivity were catalysts in transforming the Israelite social structure. The old system could not deal efficiently with the emerging new reality; only a new monarchic system that offered young people new opportunities could be effective. In two major speeches, "the rights of the king" (1 Sam 8:1–22) and his farewell speech to the people of Israel (1 Sam 12), Samuel rejected the idea of kingship. He denounced it because he tried to establish his own dynasty, and human kingship meant decline of his power and status and posed a threat to his authority. Samuel's speeches project future battles over power and authority between the prophets and the kings of Israel. Despite Samuel's objections to kingship, God ordered Samuel to anoint Saul as the first king of Israel. In the next chapter we will investigate the story of Saul's coronation and compare it to the coronation of David.

5

Samuel the King Maker

As noted, the book of Samuel is the only source from the ancient world that gives us a detailed description of how a monarchy was established. Samuel is described as a king maker—on three different occasions, he is involved with Saul's anointment. First, Saul was anointed privately and secretly at Ramah. The second time, at Mizpah, Saul was designated as king in the presence of the tribes and their representatives. A third ceremony took place at Gilgal, where Saul was officially declared king. These different versions have provoked much debate among modern scholars. Questions have been raised as to whether the three different versions of Saul's coronation actually took place. It has been pointed out that the three versions are problematic and difficult to reconstruct. What stands behind each story, and what did the narrator try to achieve by telling three different coronation stories? More so, are there any links between the different stories? Following chapters 13–14, which include stories of Saul and Jonathan's battles against the Philistines, God rejected Saul and found "a man after his own heart" to replace him (1 Sam 13:14). This rejection became more apparent after Saul's battle against the Amalekites (15:26–27). Samuel was ordered to anoint David, one of Jesse's sons, and so for a second time Samuel is a king maker. Examination of David's anointment story reveals that it is very similar to Saul's anointment; the stories share common motifs, thus, how close are these stories? Did the author intentionally describe similar stories and for what purpose? In addition, how is Samuel portrayed in Saul and David's anointment stories?

THE LOST DONKEYS OF KISH

The story of Saul searching for the lost donkeys of his father, and then founding the kingship was termed by scholars as a *legende*.[1] The story describes ancient events directed by God. In other words: God chooses the king, and the prophet anoints the king. But the Bible does not explain why God picked Saul. Similarly, when God chose Abraham, no detail of his past life is given—his first seventy-five years are ignored. The same pattern occurred with Gideon, David, and Samson—no explanation for their selection is provided. This evidently troubled the sages who tried to clarify the rationale for the selection of Saul. According to them, Saul was known for his bravery in the battle of Eben-Ezer, where he snatched the tablets from the hand of the Philistine warrior Goliath and brought them to Shiloh.[2]

Scholars point to several layers in the account, which includes the story of the lost donkeys and the anointing of Saul. However, they disagree on the subject of which verses to assign to each story.[3] Recently, several studies point to a single account that has been revised and expanded during the process of transmission.[4] The earliest part of the tale belonged to the folkloristic story, describing Saul searching for his father's donkeys.[5] While searching, he encounters a seer, or a "man of God," who indicates his future greatness. The story of Samuel anointing Saul as a prince was inserted into this story.[6] The editor who inserted this section was influenced by a "call narrative" which is found in stories about Moses, Gideon, and several prophets.[7]

1. Wildberger, "Sage and Legende," 1641–44; Fohrer, "Die Sage," 60.
2. *Midr. Sam.* 11.1; *Midr. Ps.* 32.
3. Birch, "Development," 55–68; Klein, *1 Samuel*, 84; Miller, "Saul's Rise," 157–61; Mettinger, *King and Messiah*, 80–98.
4. Schunck, *Benjamin*, 86–89; Schmidt, *Menschlicher Erfolg*, 58–102.
5. Klein, *1 Samuel*, 84.
6. Klein, *1 Samuel*, 84.

7 Birch thus points to the existence of the "call form," which includes the following elements: Divine confrontation (9:15), an introductory word (9:16–17), commission, (10:1), objection (9:21), reassurance (10:7b), and sign (10:1b, 5–7a). Habel points out that there is a different order in the Saul episode from the standard "call form." He explains this discrepancy by asserting that the call was attached to the pre-existing story of

Saul first appears as a young man sent by his father to search for lost donkeys. The Bible describes him as: "an excellent young man (*bāhûr*); no one among the Israelites was handsomer than he; he was a head taller than any of the people" (1 Sam 9:2). The Hebrew term *bāhûr* suggests that he was a young man, about to enter adult life. In other words, Saul had reached his maturity and was ready to assume adult responsibilities. Meanwhile Richter suggests that the term means one who can fight in war, receive inheritance, and was of marriable age.[8]

The second detail about Saul was his was physical attraction. The rabbis stress his physical stature, noting that he was one of the biblical personalities who was created in God's likeness.[9] Describing an Israelite hero as attractive is a biblical staple, e.g., Joseph (Gen 39:6), Moses (Exod 2:2), David (1 Sam 16:12), Absalom (2 Sam 14:25), and Esther (Esth 2:7). Eissfeldt claimed that God chose Saul because of his height: "he was taller than all the rest of the people from his shoulder upward" (1 Sam 10:22).[10] This is unlikely, since God tells Samuel: "For it is not as a man sees that God sees: a man looks into the face, but God looks into the heart" (16:7).[11]

Saul's father, Kish, loses some donkeys and enlists Saul to hlp him find the lost animals.[12] The search for the lost donkeys leads Saul and his servant across the hill country of Ephraim. Failing to find them, Saul becomes discouraged and resolves to turn back. At this point, the servant urges Saul to seek the help and advice of the man of God who will inform them

---

the search for the donkeys. In addition, he points to the function of Samuel, who serves as the human mediator of the call. None of this is attested to in the Bible. In contrast to Habel, Richter sees parallels between the call of Saul to the calls of Gideon and Moses. He points to the following elements: (1.) "I have seen the affliction," 9:16, Exod 3:7; (2.) "Their cry has come to me," 9:16, Exod 3:9; (3.) The sending, 9:16, Judg 6:14–15; Exod 3:10, 15; (4.)The anointing as prince, 9:16; 10:1; (5.) Savior formula, 9:16, Judg 6:14–15; (6.) Objection, 9:21, Judg 6:15, Exod 3:11; 4:1, 10; (7.) The formula "God is with you," 10:7b, Judg 6:16, Exod 3:12; 4:12. (8.) Giving of the spirit, 10:6, Judg 6:34. See Richter, *Die sogenannten*, 50; Birch, "Development," 55–68; Klein, *1 Samuel*, 84; Habel, "Form and Significance," 297–323

8. Richter, *Die sogenannten*, 30.

9. Soṭah 10a.

10. Eissfeldt, *Die Komposition*, 7

11. In the Koran, the name that was given to Saul was *Ṭālūt*, which is an allusion to his exceptional height. This name was probably influenced by the name given to Goliath, Jālūt. See Surah 2:248

12. Gordon compares Saul with King Agamemnon, whom Nestor encountered wandering at night, and he asks if he is looking for one of his mules or comrades (*Iliad* 10:84); see Gordon, *Before the Bible*, 229

correctly about their journey. The Hebrew word used for advice is *yaggîd*, from the verb *higgîd* ("inform/make known"), which is related etymologically to *nāgîd*, the title that Samuel subsequently bestows on Saul in 10:1. Ironically, Saul asks the man of God to tell him, *higgîd*, about the lost donkeys, but he informs him that he will be king, *nāgîd*, of Israel.

It was customary to pay the man of God for advice; hence, Saul was dispirited because of his inability to compensate the man of God with a gift. Shalom Paul calls it an "interview fee." Indeed, we read about Jeroboam's wife, who took gifts when she visited Ahijah (1 Kgs 14:3), gifts for Elijah (2 Kgs 4:42), and prophetic fees for Amos 7:12 and Micah 3:5.[13] Gifts were vital in establishing good relations and were part of social interaction in the ancient world. After a long journey, a traveler was especially expected to return bearing many gifts.[14] As mentioned above, Saul was dejected because he bore no gift for the prophet.[15] Later, coincidentally, we read that Saul's servant found a quarter of a shekel of silver to give to the prophet. The servant is the dominant character here. First, he urged Saul to consult the prophet after he abandoned his search for the donkeys. Then, after Saul was disheartened for not having a gift, it is the servant again who rescued him with a quarter shekel of silver.

THE MEETINGS

The narrative records a meeting between Saul and the maidens at the well, even before Saul meets with Samuel. This resembles previous meetings at wells, including Abraham's servant with Rebecca, Jacob with Rachel, as well as Moses with Ziporah. All of these meetings result in marriages, but in this meeting, the girls direct Saul to Samuel, who would anoint Saul as king. The girls knew of the prophet's arrival, where he was staying, and about the sacrifice. They were heralds who directed Saul to his destination. Similarly, when Joseph sought his brothers, he encountered a man in the field who had seen them and knew their destination. In both episodes, one senses

---

13. Paul, "I Samuel 9:7," 542–44.

14. Gordon, *Before the Bible*, 272–73; Homer, *Odyssey* 11:355–361.

15. The word for gift here is *těšûrâ*—a *hapax legomenon*. It probably comes from the verbs *šewr*, to see. Thus *těšûrâ* is a "gift of greetings." Interestingly, the man of God is called *rō' eh* which was an old name for the word prophet. *Rō' eh* means "seer" and is a participial form of the Hebrew verb "to see." Thus, there is a link between the gift and the prophet. See Cohen, *Biblical hapax legomena*, 24.

God's guiding hand, acting behind the scene, and directing events. The sages point out that Saul asked the girls a brief question, "Is the seer here?" however, the girls replied at length. The Gemara comments: "Because women are talkers," and as another answer, Shmuel said: "They delayed in order to gaze upon Saul's handsomeness. As it is written about Saul: *from his shoulders up, he was taller than any of the people.*"[16]

Saul did not anticipate the meeting, but Samuel knew about it in advance (9:15–16). God revealed Saul's arrival to Samuel and instructed him to anoint Saul. Ironically, when Saul meets Samuel, he asked him *haggîdâ-nā* "tell me," the reader already knows that Samuel has to designate him as *nāgîd* king. Therefore, when Saul asks Samuel *haggîdâ-nālî*, "tell me," might mean "designate me." Samuel asks Saul to dine with him, at which time he tells him everything that is on his mind. The narrator does not tell us that Saul asked about the donkeys *per se*, but we learn that they have been found. In addition, Samuel told Saul: "And to whom do the riches of Israel belong if not to you and to your father's house?" (9:20). Saul understood it as a reference to kingship. The people of Israel knew that Samuel was looking for a king. Therefore, Saul said: "Am I not a Benjaminite, from the smallest tribe of Israel and from the humblest clan of all the tribe of Benjamin? Then why have you spoken to me this way?" (1 Sam 9:21). Saul claims he is unworthy, a typical response by people called upon for a mission by God, as did Moses (Exod 3:11) and Gideon (Judg 6:15).[17]

Saul is God's anointed one; therefore, Samuel brought him to a sacrificial meal, placing him at the head of thirty guests. The number thirty is typological and appears often in Judges and Samuel.[18] The LXX and Josephus have seventy guests.[19] Seventy is an artificial number, identifying the guests with the institution of the "elders of Israel" which the Torah numbers seventy (Exod 24:1; Num 11:16, 24). Additionally, Adonijah held a banquet-sacrifice when he planned to succeed his father David as a king, while Absalom invited two hundred people to a banquet-sacrifice as part of his plan to become king (2 Sam 23:13, 18).

Saul sat at the head of the table as a form of introduction. Saul was introduced to those who would be his subjects. Similarly, when Moses introduced Joshua as his successor, it reads: "Have him stand before Eleazar

---

16. *Ber.* 48b
17. Gordon, *1 & 2 Sam*, 115.
18. Judg 10:4; 12:9; 14:11–13, 19; 20:31, 39; 1 Sam 19:21.
19. Josephus, *Ant.* 6.4.1.

the priest and before the whole community, and commission him in their sight" (Num 27:19). At the meal, Saul received the "thigh of consecration"—that part of the sacrificial animal reserved for the priests and their families.[20] He is the only king who received this "thigh of consecration," and is treated as a priest as he is given the priestly share of the sacrifice (1 Sam 10:4). Leviticus (8:32) states that only Aaron and his sons can eat from this sacrifice, and what was not eaten had to be destroyed. C. H. Gordon points out that all guests were not equal in rank, which was indicated by the amount and quality of their serving. He terms it a "proportionate feast" with parallels in the Odyssey 8:98 and 11:185.[21] By giving Saul the "thigh of consecration" Samuel indicated Saul's future role.

The encounter between Saul and Samuel contains several motifs found in other prophetic stories. Samuel appears as a prophet; he knows what will happen to Saul on his return journey and whom he will meet (1 Sam 10:2, 3-4, 5-6, 10-11).[22] Samuel prophesied that Saul would meet a band of prophets and prophesy along with them (1 Sam 10:5-6). Thus, like prophets, Saul becomes God's messenger.

SAUL'S ANOINTING

At the break of day, Samuel secretly anointed Saul. The servant is dispatched. Saul is left alone with Samuel. In biblical literature, a divine call is depicted as a private experience. Samuel anointed David among his brothers (1 Sam 17:3-5, 13), Jehu was anointed by one of the disciples of the prophet Elisha (2 Kgs 9:10), and Ahijah the Shilonite told Jeroboam that he would become the king when they were outside of Jerusalem (1 Kgs 11:29). On the other hand, the Bible reveals that the coronation ceremonies of Solomon (1 Kgs 1:32-39) and Joash of Judah (2 Kgs 11:12, 14) were public. The high priest, dignitaries, and representatives of the people participated. The anointing was done by the high priest while the people shouted praises.[23]

Samuel anointed Saul, which consisted of rubbing or smearing with oil. This act, it was believed, transferred the sanctity of the national god to

---

20. Milgrom, "Alleged Wave Offering," 33-38.

21. Gordon, *Before the Bible*, 241.

22. Similarly, Elijah directed Ahab on his journey from Carmel to Jezreel (1 Kgs 18:45-46). Elisha prophesied to Kings Jehoram and Jehoshaphat what would take place in their military campaign to Moab (2 Kgs 3:19, 25).

23. 1 Sam 10:24; 1 Kgs 1:39; 2 Kgs 9:13; 11:12.

Samuel the King Maker

the king. Anointment symbolized a covenant between God and the king indicating that God would protect the king, and it bestowed legitimacy. The anointing of Saul was done secretly and privately, because there are two stages of the election depicted here. The first stage entailed divine designation before the proper enthronement ritual. Many times, the chosen person was young, weak, and felt unworthy. A private ceremony could encourage him and instill confidence in his ability to carry out his task successfully. The two-stage election is manifest with Jeremiah, who says that he was selected from the womb, and later when he was young, was sent on a mission (Jer 1:5–6).[24] Parallels exist in Egyptian and Mesopotamian traditions. Thut-Mose III claimed that the god Amon said that he would be upon his throne while he was still a nestling. Later it was Re who established his throne.[25] Thutmose IV claimed that Re told him in a dream that he shall bequeath the kingdom to him long before he ascended to the throne.[26] Mesopotamian literature tells of kings like Assur-rêsh-ishi, Asshurbanipal and Nabonidus who claimed to be designated in the womb.[27]

In the biblical story, the first stage takes place in Ramah, where Saul is designated as future king. In Mizpah, where Saul is crowned before the whole nation, the second act occurs.

Saul's anointing also includes a message from Samuel: Saul would liberate the Israelites from their enemies. Samuel gives Saul signs that God has anointed him as a king of Israel. These *three* signs would occur in three different locations. The first will take place at Rachel's tomb, where he will meet two people who will tell him *three* things: the donkeys were found, his father had given up on finding the donkeys, and his father is worried about him. The second will take place at the Oak of Tabor, where he will meet *three* people. One will carry *three* kids; one will carry *three* bags of bread; and one will carry a jug of wine. They will greet him and offer him two wave offerings of bread, which he will accept. The bread is intended for God, but Saul is instructed to accept it.[28] The third encounter will occur at the Hill of God where the Philistine prefect was located. Saul will encounter a band of

---

24. Halpern, *Constitution*, 127–28.
25. Willis, "Divine Nomination," 446–47.
26. Willis "Divine Oracle," 449.
27. For Assur-rêsh-ishi and Ashurbanipal see Luckenbill, *Ancient Records*, 1:209; 2:765; for Nabonidus, see Langdon, *Die neubabylonischen Königsinschriften*, 218.1:4–5.
28. Afterwards, David, to Saul's displeasure, will accept bread from the priest of Nob (1 Sam 21:7).

prophets who will have harps, tambourines, clarinets, and lyres in front of them, and they will be prophesying with musical instruments.

Samuel predicted that the encounter with the band of prophets would change Saul, as "the spirit of God will rush upon" him, and he would prophesy (1 Sam 10:6).[29]

THE CORONATION AT MIZPAH

Contrasting the private, secretive anointing of Saul, the coronation at Mizpah is public. Saul was anointed by Samuel first as *nāgīd*, now he is elected a king.[30] As Herzberg pointed out, Saul's rise to power was narrated in different ways in different places. However, he acknowledges the general agreement that God directs the events and uses Samuel as his instrument.[31]

Here, Saul is chosen king by a "lot." The Hebrew Bible maintains that a lottery was used to determine an unknown offender. In the Achan story, a lot was cast to find the person who did not follow the laws of the ban (Josh 7:1). Later a lot was cast to find out who broke Saul's vow (1 Sam 14:24–29). In each case, the reader knows who will be caught. It is not clear why a lot was cast to identify the king of Israel, since Samuel had already anointed Saul. Moreover, the fact that a lot was cast to find the king of Israel gives the impression that Saul might be guilty of something. The feeling arises that things will turn deleteriously. According to McCarter, "There is a clear, if subtle, implication that he is an offending party by the virtue of the election itself."[32] The word "lot" is not used but is inferred. Instead, the writer uses the word *hiqrîb*, "present," which also means sacrifice. Since Saul was not found, Samuel again asked YHWH. There is a play on words: the verb *šā' al*, "ask, inquire," and the name Saul (*šā' ûl*). Saul was hiding the entire time the casting of the lot took place, but it does not say why Saul was

---

29. This is a typical expression in the stories of Samson and Saul where the hero is empowered by God's spirit to perform heroic actions (Judg 14:6, 19; 15:14; 1 Sam 11:6). Saul started to prophesy by musical inspiration the same way Elijah prophesied by music (2 Kgs 3:15). As the spirit rushes upon he changed (1 Sam 10:9).

30. When Saul was anointed, he was not termed "king" (*melek*), but is given the title *nāgīd*. This led scholars to believe that Samuel and the tribal leaders never intended to elevate Saul to the kingship. However, the term *nāgīd* means a person chosen by God for kingship. See Alt, *Kleine Schriften*, 2:2324; Noth, *Geschichte Israels*, 156n2; Bright, *History of Israel*, 185.

31. Hertzberg, *I & II Samuel*, 87.

32. McCarter, *I Samuel*, 196.

Samuel the King Maker

hiding. Was it modesty or shyness? The Talmud commentating on this passage asserts that Saul was a model of humility. This detail is significant in understanding the different stages in Saul's coronation. Saul's hiding proves that there was a link between Saul's secret anointing and the anointing in Mizpah. Why does Saul hide? How did he know that he would be chosen? Evidently, one tradition holds that there were two stages of Saul's anointing. Therefore, he concealed the matter of his kingship from his uncle (1 Sam 10:17), and he hid because he already had been anointed by Samuel, suggesting that he knew he would be chosen by lot.

When Samuel brought Saul forth from his hiding place, the narrator repeats some of the details mentioned previously in the anointing story. Once again, we are told that he was taller than the rest of all the people, yet this will be repudiated later in the story (1 Sam 16:7).[33] Further repeated details are that Saul was the son of Kish from the tribe of Benjamin, and that he was modest and shy. Modesty is a quality associated with Moses (Num 12:3), Gideon (Judg 6:15), David (1 Sam 18:23; 2 Sam 7:18–21), and Solomon (1 Kgs 3:7). In Saul's anointing and coronation ceremonies, his modesty is stressed. It is mentioned first in connection with Saul's appearance (1 Sam 9:21), then when Saul was elected by lot (10:22), again when Saul concealed the kingship from his uncle (10:16), and lastly when Saul already was the king of Israel (15:17).

Saul was presented as YHWH's chosen one. This reflects the belief that the king is God's elected one and the elected one of the people. Samuel shortly tells the people of Israel: "And now here is the king you have chosen! YHWH has appointed a king over you" (12:13). Likewise, we read that Hushai justified his support for Absalom, saying: "No, the one chosen by the Lord, by these people, and by all the men of Israel" (2 Sam 16:18). The belief that the king is the one chosen by God and the people is also known from ancient Near East texts. In the Hebrew Bible the preeminently chosen one of YHWH is David, but at the early stages of the monarchy, Saul was seen as the chosen one. By shouting "Long live the King!" the people of Israel recognized Saul as king. This phrase is repeated throughout the historical books of the Bible to express approval for the king (1 Kgs 1:25, 34, 39; 2 Kgs 11:12). P. R. Gordon points out that "for the first time since his

---

33. This is similar to the story of Athtar in the Baal myth, where we read: "[He] sits on Mighty Ba'lu seat. (But) his feet do not reach the footstool; his head does not reach the top (of the seat)." Thus, because he was short, he was rejected as king. See Pardee, "The Ba'lu Myth," 269.

introduction in 9:1f, Saul is called 'king' significantly; it is the people who acclaim him so."[34]

In spite of Saul's election by God and his recognition by the people, some people did not accept Saul as a king. The Bible mentions two groups, stalwart men and worthless men. The former refers to soldiers or warriors and connotes loyalty. They were part of the army that Saul gathered (1 Sam 14:52). The second group refers to disloyal traitors. They expressed their contempt to the new king by words and actions. They asked, "How can this fellow save us?" (14:27). They spurned him and tendered no gifts. No evidence exists for giving a gift following a new king's election; nevertheless, the biblical narrator stressed that fact. Gift-giving by a vassal to a king was considered a sign of recognition and loyalty to the king.[35] The same people's contempt towards Saul will be mentioned after his victory over the Ammonites.

SAUL PROCLAIMED KING AT GILGAL

After the victory over the Ammonites, Samuel asked the people to join him in renewing the kingship at Gilgal (1 Sam 11:14). The people went to Gilgal and, in the presence of YHWH, crowned Saul as their king. There they sacrificed to YHWH, and Saul and all of Israel rejoiced. Medieval commentators, such as Rashi and Radak raised the question: why was a third coronation needed in Gilgal? They claimed there was disagreement about Saul. Many people rejected him, believing he could not save them (10:27; 11:12). After he proved his military ability, a need arose to renew his kingship.

As mentioned, modern scholars have debated the existence of the three different and problematic versions of Saul's coronation. According to McKenzie, the three stories came from three different sources that were available to the Dtr. Instead of choosing one of them, the Dtr merged the three stories through a series of editorial additions.[36] Mettinger says that Saul's rescue of Jabesh-gilead is the most reliable tradition describing the events that led to Saul's coronation. This tradition is unfamiliar with the casting of a lot at Mizpah, and so he believes that 1 Sam 11 is an independent tradition and never had any connection with the Mizpah version.[37]

34. Gordon, *1 & 2 Samuel*, 121.
35. 1 Kgs 5:1; 2 Kgs 3:4; 17:3–4.
36. McKenzie, *King David*, 29.
37. Mettinger, *King and Messiah*, 83–84.

Edelman does not accept the view that Saul's rescue of Jabesh-gilead led to his coronation. According to her, Saul's ability to lead his people in a battle after defeating the Ammonites is historically implausible. This battle must have taken place only after Saul became a king with a strong army.[38]

Perhaps the confusion and disagreement among scholars for why a third ceremony was needed at Gilgal derives from the scholars' failure to discern the meaning of the Hebrew word *ûněḥaddēš*. This word is usually translated to "renew, restore." In other words, the people wanted to renew Saul's kingship.[39] But examination of the Hebrew word shows that it has a second meaning, "to strengthen." According to 2 Chronicles 24:5, 12, King Jehoash decided to renovate the temple. There we read that the word *leḥaddēš* is parallel to *leḥazzēk*, which means "to strengthen."[40] Thus, the ceremony which is described at Gilgal strengthened Saul's rule. One purpose was to strengthen his kingship by bringing the Israelite tribes in Transjordan under the authority of the new king. Having freed the Israelite tribes from the oppression of the Ammonites, it was the right time to make Saul the king.[41]

The location of the coronation in Gilgal was not accidental. It was east of Jericho and close to the Jordan crossing; thus, it was convenient to the tribes from both west and east to meet and strengthen the king's rule. There is also a possibility that this location was chosen because of a preexisting altar that symbolized the connection between the tribes of Transjordan and the tribes of the west (Josh 23). The place was called Glilot and an altar was built there, therefore it is probably Gilgal. In contrast to the past two ceremonies, here at Gilgal we are told that Saul and all the men of Israel celebrated exuberantly.[42] Klein balanced the statement of celebration with critical comments about kingship from the book of Hosea: "They

---

38. Edelman follows Halpern, who pointed to a three-part designation; the search for a candidate, his anointing which showed divine approval, and public acclamation, expressed by the phrase "Long live the king." She believes that those three stages were followed by a testing stage. However, the rescue of Jabesh-gilead could not have been the catalyst triggering the foundation of the monarchy. See Diana Edelman, "Saul," 5:993; Edelman, "Saul's Rescue," 195; Halpern, *Constitution*, 127, 130, 134.

39. *BDB*, 293–94; *HALOT*, 1:294.

40. Elat, *Samuel*, 124.

41. Interestingly, the author of 1 Chronicles 29:22 uses the word *šēnît*, meaning "again," and not *leḥaddēš*, to describe Solomon's second coronation.

42. Another place we read that Saul rejoiced is after the victory against Goliath. But this is indirectly described by Jonathan (19:5).

have made kings, but not by my sanction" (8:4), and "All their misfortune [began] at Gilgal, for there I disowned them" (9:15).[43] This is not surprising, since the text echoes Samuel's prior rejection of kingship. And the arrival of kingship would signal a decline of prophetic power.

Following the victory against the Ammonites and before the celebrations at Gilgal we read that Saul had already been accepted by the people of Israel. Evidently, his victory removed any doubt about his leadership abilities. Thus, when the people of Israel asked Samuel, "Who was it who said, 'Saul shall not reign over us?'"(1 Sam 11:12), they turned to Samuel, who was still perceived as a judge, and demanded these people be put to death. But Saul interfered and declared that no one would be slain. Here Saul appropriated the authority to judge from Samuel; after this episode, Samuel's decline began. By taking the authority to judge, Saul became like the other kings of the ancient Near East who judged their people.

The proclamation of Saul's kingship was done by all the people. Interestingly, Samuel is not mentioned as taking part in the celebration. This has led scholars to suggest that the initiative to make Saul a king was from the people. It was suggested that the early kings were crowned by the people and the prophetic material, which describes the role of YHWH in electing the king, represent reinterpretation of the tradition.[44] In 2 Samuel 2:4 and 5:3, David was anointed by the people, and the tradition that he was anointed by Samuel in 1 Samuel 16:13 is a result of later prophetic influence. It appears that we have here an older tradition of Saul's accession to kingship as a result of the people's initiative, which coincides with the elders' request for a king in chapter 8. Nevertheless, it was Samuel in verse 14 who said, "Come, let us go to Gilgal and there inaugurate the monarchy." What emerges from this description is that Samuel's power is on decline; it is the people who took a decisive role here. They made a peace offering to God and held a great celebration with Saul. They were happy to have a king like Saul.

THE ANOINTING OF DAVID

David is mentioned more times than any other character in the Hebrew Bible. In fact, several books are devoted to him, which shows his importance. We read about him from 1 Samuel 16 through 2 Samuel 24, and in 1

---

43. Klein, *1 Samuel*, 109.
44. Knierim, "Messianic Concept," 28.

Kings 1–2, 1 Chronicles, and Psalms. The stories in Samuel and Kings are the most significant. They contain the largest and most detailed version of David's life. They are the basis of information about him in both Chronicles and Psalms.

There is a great similarity in the stories of the anointment of Saul and David. God instructed Samuel to anoint a man from the territory of Benjamin (1 Sam 9:16). Later, God ordered Samuel to go and anoint one of Jesse's sons to be a king. In both incidents the identity of the king is not revealed at first. God tells his servant Samuel his plans for the future, which is a reminder of the words of Amos 3:7: "Indeed, My Lord God does nothing / Without having revealed His purpose / To His servants the prophets."

God ordered Samuel to fill his horn with oil and to go to Jesse of Bethlehem. There among the sons of Jesse was one whom God had already selected to be the next king. Samuel expressed fears for doing so, which is quite puzzling. It is possible that Samuel was afraid because anointing a rival successor could be seen by Saul as an act of rebellion, and as a king Saul had the right to execute rebels. Samuel had to go from Ramah to Bethlehem, passing through Gibeah of Saul. He was probably afraid of being exposed to surveillance by the king. Samuel showed here lack of faith in God; he should have known that God would protect him if necessary. In response to Samuel's fear, God told him to take a heifer for sacrifice. According to Herzberg he took the heifer "as authentication in case the king noticed anything."[45] The sight of Samuel arriving led to a trembling among the elders of the city; they went with apprehension to meet him. According to Radak and Abravanel (Rabbi Don Isaac ben Judah Abravanel, 1437-1503), the elders feared that Samuel had heard of a sin that took place in their city but that they were unaware of. That is why they asked him if he came in peace or to chastise them. Malbim (Mein Loeb ben Yehiel Michael, 1809-77) explained that when they saw that Samuel came with a heifer, they feared that a corpse was found on the outskirts of the city and Samuel had come to carry out the ritual of the decapitated calf (Deut 21:19). Alternatively, the elders were aware of the rift between Saul and Samuel and did not want to be involved in trouble, as happened later to the priestly city of Nob.[46] Samuel reassured them that his visit was peaceful in nature, and he invited them to a feast. The elders are only mentioned in chapter 16, verses

---

45. Herzberg, *I & II Samuel*, 137.
46. Herzberg, *I & II Samuel*, 137.

4b and 5a after that the focus is on Jesse and his family. The reason for Samuel's visit remains hidden from the elders and the sons of Jesse.

Samuel blessed Jesse and his sons and invited them to the feast. Before the feast Jesse's sons appeared one after another before Samuel. When Samuel laid his eyes on Eliab, he thought that he was God's chosen. He probably chose Eliab because he had a physique similar to that of Saul, but it turned out he was not the one God had elected. The explanation that is given for his rejection is that God does not look at what is externally visible but what a man is like within. According to Malbim, when Saul was chosen, his appearance was important because people demanded a king, and he had to look the part. Now God wanted a king that would be personally worthy; therefore, Eliab's appearance was not important. Jesse presented all his sons before Samuel, and each time the son in question was not chosen by God. At this point Samuel asked if there was another son, and he found out that there was another younger son who was shepherding the flock. The choice of the younger son who passes over his older brother is a well-known motif in the Hebrew Bible, with Jacob over Esau, Ephraim over Manasseh, and Perz over Zearah.

In both the Saul and David stories a sacrificial meal prior to their anointment was organized by Samuel. Saul was placed at head of a table that included thirty invitees and was given a priestly portion. The following day he was secretly anointed. Similarly, David's family along with the elders of the city of Bethlehem were invited by Samuel to a sacrificial feast. It is not clear, however, if the elders indeed took part in the planned sacrifice. David had not been mentioned by name until this point; according to Smith, "this is probably intentional, to heighten the effect."[47] During the anointment, only the brothers were present. However, we believe that David was anointed in secret, like Saul. This is evident from Eliab's rebuke of David when he arrived at the valley of Elah (1 Sam 17:28–29). Eliab evidently was not aware of his brother's new status; therefore, we should have here instead of *beit* (בקרב), *mem* (מקרב). Thus, the text should read: "Samuel took David *from among* his brothers and anointed him" (1 Sam 16:13). We should point out that the difficulty does not exist in the LXX, which omits the verses describing David's arrival to the battlefield to meet his brothers (1 Sam 17:12–31), which include Eliab's rebuke.

Neither Saul nor David was present at the time of their election. Saul was hiding and had to be brought to his coronation (10:22–23). Likewise,

---

47. Smith, *Critical and Exegetical Commentary*, 145.

David was tending the sheep and was brought to his anointment (16:11–12). Equally Saul and David are depicted as small and unworthy for the task. Saul said: "But I am only a Benjaminite, from the smallest (מקטני) of the tribes of Israel, and my clan is the least of all the clans of the tribe of Benjamin!" (9:21). Meanwhile, David is described as the "youngest" (16:11) (הקטן). In both stories a young man (נער) is directing the events unintentionally. In the first story, the young man is guiding Saul to meet Samuel who later anointed him. In the second tale, it is a young man who advised Saul to bring David to his house. Saul asked for a person who can play music well (the harp) but the young man brought a person who has many attributes such as "stalwart fellow and warrior, sensible in speech, and handsome in appearance, and the Lord is with him" (16:18). At first glance, it appears that David's characteristics are irrelevant in our text and did not answer Saul's need for a musician. However, those characteristics are mentioned here to give the reader a broader perspective of David and will be displayed later in the ensuing conflict between Saul and David.

A. Rofé has discussed the relative lateness of stories about the hero's beginning which is a known phenomenon. He pointed to the story of the anointment of David. According to him the story is a late composition and has no organic connection with the narrative at hand. The story belongs to the genre of the hero's setting out and is relatively late. To strengthen his argument, he points to the fact that the story is not even mentioned once in the book of Samuel, even though legitimization was important to David. Moreover, there is no mention of it in the book of Chronicles. The first reference to it can be found in the late apocryphal psalm no. 151, found in Cave 11 at Qumran.[48] Thus it appears that David's secret anointing is a late story designed to confer legitimacy on David's kingship.[49]

The moment that David was anointed, the divine spirit rested upon him and departed from Saul because David replaced him as God's anointed. There can be only one king with supernatural powers. David had the supernatural powers, but Saul was still the legal ruler. Saul was the king for several years, but without divine legitimization. In contrast to David, an evil spirit from the Lord seized Saul and began to terrify him. Saul was not aware that the spirit departed from him; similarly we read about Samson: "For he did not know that the Lord had departed from him" (Judg 16:20). The evil spirit that is mentioned here is like the evil spirit that was

---

48. Rofé, *Prophetical Stories*, 46n16.
49. For further study see Stoebe, *Das erste Buch Samuelis*, 302–03.

sent by God between Abimelech and the citizens of Shechem (9:23). Some say that Saul suffered from mental illness and paranoia, but according to Hertzberg, "Saul's suffering is described theologically, not psychopathically or psychologically."[50] However, we believe that the evil spirit was probably visions and dreams that were sent by God: "You frighten me with dreams, and terrify me with visions" (Job 7:14).

David's arrival to King Saul's court resembles the signs the Saul received after his anointment. On that occasion Samuel told him that the asses were found, and that he would meet three people who would make pilgrimage to God at Bethel: one with kids, one with bread, and one with a jar of wine. Later he would encounter a band of prophets who proceeded with lyres, timbrels, flutes, and harps. Similarly, in the section which describes Jesse sending his son David to Saul, we read that he took an ass and sent him with bread, a skin of wine, and a kid (1 Sam 16:20). Afterward, when the evil spirit came upon Saul, David took a lyre and played it. We can see there is a great similarity in the stories of the anointment of Saul and David. This is not a coincidence; it is to stress that it is David who is the legitimate king instead of Saul. David is now God's chosen one and not Saul.

In conclusion, in the stories of both Saul's and David's coronations, Samuel appears as a prophet who knows what will happen. He delivers the words of God and he is the king maker. God directs the events and uses Samuel as his instrument. Samuel anointed Saul as the first king of Israel and later anointed David. There are different versions of Saul's coronation: first, Samuel secretly anointed Saul at Ramah; then, at Mizpah, Saul was designated as a king following the casting of lots. This was done in the presence of the tribes and their representatives. Following the victory against the Ammonites, a third ceremony took place where Saul was declared king. While Samuel played a pivotal role in the first two coronations, at the third ceremony in Gilgal he is overshadowed by Saul and the people of Israel. In Gilgal it was Saul who made the judgment in the sacred legal realm. It is the first signs of Samuel's decline in prestige and status.

The story of David's coronation is like Saul's coronation, and they share common motifs. There is a sacrificial meal prior to both coronations, neither is present at the time of their election, and both were anointed in secret. Equally, Saul and David are depicted as small and unworthy for the task. In both stories a young man is directing the events unintentionally. When Saul was anointed the spirit of God rested on him. However, when

---

50. Hertzberg, *I & II Samuel*, 141; Smith, *Critical and Exegetical Commentary*, 148.

David was anointed the spirit of God rested on him but departed from Saul. David's arrival to King Saul's court resembles the signs that Saul received from Samuel after his anointment. This resemblance in the stories is not accidental; it appears to stress that David is the chosen king instead of Saul. Samuel is the king maker who delivers God's words and anoints Saul and later David. However Samuel is no longer the person who leads the nation; there is a new reality, and there is a king Saul. In the next part of our work we will look into chapter 12, which contains a farewell address by Samuel. What are the main convictions and ideas this speech tries to convey? What can we learn about Samuel's personality and the relationship between the prophetic office and the kingship?

6

Samuel's Farewell Speech

SAMUEL LISTENED TO THE people's request, and in obedience to YHWH's command anointed Saul as the first legitimate king of Israel. Now, after the renewal of Saul's coronation at Gilgal, it is time for Samuel to step down. Samuel represents the past, while king Saul is the present and the future. Therefore, Samuel addressed the people of Israel in a farewell speech. This speech is similar to other speeches in the Hebrew Bible where leaders addressed their people at the end of their assignment. The speeches contain a call to follow the covenant, and to obey God, who would deliver the Israelites from their enemies. These motifs are found in Moses' speech in Deuteronomy 31:1–34:12, which is set on the eve of his death, and Joshua's speech after the conquest of the promised land before his death (Josh 23; 24:29–30).

To mark the end of an era, and to signal the beginning of new one, the biblical narrator outlined and summarized his views on past and future events. This type of summary, found in 1 Samuel 12, is also found in the book of Judges (2:6–3:6) and in the second book of Kings (2 Kgs 17:7–23).[1] Hertzberg has pointed out that the judges period begins and ends with sermons: statements were made before the arrival of the first judge (Judg 2:6-3:6), and following the activities of Samuel as the last judge (1 Sam 12).[2]

---

1. To this type of category scholars have added more speeches; see McCarthy, "II Samuel," 131–38.

2. Hertzberg, *I & II Samuel*, 97.

Wellehausen suggested that Samuel's speech is not an integral part of the original rejection of human kingship but was written by the editor of the book of Samuel who lived many years after the events took place.[3] Noth proposed that the whole of chapter 12 is the work of the Deuteronomist, who created the chapter as a farewell speech.[4] The speech expresses the author's denunciations of kingship and contains typical Deuteronomistic expressions.[5] Buber, on the other hand, says the original material of the chapter is found only in verses 1–5 and 24–25. This is because the statements which are hostile to kingship could not be original.[6] Strangely, Saul is not mentioned by name in the chapter. Although the speech is considered the "farewell address" of Samuel, he still continued to be a prophet and a king maker. The chapter contains older material which is different than what is recounted by Deuteronomist. The names of the enemies, for example, appear in reverse order to what is described in Judge; also the chronological order of the names of the deliverers is incorrect.

In 1 Samuel 11, the people of Israel held a great celebration proclaiming Saul as king, while in the following chapter, 12, the demand for a king is seen as sinful. Evidently, chapters 11 and 12 were not written by the same author. The theme of Samuel's speech corresponds exactly to chapter 8, where the people of Israel made their first demand for kingship. Thus, the inevitable question is: What are the main ideas the speech tries to convey? Who wrote the speech and in what era was it written? Since there was already a king in Israel, what did Samuel try to achieve with his speech?

SAMUEL ESTABLISHES HIS INTEGRITY

Samuel declared that Saul's monarchy was the result of the people's request (verse 1). The demand to have a king was due to his old age and his sons' misconduct, which was already mentioned in chapter 8:1–5 and is repeated here in verse 2. The sons are mentioned here but not their misdeeds. Samuel is reluctant to criticize his sons' misbehavior. Instead, he says, "but my sons are still with you" (12:2). He reminds the people that he was leading them to this day, and now it is the king who is leading them. The contrast between Samuel and the king signals a transition from a prophet to a king.

---

3. Wellhausen, *Die Composition*, 240–43.
4. Noth, *Überlieferungegeschichtliche Studein*, 5, 59–60.
5. Noth, *Überlieferungegeschichtliche Studein*, 5.
6. Buber, "Die Erzählung," 113.

Samuel listened to the people's demand for a king and obeyed God: "Heed their demands and appoint a king for them" (8:22).

It is not clear why, for a second time, Samuel had to denounce the office of kingship; there was already a king, and his name was Saul. Ehrlich pointed out that in the premonarchic days a judge was like a king. Not surprisingly Samuel appointed his sons as judges; he was expecting that they and their descendants would rule after him. As noted before, he tried to create his own dynasty. However, his sons misbehaved, which led the people to request a king. This upset Samuel greatly and he never got over it for the rest of his life. Since he could not pour out his anger on the people, he transferred it onto Saul, hating him. According to Ehrlich, Saul was the man who was given what he believed belonged to his sons: "And woe to the man that a holy man hates. And so, David was anointed king only because Samuel hated him [Saul]."[7] In addition, Ehrlich says that Samuel's bitterness is similar to the later prophets who did not get along with the kings and were as painful as thorns to the kings. "And the first of the prophets transferred Israel's monarchy [for personal reasons] because of his love of his evil sons and his hatred of a righteous man who had been given their place."[8]

Samuel declared his innocence before the Lord and his anointed king. Declaration of innocence does not appear in other farewell speeches and is unique to Samuel's. The king who is mentioned here serves in his legal capacity, which might point to Samuel retiring from his office. This is in contrast to the king who is described as taking from the people (8:11–17). Samuel, in a series of negative statements, declares that had not defrauded, oppressed, or taken anything. The people are summoned to testify against him in case he committed any wrongdoings. He puts himself on trial with the knowledge that he is innocent. Samuel enlists God and the new king as his witnesses. His words here are similar to Moses', who responded to claims by Dathan and Abiram by saying: "I have not taken the ass of any one of them, nor have I wronged any one of them" (Num 16:15).[9] Elat suggested that Moses make his plea to God not only to say that Korah was guilty in committing a sin but also to convince him that he deserved to lead the people in the future: "By this you shall know that it was the Lord who sent me to do all these things; they are not of my own devising" (16:28). To

---

7. Ehrlich, *Mikrâ ki Pheschutô*, 2:125; Drazin, *Who Was*, 102.
8. Drazin, *Who Was*, 102.
9. This was noticed by Josephus, *Ant.* 4:46–50; *Ned.* 38a.

SAMUEL'S FAREWELL SPEECH

bolster his study, he gives an example from the ancient Near East where this type of declaration did not come to summarize a man's life but to convince the audience that he deserved their trust in the future.[10] Similarly, Samuel declared his innocence by asking God and the new king to judge between him and the people of Israel who did not want his leadership anymore. This request came to convince them that he is worthy to be a leader in the future.[11]

The call for God to pass judgment is a recurring motif in the Hebrew Bible. David did not harm Saul and spared his life because Saul was anointed by the Lord. In the exchange between them David said, "May the Lord be arbiter and may He judge between you and me! May He take note and uphold my cause and vindicate me against you" (1 Sam 24:15). A call for judgment is also found in the story of Jephthah the Gileadite in his feud with the Ammonites: "May the Lord, who judges, decide today between the Israelites and the Ammonites" (Judg 11:27).

THE WITNESS OF HISTORY

The people exonerate Samuel from all the charges, and now Samuel calls God as witness against the people. Sin, oppression, cry to YHWH, and deliverance are patterns that are repeated in Samuel's summary. These types of themes appear in farewell speeches (Deut 31:4–8; Josh 23:4–5) as well as in covenant formulas (Exod 19:3–6; Josh 24:2–13; Neh 9). According to Gordon: "Such summaries of salvation-history were an integral part of Israel's worship."[12] Their aim was to encourage the Israelites. As God showed mercy to his people in the past and delivered them from oppression, he will continue to deliver them in the future as long as they obey and follow him. The Exodus from Egypt, which was a pivotal event in the history of Israel, is mentioned first. God promised to bring the Israelites back and make them into a great nation (Gen 46:3).[13] These promises are fulfilled through God's mediators, Moses and Aaron, who are portrayed here like the saviors in the book of Judges that God sent.

The second period that is mentioned is the judges period. The Israelites forgot God; they showed their ingratitude, so he abandoned them

---

10. Elat, *Samuel*, 132–35.
11. Elat, *Samuel*, 136.
12. Gordon, *1 & 2 Samuel*, 127.
13. Joshua in his summary mentioned all the three patriarchs (Josh 24:2–4).

to their enemies. The calamities that the people suffered were the result of their own sins. Samuel mentions the enemies that God has sent against Israel. The enemies listed are not recorded in chronological order. Sisera, Philistines, and the king of Moab are referred to as the enemies who oppressed the people of Israel. The Israelites cried to the Lord, admitted their sins for abandoning God and serving the Baals and Ashtaroth. This description contains terms which recall the book of Judges (Judg 10:10). It is similar to Samuel's previous call to the Israelites to remove the foreign gods and to repent (1 Sam 7:3). The reference of Sisera, Philistines, and the king of Moab are classic examples. They serve as an illustration of the whole period of the judges. The Israelites forgot God, and so he punished them and delivered them into the hands of their enemies.

In addition to the enemies Samuel also mentions some of the most important judges that were sent to deliver the nation of Israel. Jerubbaal, Bedan, Jephthah and Samuel are listed. By mentioning Jerubbaal and Samuel, he creates a time frame from the first judge to the last one. In the middle are Bedan and Jephthah, who represent those mediators who were sent to deliver the Israelites. Jerubbaal (Gideon) saved the nation from the Midianites' oppression (Judg 6–8). Bedan is not mentioned in the book of Judges, but *Tg. Jon.* has identified Dan with Samson. Likewise, we read in the Talmud: "And why is he called Bedan? Because he comes from the tribe of Dan," in other words, Bedan is the contraction of "a son of Dan," which refers to Samson.[14] Jephthah, who defeated the Ammonites, is also mentioned. How odd is the occurrence of Samuel's name among the names of the judges who delivered the Israelites? He mentions himself in the third person. The LXX and Syr. read "Samson," but this is unlikely since the mention of Samuel as one of the saviors coincides with the context of his speech. According to Goldman: "Samuel the accuser dissociates himself from Samuel the savior, who is cited as evidence against his people."[15] Herzberg believes that the mention of Samuel is not "a slip of a pen"; the whole period of the judges including the time of Samuel is under review here.[16] It

---

14. *Roš Haš* 25a; the LXX and Peshitta have "Barak"; Zakovitch says that Bedan in 1 Chronicles 7:17 is like Jephthah. He suggests that "Bedan" and "Jephthah" are alternate names for the same person. See Zakovitch, "יפתח=בדן," 123–25.

15. Goldman, *Samuel*, 65

16. Hertzberg, *I & II Samuel*, 99.

comes to make his case relevant to the existing situation and the request for a king.[17]

Another reason for the people's demand for a king is stated. The attacks of Nahash the king of the Ammonites led the Israelites to request an earthly king instead of God who was their king. This reason was not mentioned in chapters 8 or 11. It was suggested that the Deuteronomistic author knew of a tradition which was different from the events narrated in chapters 8 and 11, or he made a free interpretation of the present materials.[18] While, according to Vannoy, "Samuel's statement in 1 Samuel 12:12 is thus compatible with chapters 8, 10, and 11, more importantly it reveals his own analysis of the motivation behind the initial request of the elders for a king."[19] Instead of a cry for God's help, the people demanded an earthly king that shall rule over them. Samuel sees their request as a rejection of God who delivered them from their enemies time after time. Samuel is portrayed here as a loyal servant to YHWH who does not accept the people's demands for a king. Acceptance of the people's demands meant a decline in his status as mediator between the people and God.

Since God sent the Israelites a king, Samuel underlines the conditions on which the new political establishment will function. The Israelites can follow and serve God. The earthly kingship is approved and God's kingship over Israel will last. They will continue to have God's help and the blessing of the covenant (Deut 28:11). Or they can rebel against God and the commandments and God will punish them. The author uses the same language, "hand of YHWH," which describes the overwhelming action against the Philistines which now will turn against monarchic Israel. Some scholars suggests that verses 14–15 are a representation of the covenant of blessing and curse which Israel is now offered.[20] It corresponded to the blessing and curse sections which are found in the Hebrew Bible (Deut 12–26; Josh 24:14). Obedience would continue the bond between Israel and God; disobedience would lead to a break; God would be their enemy. The disobedience foreshadows the future kingship in Israel where we have a similar description of the kings of Israel. According to Herzberg, except for Hezekiah and Josiah, the other kings of Israel failed to follow God's first commandment. Had they not done so the events of 587 BCE would not

---

17 Hertzberg, *I & II Samuel*, 99.
18 Noth, *Überlieferungsgeschichtliche Studien*, 60; McCarter, *1 Samuel*, 215.
19 Vannoy, *Covenant Renewal*, 39.
20 Muilenburg, "Form and Structure," 363; Vannoy, *Covenant Renewal*, 46.

have taken place.[21] However, the text is not a covenant or covenant renewal because there are no commandments given by Samuel or a commitment by the people to follow them. The instructions that were given by Samuel (1 Sam 12:20b–22) are general in nature and convey Deuteronomistic language that was added by the editor.

THE PEOPLE ACKNOWLEDGE THEIR ERROR

Samuel told the people to attend and witness God's response to their demand for a king. Samuel called God and he answered him. In the book of Psalms, we read: "Moses and Aaron among his priests, Samuel, among those who call on his name when they called to the Lord, he answered them" (Ps 99:6). Moses called God many times and prayed for the people of Israel; Aaron is also mentioned with Moses as praying for Israel (Lev 9:23). Similarly, Samuel called to God and God answered (1 Sam 7:9). Samuel appears here as Moses, who leads Israel to a new relationship with God. In the past, it was the miracle of the Red Sea that led the Israelites to fear God and to believe in him and his servant Moses. Now, Samuel asks God to send thunder and rain during the wheat harvest period so they will fear him and God. The time of wheat harvest in the land of Israel is May to June. During this period of the year rain is unknown. The unnatural occurrence of this phenomenon came to convince the people of their sinfulness in asking for a king. According to the book of Deuteronomy God promised to grant rain in the appropriate season (Deut 11:14). If rain comes at the wrong season it is impractical and harmful. Early or late rain can extend or shorten the growing season, delay the harvest, or cause it to rot.[22] In the Talmud we read of fasting in the case of rain delay, and when it rains after the typical season it was considered a curse.[23] Longman suggested that chapter 12 is a covenant renewal ceremony. The thunderstorm was part of the covenant curse, as it damaged the crop.[24] This is unlikely, because as a result of the thunderstorms the people realized their demanded for a king was evil in the Lord's eyes. It is Samuel who calls God for rain and thunder, and God answered him. God is listening to his servant Samuel who serves here as intermediary between the people and God. Samuel is a legitimate channel between man

21. Hertzberg, *I & II Samuel*, 100.
22. Arden-Close, "Rainfall of Palestine," 122–28; *Lev R.* 35:12; *Tg. Jon.*; *Ta'an*.19b.
23. *Ta'an.* 1:7.
24. Longman, "1 Sam 12:16–19," 168–71.

and God. As mentioned above God responded to him already in 7:9–10. This foreshadows the prophetic movement where the prophets intercede on behalf of the people. Moreover, the book of Deuteronomy states that God will raise up a prophet like Moses—someone who the people would listen to (Deut 18:15).

The scene of the thunder and rain led the people to fear Samuel and God. Similar language is mentioned with Moses after God's wondrous powers were displayed in Egypt: "the people feared the Lord; they had faith in the Lord and His servant Moses" (Exod 14:31). When Moses descended from Mount Sinai the people were afraid to go near him (34:30). Fear is also mentioned with Joshua: "so that they revered him all his days as they had revered Moses" (Josh 4:14). The fear led the people to ask Samuel to pray for them to the Lord. It was the prophet's role to call on the Lord to receive and proclaim his message. The prophet was a spokesman for God and man; he interceded in helping people. Abraham, who is called a prophet in Genesis 20:7, pleads for Abimelech. Moses, Amos, Jeremiah, and also Samuel act in this capacity. Pleading to Samuel the people referred to themselves as "your servants," which shows humility. They were afraid that they would die; the thunder and rain served as a sign of God's displeasure; it was a bad omen. In the Hebrew Bible these forces serve as a display of God's power. This happened as a direct result of Samuel's prayer, which shows the strength of his ties with God.

People were afraid of divine manifestation, as these encounters were terrifying experiences full of dread. Jacob after his encounter with the mysterious assailant said: "I have seen a divine being face to face, yet my life has been preserved" (Gen 31:31). Moses at the burning bush hid his face, "for he was afraid to look at God" (Exod 3:6). Realizing that they saw an angel of God, Manoh, like Gideon (Judg 6:22), expected that he and his wife would die. The scene of the miraculous thunder and rain led the people to realize that God was displeased with their request for a king. The manifestation of the divine power led them to admit their sins to Samuel. Among their sins, the request for a king is mentioned. Before it was Samuel who called the request for a king a sin; now the people agree. But above all, this demonstration of the divine power exhibited the people's need for Samuel's service as a mediator to pray on their behalf. Interestingly, when they ask Samuel to pray on their behalf, they say: "Intercede for your servants with the Lord your God" (verse 19). They speak here of YHWH as Samuel's God.

According to Vannoy, they recognized that their request alienated God.[25] Previously in 7:8 the people asked Samuel to cry to "YHWH our God." Evidently, after they rejected him, they believe they lose the right to call YHWH "our God."[26]

SAMUEL ENCOURAGES THE PEOPLE

Samuel allays the people's fear. "Fear not," a phrase which is similar to what Moses said to the Israelites: "Be not afraid" (Exod 20:17). The phrase "fear not" appears several times throughout the Bible and is used by God. It is also found in extrabiblical sources and is known as an "oracle of assurance."[27] Here, it's Samuel who uses this phrase in his role as intercessor, which was one of the duties of the prophet. The people already did all this evil, which probably referred to the demand for a king. Now Samuel cautions them not to "turn away from the Lord" but to worship God and serve him with their whole hearts, a demand that Samuel had already stated (1 Sam 7:3). The phrase "turn away from God" is a typical Deuteronomistic phrase, and it is used to describe apostasy in a Deuteronomistic context.[28] Samuel repeated the phrase "turn away" without mentioning the Lord (12:21). The phrase "turn away" precedes the particle *kî* for emphasis. He told them not to follow *tōhû* vain things (Isa 44:9). The Hebrew *tōhû va-vohu* appears in the story of creation (Gen 1:2), and appears later in Jeremiah's prophetic vision which describes the primal chaos (Jer 4:23–27). In other words, Samuel told the people to follow God the creator of heaven and earth and not false gods, which are described as *tōhû*.

Samuel's warning turned to encouragement, and God's faithfulness is emphasized. God would not abandon his people; they are his chosen ones. This idea is displayed in the book of Psalms: "For the Lord will not forsake his people; he will not abandon his very own" (94:14). It would lower his honor in their eyes if he abandoned them: "It would reflect badly on his own reputation if he were to cast them off."[29] God keeps faith with the descendants of those who are loyal to him (Deut 7:7–8). As Moses reminded the people, it was part of God's promise to Israel's ancestors that its future

25. Vannoy, *Covenant Renewal*, 52.
26. Vannoy, *Covenant Renewal*, 52.
27. Sarna, *Genesis*, 112.
28. Weinfeld, *Deuteronomy*, 339
29. McCarter, *I Samuel*, 217.

depends on following God's commandments. After instructing the people, Samuel outlines his own responsibilities. He promises to continue his task as a religious leader of the people. He undertakes to keep Israel on a good and upright path. In his commitment he mentions two elements: to pray and to teach. Samuel intends to do so even after the inauguration of the kingship.[30] His failure to carry out these duties would be a grave sin. As we read in the Talmud:

> Raba b. Ḥinena the elder said further in the name of Rab: If one is in a position to pray on behalf of his fellow and does not do so, he is called a sinner as it says, *moreover as for me, for be it from me that I should sin against the Lord in ceasing to pray for you*.[31]

Samuel promised to continue to lead and instruct the people as a religious teacher in the practice of what is good and right. This kind of language is mentioned in the book of Deuteronomy (6:18; 12:28) and is associated with obeying God's commandments (Exod 15:26; 1 Kgs 11:38). He charged the people to fear and serve God (1 Sam 12:24). Fear, serve, and obey appeared already in verse 14, and the phrase "with all your heart" in verse 20; the repetition here serves as inclusion. Similar language was used by Joshua in his farewell speech: "Now, therefore, revere the Lord and serve him with undivided loyalty" (Josh 24:14). Samuel calls the people to see all the great things that God did for them. This can be explained as all of God's gracious dealings with his people (1 Sam 12:7). It is also reminiscent of 7:10; as Radak explained, this is a reference to the miracle of the thunder and rain, which is described in verse 16. God on his part provided them with a choice, and it is up to the king and the people to keep it or not.

Despite all of Samuel's prayers, if the Israelites would do "wickedly," which is mentioned in verses 17, 19, 20, the Israelites and their king shall be swept away. The language of "swept away" is a reminder of the destruction of Sodom and Gomorrah, where the sins of the people was so grave (Gen 18:23–24; 19:15, 17). It is suggested that Samuel speaks here about the near future. Saul would be rejected from being king over Israel and he and his sons would die on Mount Gilboa.[32] But Saul is not mentioned by name in chapter 12, nor is his kingship questioned or criticized. Therefore, this might refer to a later period in Israelite history, a period following the exile

---

30. Balentine, "Prophet as Intercessor," 161–73
31. *Ber.* 12b.
32. Thornton, "Studies in Samuel," 421.

of 597 and 587 BCE. Exile was the result of sins that were committed by the Israelites and their kings.

THE PURPOSE OF CHAPTER 12

This chapter marks a transition between the end of the judges period and the beginning of the monarchic era. Samuel relinquishes his office and calls the people to remind them of their covenant with God. This act is similar to a call by Moses and Joshua who, on the eve of their death, gathered the people of Israel and delivered a farewell speech. It is the changing of the guards; the old one, Samuel versus the new king. Samuel is portrayed as saying, "I have grown old and gray . . . and I have been your leader from my youth to this day" (verse 2), versus the king: "Here is the king that you have chosen, that you have asked for" (verse 13). In his speech, Samuel insists that kingship was a bad choice for Israel because God is their king (verse 12). By asking for a king, the Israelites showed their ingratitude for all the kindnesses that God has done for them. Nevertheless, God granted their request. As we read in the Talmud: "In the way that a person wants to go, he will be led."[33] For the first time the people recognized their sinfulness for asking for a king. Still, the kingship would last as long as the people would worship God and serve him with their whole heart (verse 24).

From chapter 7 through chapter 12 the kingship that is held by Saul is viewed in a positive manner. Saul is anointed by Samuel per God's instructions (1 Sam 9:16). The spirit of YHWH rested upon Saul and he prophesied among a band of prophets (10:10). Later the spirit of YHWH helped him to deliver the people of Jabesh-gilead (11:6). After the victory the people renewed Saul's kingship in Gilgal. When the people asked Samuel for a king, they wanted the king to be responsible for ministering justice and to fight against their enemies. The law in Deuteronomy does not assign these duties to the king. The law says nothing about his rights or authority or obeying him. What the book of Deuteronomy says is that the king should revere the Lord and observe his laws (17:19). The law in Deuteronomy limits the king's powers; the king and the people are subject to God's law.[34] This outlook is repeated in chapter 12, which stresses several times that obedience to God and his laws will guarantee the continuation of kingship (1 Sam 12:14, 24).

---

33. *Mak.* 10b
34. Tigay, *Deuteronomy*, 166.

In contrast to favorable assessments of kingship, there is also criticism of the institution. Samuel criticized kingship and warned the people of the hardship the kingship would bring (8:10–17). He viewed kingship as a rejection of YHWH as a king (8:7; 10:19). Nevertheless, this assessment is balanced by YHWH's command to make a king (8:7, 2) and the positive understandings of kingship which is presented in this chapter (12:14, 24).[35] According to Klein, Samuel and God are shown to be innocent in two legal procedures (verses 1–5, 6–15), and the demand for a king was a failure since the people should have looked for God's help. God, with his love for his people Israel, gave them the gift of kingship. If the people would be obedient and follow God, this gift would be a blessing. On the other hand, if they would be rebellious and disobedient, this would become a curse.[36]

As mentioned above, Samuel's speech has some features which are found in Joshua 24. It was suggested that the entire chapter 12 is a covenant—a renewal ceremony. According to Vannoy, 1 Samuel 11:14–12:25 is "the record of a covenant renewal ceremony held for the dual purpose of providing for covenant continuity at the time of transition in leadership and covenant restoration after abrogation."[37] However, when Samuel addessed the people, they did not swear to uphold his instruction. Moreover, there is no mention of a covenant ceremony which exists in the other biblical texts. Knutson admits that there are some parts in chapter 12 which are similar to treaty elements, but he does not accept the existence of treaty structure or covenant language in chapter 12.[38] Tsumura follows him and suggests that what we have here is a "negative confession," Samuel justifying his past behavior.[39] It is between Samuel and the people and not between the people and God or the king. He believes that the aim of the chapter is to depict Samuel's new role and his relationship with the people rather than God's covenantal relationship with the people.[40]

In this chapter are Samuel's declaration of his innocence (12:2-6), his mentioning of historical events, the part he played in initiating the miracle (verse 7), the leading of the people to confess their sins (verse 19), and his demand for a new role in the era (verse 23).

---

35. Klein, *1 Samuel*, 120.
36. Klein, *1 Samuel*, 120.
37. Vannoy, *Covenant Renewal*, 178.
38. Knutson, "Literary Genre," 2:171–73.
39. Tsumura, *First Book of Samuel*, 315.
40. Tsumura, *First Book of Samuel*, 315.

SAMUEL

These kinds of themes are not usually found in the Bible when it summarizes the life of its leaders.[41] Samuel's speech exhibits his desire to continue to lead the people and to increase their trust in him. The people's fear grew as a result of the miracle, and hence Samuel declared that he would continue to intercede on their behalf and instruct them in the practice of what is good and right (12:23). In this interchange he tried to convince the people that all their past victories were the result of God's doing and they sinned by asking for a king. He ended his speech by asking for a role under the king's leadership, so he would be able to intercede, instruct, and teach the people the duties that he already fulfilled.[42]

Samuel's speech reveals the contrast between his conduct and the king's rights (1 Sam 8:11–17). The king makes demands from the people, while Samuel declares his innocence before the Lord and his anointed king. In a series of negative statements Samuel declares that he did not take anything from the people. Samuel stresses the bond between God and his people. God will not forsake his people Israel, his chosen nation. He uses similar language to what Moses and Joshua used, but in a more caring and sympathetic way. Moses said: "He forsook the God who made him and spurned the Rock of his support" (Deut 32:15). Samuel says that God would not abandon his people. Joshua said, "And what will You do about Your great name?" (Josh 7:9), whereas Samuel says, "For the sake of His great name" (1 Sam 12:22). Samuel's activities in chapter 12 are comparable to his deeds in chapter 7 when he started to serve the people of Israel. In chapter 7, he demands that the people remove their foreign gods and only worship and serve God (verse 3). In chapter 12 he repeats his warning that turning away from God and worshiping other gods is hopeless (verse 15). It would not save the people and would only would bring calamity and destruction (verse 21). As in chapter 7 he demands that the people serve and worship God with all their heart (12:24). Of note, chapter 7 includes "the Lord thundered mightily" (verse 10) and chapter 12 reads, "and the Lord sent thunder and rain" (12:18). These shared elements, which appear at the start of Samuel's mission and on the eve of his departure, obviously have a purpose. It signals the end of an era in Israel's history, with the closure of the judges period and the inauguration of the monarchic period. Samuel was the last judge in Israel; he was also a prophet and a teacher who instructed the law to the people. Now, with the emergence of kingship, he

41. Elat, *Samuel*, 140.
42. Elat, *Samuel*, 140.

disowned his responsibility as a judge but continued his call as a prophet and a teacher "As for me, far be it from me to sin against the Lord and refrain from praying for you; and I will continue to instruct you in the practice of what is good and right" (verse 23).

The Deuteronomistic editor interpolated and added into this story the phrases and ideas which coincided with his theology (10b, 14–15, 20b–22, 24a). In his expansion he tries to convey his thoughts about the relationship between God, Israel, and the kingship in the past and the present. According to his views the main sin committed by the Israelites was forsaking the Lord, and worshipping Baalim and Ashtaroth (verse 10b):[43] "Do not turn away to follow worthless things, which can neither profit nor save but are worthless" (verse 21). These themes have no link to the other stories about the establishment of the monarchy.[44] Samuel demanded from the people, "revere the Lord" (verse 14, 24), "serve the Lord with all your heart" (verse 20, 24), "obey the Lord" (verses 14–15), and "seeing that the Lord undertook to make you His people" (verse 22). These ideas do not refer to a specific period of time, whereas Samuel's dialogue about his conduct is limited to his lifetime. The expansion by the Deuteronomist, which includes warnings against worshiping other gods and the demand to serve God and obey his commandments, are timeless.[45]

Combining his views and Samuel's thoughts about the difficulties that arose in his days, the Deuteronomistic editor created a speech that is set on the eve of monarchic period. Accordingly, the worship of other gods and the failure to follow God's commandments led ultimately to the fall of the Israelite monarchy. The speech was inserted to indicate the end of the judges period and to introduce the monarchic period. To announce this new era the editor used similar language that describes the kings of Israel and Judah, which is found in 1 and 2 Kings. Therefore, we read "Saul was... years old when he became king, and he reigned over Israel for two years."[46]

More than likely, the editor of chapter 12 added and expanded Samuel's speech. The speech originally dealt with a specific event. He introduced themes and ideas which coincided with his own views about the nature of the covenant between God and Israel. By doing so the editor gave it a

43. Weinfeld, *Deuteronomy*, 320:2a.
44. Elat, *Samuel*, 142.
45. Elat, *Samuel*, 143.
46. See for example 1 Kgs 14:21; 15:1–2, 9–10, 25; 2 Kgs 3:1; 8:17, 26; 9:29.

different meaning from its original setting.[47] As a farewell speech, Samuel's speech is not similar to the speeches of Moses and Joshua. In these speeches there is a summary of their life and their activities before their deaths. Not so with Samuel, who did not end his calling and continued to be involved with the affairs of the state. He demanded that sacrifices be made before the battle against the Philistines (13:11), delivered God's message to fight the Amalekites, and enumerated all that belonged to him (15:3).

In conclusion, Samuel's farewell address contains his thoughts about the difficulties that arose during his days regarding the monarchy. He insists that a king is a bad choice for Israel because God is their king (verse 12). Because of his love for his people, God gave them the gift of kingship. If the people would be obedient and follow him, this gift would be a blessing. The speech is delivered on the eve of the monarchic period. Samuel appears as a mediator, much like Moses and Joshua. He exhibits a desire to continue to lead the people as a prophet and a teacher. With the establishment of the monarchy there is a steady decline in Samuel's stature. Therefore, Samuel tries to restore and increase his trust among the people as their leader. The new reality of the existence of a king and a prophet side-by-side led to clashes between these two forces. The boundaries between them were not set. Samuel tries to maintain his power. The speech was expanded by the Deuteronomist, who uses phrases and ideas which coincide with his theology. It appears in the form of a direct address by Samuel and emphasizes that the worship of other gods and the failure to follow God's commandments would lead to grave consequences, which is a timeless addition. What emerges here is that Samuel vehemently opposes kingship. The kind of relationship that existed between Samuel and Saul, and between Samuel and David, will be the subject of our next chapter.

---

47. Elat, *Samuel*, 143.

7

Samuel, Saul, and David

THE PEOPLE'S DEMAND FOR an earthly king who would lead them in war displeased Samuel, who had devoted his entire life to serving the nation. Samuel strongly denounced kingship because he viewed himself as God's instrument on earth. By demanding a king, the people of Israel rejected YHWH's leadership in war. They wanted a king to lead them in their wars, not YHWH's wars.[1] God perceived the demand for kingship as rejecting of him and not Samuel. It was a denunciation of the eternal, an act of disloyalty. Samuel, despite his reservations as a loyal servant of the Lord, obeyed God's order and anointed Saul as the first king of Israel. Later he would anoint David as a king instead of Saul. Examination of the biblical text reveals that from the start there are clashes between Samuel and Saul. First, during the war against the Philistines (1 Sam 13:7–15) and following the war against the Amalekites (1 Sam 15), Samuel condemned Saul's dynasty, rejecting his rule. So what were the reasons for Samuel's harsh judgment against Saul? Did Saul commit grievous sins that necessitated his removal? Was Samuel only delivering God's judgment on Saul, or was there, perhaps, a personal motivation behind his condemnation? On the other hand, we read: "But Samuel grieved over Saul because the Lord regretted that He had made Saul king over Israel" (15:35). Did Samuel grieve over the rejection of Saul and feel sorry for him?

---

1. Klein, *1 Samuel*, 78.

Not much is said about the relationship between Samuel and David. We are told that Samuel anointed David, but there is no exchange between them. Later, after Saul attempted to capture David, he fled to Samuel. There, for the first time, David spoke to Samuel, and told him everything that Saul had done to him. Is there any conceivable reason for this laconic account and what the narrator tried to achieve by doing so? In this chapter, the relationships that existed between Samuel and Saul and Samuel and David will be examined. This will shed more light on their different personalities and the dynamic that existed between them. In addition, we will try to see if Samuel's views about the institution of kingship influenced his dealing with Saul and David and how Samuel rationalized his views on the institution of kingship with God's demand.

SAUL AND SAMUEL'S FIRST CLASH

The feud between Saul and Samuel started during the conflict with the Philistines, which is described in chapter 13. Saul's fighting with the Philistines is interrupted by the insertion of verses 7b–15a, which is an account of Samuel's accusations of Saul. Some scholars include 13:8 and 10:8, when Samuel instructed Saul to wait for him at Gilgal for seven days.[2] However, in chapter 10:8, Saul was a young shepherd who was still living in his father's house; here, he is the king of Israel, who had already defeated the Ammonites. Chapters 13–14 suggest that wars were conducted by a mature Saul with a grown son. Nevertheless, there are several similarities between 10:8 and 13:8–9. In both, Saul is instructed to wait seven days until Samuel comes; also mentioned are the sacrifices of burnt offerings and peace offerings. On the other hand, it was suggested that the reference to 10:8 and 13:8 is not necessarily about the same occasion: "People could 'wait on God at Gilgal for seven days' on many occasions."[3] We should also point out that the Hebrew word for "days" sometimes also means a year (Gen 38:12; 40:4).

It has been suggested that verses 9–14, which contain Samuel's rebuke of Saul, are a late addition that did not belong to the original narrative and are secondary.[4] Duplication exists in our verses, as well as in chapter 15. Both involve Saul and Samuel, and both took place at Gilgal. In both chapter, we read about a sin that Saul committed and a rebuke of Saul by the

2. Yonick, "Rejection of Saul," 29–50; Donner, "Basic Elements," 40–54.
3 Tsumara, *First Book of Samuel*, 341.
4. Miller, "Saul's Rise," 157–74; Klein, 1 *Samuel*, 123.

prophet Samuel.⁵ Together, the two stories demonstrate the violations of sacred traditions dealing with a holy war. Thus, the question arises: why does the author tell the story of Saul's rejection twice? The author is giving the same reasons in both stories. However, we should point out that Saul's sin is an integral part of the story. By reiterating the narrative of sin, the author distinguishes the personal character of Saul and Jonathan by creating dissimilarity. Saul does not trust God, while Jonathan does.⁶ Moreover, the condemnation of Saul's dynasty and his rejection are two separate subjects. Therefore, verses 13:7b–15a and 15:1–34 are stories written by the same author who gave different reasons for each account. In the first account, only Saul's dynasty is discontinued (13:14); while in the second, Saul himself is rejected, leading to David's anointing.⁷

Saul is described in an unflattering way. He is under pressure because Samuel did not arrive on time. The people started to leave Saul. Saul is frightened—he was indecisive, did not act, and feared that the Philistines would come to capture him. As a result, he disobeyed Samuel; he did not wait for the prophet and offered a sacrifice by himself. Saul's sin can be explained in two ways. According to one explanation, he sinned because he disobeyed Samuel's order to wait for him for seven days. Saul lost his patience, and therefore did not wait for the prophet who was delayed. The second explanation is that Saul did not have the authority to make the sacrifice.

Samuel rebuked Saul for these actions. Saul apologized by describing the events that led him to his actions. The people had left him, and the Philistines were moving forward in his direction. Interestingly, Samuel did not react to Saul's apologies and explanations. The narrator thought that Saul failed because he did not put his trust in God. He should have avoided military actions and trusted in God to deliver him from his enemies. By disobeying Samuel and not waiting for him, Saul disobeyed God and violated the terms of his appointment as king. Kingship required obedience; thus, the kingship would no longer go to Saul's son but to a man of God's choosing.

We should point out that Saul did wait the seven days for Samuel as he was instructed. Ironically, Samuel arrived just when Saul was finishing his sacrifice for the peace offerings. From the description of the ensuing events,

---

5. Brooks, *Saul and the Monarchy*, 55.
6. Garsiel, *First Book of Samuel*, 86–87.
7. Birch, *Rise of Israelite Monarchy*, 105–08; McCarter, *I Samuel*, 270–71.

Samuel

Saul did what was permissible to him. The army started to drift away, and the Philistines were gathering at Michmas. Saul was afraid; he was left with no option but to turn to God. Indeed, sacrifices were offered before a holy war (1 Sam 7:9); God's permission was frequently sought (Judg 20:23, 27; 1 Sam 7:9; 14:8–10; 14:37; 23:2, 4; 28:6; 30:7–8; 2 Sam 5:19, 23). The sacrifice of whole burned offerings, or "holocaust," was considered as pleasing to YHWH. What Saul did was essentially permissible for him to do. There was no law prohibiting him from performing sacrificial rites. Later we read that David at Jerusalem (2 Sam 6:13, 17–18; 24:25) and Solomon in Gibeon (1 Kgs 3:4, 15) offered sacrifices. As a commander-in-chief, he was left with no options after his men scattered. If anyone is in the wrong here it is Samuel and not Saul.[8]

Samuel acted here by his own initiative: "He alone declares that the king of Israel is in breach of YHWH's commandment. He alone announces that YHWH has rejected Saul."[9] Saul acted as a king, to do whatever he saw fit, since God was with him (1 Sam 10:7). He found himself in a desperate position and consequently took action. Saul tried to act as a king, but Samuel, who represented the older order, did not like that Saul acted independently. An independent king was a threat to his authority.

Later, on the eve of his last battle against the Philistines, Saul found himself in an identical situation. The Philistines were assembling their forces, Saul became afraid and tried to communicate with God, but God did not answer him, either by prophet or dreams. Left with no choice, Saul turned to the witch of Endor, who raised Samuel from his grave. Like the first episode, Samuel rebuked Saul, but this time for bringing him from the realm of the dead. His message was clear: Saul and his sons would join him the following day. This was a fulfillment of Samuel's previous message to Saul that his kingdom would not last. Saul, both in 1 Samuel 13 and the following chapters, is portrayed as disobedient, with no patience and no faith. The clash between Saul and Samuel was the first between a prophet and a king; it was the beginning of many feuds between the kings of Israel and the prophets. Historically speaking, Saul had differences with Samuel, who was the last judge. These differences stem from the fact "that the relationship between the king's sacred and secular functions was ill-defined, and the

---

8. Hertzberg, *I & II Samuel*, 106.
9. Jobling, *I Samuel*, 86.

secular requirements of the monarchy conflicted with the ancient sacred traditions."[10]

SAUL AND SAMUEL'S SECOND CLASH

The second quarrel between Saul and Samuel took place following Saul's failure to carry out the order to destroy Amalek. Saul spared King Agag and the best of the livestock. This was the last conversation between the two, and it was a long one (1 Sam 15:13–30). Each person spoke six times. Samuel led Saul step by step to admitting his guilt. To Samuel's question, "[What] is this bleating of sheep in my ears, and the lowing of oxen that I hear?" (verse 14), Saul responds like a person who is caught in a lie. He immediately tries to separate himself from the people to save face; he blames the people. Interestingly, there is a similarity between Saul under interrogation and Adam under interrogation. Each blamed a second party for his failure, and each was punished harshly, escaping immediate death. Saul still tries to justify the people's actions by claiming that they reserved the best of the animals for sacrifice to God who was with them in the war. When referring to God, he tells Samuel, "*your* god." Saul does not speak here of God as his God, instead, he refers to Samuel's God, and by that, "he tries to lighten his own responsibility as the representative of the people."[11]

Samuel's response to Saul's excuse was harsh. He told the king to stop, and to wait, to let him deliver God's message from last night. This mention of time is a hint about Saul's death. Samuel uses sarcasm here. He repeats Saul's own words that refer to the period before he was anointed as a king: "But I am only a Benjaminite, from the smallest of the tribes of Israel" (9:21). In other words, Samuel tells Saul that, since he was anointed as a king, he must take responsibility for his people's actions. Neither humility nor lowering of his self-image can remove him from responsibility.[12] Samuel also repeats his instructions concerning the destruction of Amalek, which Saul did not execute. He rebuked Saul for not listening to God. The word "listen" is a keyword here and is repeated in the following verses (verses 20, 22). "Listen" opened this chapter, where Samuel instructed Saul, "listen to the Lord's command" (verse 1). But Saul did the opposite; he did not listen.

---

10 Noth, *History of Israel*, 175–76.
11. Tsumara, *First Book of Samuel*, 399.
12. Mauchline, *1 and 2 Samuel*, 124.

SAMUEL

Samuel's unforgivable response in verses 22–23 is couched in Hebrew poetry and reflects prophetical teachings. Sacrifices are contrasted with obedience; the word "listen" is repeated here. Listening to God and obeying his commandments is preferable to sacrifices, which are the outcome of disobedience. Samuel is the first prophet who says that obedience to God is more important than sacrifices. Indeed, the later prophets will stress values such as justice, humility, truth, and peace that are preferable to sacrifices (Jer 7:21–23).

As in chapter 13, the question of authority is manifested here. According to Samuel, the anointed king should be under the authority of the prophet and obey his commands. On the other hand, King Saul thought that he had the authority to diverge from the prophet's instructions. Indeed, we find that Saul after his coronation became more independent and less modest as he erected a monument for himself after the victory against Amalek (1 Sam 15:12).[13]

Saul's sin is described as rebellious against God. The rebellion is characterized here as apostasy, the usage of forbidden forms of divination, and the worship of idols (verse 23). We have here the denial of God's authority and recognition of magical powers distinctly apart from God. This indictment is ironic because Saul fought against the usage of magic and banned it (28:9). It was only in his desperation, the night before his last battle against the Philistines, that he was seeking a woman who consults ghosts. Saul rejected God, therefore God rejected him. After his sin in Gilgal, Samuel told Saul: "But now your dynasty will not endure" (13:14). In Gilgal, God rejected Saul's dynasty, while here he rejected Saul personally: "The Lord has this day torn the kingship over Israel away from you and has given it to another who is worthier than you" (1 Sam 15:28).

Only after his rejection did Saul confess his sin for disobeying God's command, due to his fear of the people. In his confession, he exposes his own weakness. Instead of listening to God, he listened to the people. It is the king's responsibility to lead his people and not to be led by them. Frisch pointed out the similarity between Saul's confessions "take my sin away" (verse 25) and Pharaoh's confession in Exodus 10:16–17.[14] In both, a king declares that he had sinned and asks for forgiveness. This suggests that King Saul and Pharaoh acted dishonestly. Pharaoh certainly was not truthful and changed his mind when the plague was withdrawn.

---

13. Bar-Efrat, *I Samuel*, 195.
14 Frisch, "For I feared," 98–104.

Samuel, Saul, and David

Still, it is unclear what Saul did wrong. Saul had every intention of carrying out the word of YHWH and destroying Amalek. In doing so he wanted to give more honor to God. Why waste animals when they can be offered to YHWH? He also presented Agag as an example of what God does to his enemies. We must remember that in the ancient world kings humiliated their rivals (Judg 1:7); more so, they shared with their people the spoils of the war as a reward for services and to ensure their loyalty. According to the book of Numbers, the bounty was divided equally between the combatants who engaged in the campaign and the rest of the community (Num 31:27). Later, David declared in a statute that "the share of those who remain with the baggage shall be the same as the share of those who go down to the battle; they shall share alike" (1 Sam 30:24). Hence, King Saul is judged harshly for not destroying the Amalekites while David is "praised" for setting a law that divides the spoils of war.

The story in 1 Samuel 15 is an old one, because by the time of the Deuteronomist, the Amalekites could not have been one of the nearby nations; it would have had to have been Israel that was placed under the order. Saul's war against the Amalekites protected the tribe of Judah and incorporated an important tribe into his emerging monarchy. But this original story was changed later to create anti-Saul propaganda. What started as a great victory in the south was changed to show that Saul's expedition was a failure, moreso depicting Saul as a sinner.[15]

TEARING THE ROBE

Saul requested Samuel to return with him so that he could worship God and to "pray to Him for forgiveness." Samuel refused for the same reason he expressed already in verse 23: "because you rejected the Lord's command." Samuel also repeats here the fact that Saul was rejected by God as a king, and this time he added "over Israel." We have here a reversal: before, the people of Israel had rejected YHWH as king, but now it is God who rejects Saul as a king. This verse is a reminder of Samuel's speech against kingship: "If you rebel against the commandment of Yahweh, then the hand of Yahweh will be against you and your king" (1 Sam 12:14–15).

When Samuel turned to leave, refusing to return with Saul to worship YHWH, Saul grabbed Samuel's robe and tore it. The tearing away of the edge of Samuel's robe is interpreted as an omen, severing the kingdom

---

15. Brooks, *Saul and the Monarchy*, 55.

from Saul. According to the simple interpretation, it was Saul who tore the prophet's robe. While a second interpretation suggests that Samuel tore Saul's robe, thereby signaling him that whoever severed the skirt of his robe, would reign in his place. This is what Saul said to David on the day that he severed his robe: "I know that you will reign" (24:21).

Similarly, the prophet Ahijah tore Jeroboam's robe as a sign that his kingdom would be divided (1 Kgs 11:29–31). A third possible interpretation: Samuel tore his own robe as a sign of mourning for the failure of his "sapling to thrive." We should point out that in the Hebrew Bible the tearing of cloth was a sign of mourning for the dead, a custom that still exists today. The ripping of the robe was an omen for the end of Saul's kingship and death. According to Samuel, the kingship was already given to someone else; the rejection is final. However, Samuel did not tell Saul who the worthier person was. He would tell him that on the eve of his death: "The Lord has torn the kingship out of your hands and has given it to your fellow, to David" (1 Sam 28:17).

Samuel's symbolic act finally prompted Saul to admit his sin but this time with no excuses. Although he sinned, he still asked the prophet to honor him in the presence of the elders so that he would not be disgraced during his lifetime. Saul, despite his independent actions, remained dependent on Samuel and his support (verses 25, 27, 30). Samuel, on the other hand, criticized Saul harshly but showed compassion towards the king and later would grieve for him. As God's messenger, Samuel had to criticize Saul, but on a personal level, he felt sorrow for Saul's failure. Samuel's return with Saul was the narrator's way of saying that the sinful king still retained his office for some time. His kingship was supported by the prophet before the elders and the people of Israel.[16] Finally, the departure of Samuel and Saul to different locations signifies the end of the story. The narrator adds that Samuel never saw Saul again until the day of his death; he mourned for Saul and was no longer angry with him. There is an apparent allusion to an approaching meeting of the two that took place on the eve of Saul's death.

Did Samuel grieve over the rejection of Saul and feel sorry for him? It has been suggested that Samuel, who tried to prevent kingship, still controlled King Saul. He wanted to keep him as a figurehead, that is, under his control. God, on the other hand, decided to have a new king who was beyond Samuel's reach.[17] As pointed out earlier, Samuel's stature declined

---

16. Klein, 1 *Samuel*, 154.
17. Jobling, *I Samuel*, 87.

steadily. He had no role in the establishment of the army or the recruitment of people in the war against the Philistines. Moreover, Saul assumed cultic leadership for making sacrifices. After his coronation, Saul became more independent and less modest as he started to act like a king which caused the clashes between him and Samuel. Still, despite the feuds between the two, we witness here the "other Samuel." No more a raging prophet who criticizes King Saul, but a compassionate prophet who grieved for the king of Israel.

GOD AND KINGSHIP

It was Samuel, not God, who was unhappy with the people's request for a king. Israel was a theocracy until this request; their heavenly king endowed earthly judges with charismatic powers to fight and deliver them from their enemies.

Samuel's main objection was the fear that the Israelite kingship would be similar to that of "the other nations," but Samuel had a different agenda: he tried to establish his own prophetic dynasty. God encouraged Samuel to comply with the people's request (verse 7) stating that it was not Samuel the people were rejecting but the kingship of YHWH. Similarly, Gideon interpreted the people's request to crown him as a rejection of YHWH's rule (Judg 8:22–23). Choosing a king is also considered a rejection of YHWH in other biblical passages (1 Sam 10:19; 12:12). The rejection of YHWH is a recurring theme in the Hebrew Bible, which started at the time of the Exodus and lasted until the time of the Exile. The people rejected the eternal king. Even though the Israelites abandoned God, he fulfilled their request and instructed Samuel to crown Saul as a king. It was God's love and mercy for his people that led to the coronation of Saul.

As noted previously, at the first clash between Samuel and Saul, it was Samuel who announced that YHWH had rejected Saul (1 Sam 13:13). However, a reading of the Bible reveals that at this stage God did not reject Saul. Furthermore, reading the following chapter, we find that God did not abandon him, either. God delivered the Philistines into the hands of Saul; God saved Israel (14:23). Describing the war, the narrator mentions that God sent terror and confusion to the enemy camp. The savior formula that appears in our verse is drawn from the tradition of holy war (1 Sam 4:3; 7:8; Judg 2:18; 6:37; 7:7; 10:12). Following the oath that Saul laid on his people to not eat food, and how the troops sinned by eating meat with blood, Saul inquired of the Lord, but he did not answer him. The withholding of an answer was an indication that the Lord was displeased with the actions performed at Saul's camp. Nevertheless, God later responds to Saul's lot-casting ceremony to decide who broke the oath. Therefore, it appears that at this time it was Samuel who rejected Saul, because of his personal agenda. Samuel claimed that God rejected Saul. However, at this juncture, God did not abandon Saul. He delivered the Philistines into his hand. Moreover, God responded to Saul's inquiries.

The first time that God expressed his displeasure with Saul was after the war against Amalek. God regretted that he made Saul a king. This regret expressed by God is similar to God's regret after the creation of man (Gen 6:6). As king, Saul was supposed to carry out God's words, but he failed and turned away from following God. It was only after the war against Amalek that God instructed Samuel to anoint David as a king. Interestingly, Samuel was very angry and cried to the Lord all night (1 Sam 15:11). The fact that he was angry at Saul can be understood in light of his personal agenda. But what is not clear is why Samuel cried out to the Lord all night. It has been suggested that the prophet of the Lord feels God's inner feeling. Indeed, it was Heschel who interpreted the experience of the prophet of Israel as "a fellow-ship with the feeling of God, a sympathy with the divine pathos, a communion with the divine consciousness which comes about through the prophets' reflections of, or participation in, the divine pathos."[18] Samuel did as the Lord ordered, reporting God's words to Saul. But an examination of Samuel's words to Saul reveals that the prophet Samuel said far more to Saul than what was reported in the words of the Lord in verse 11. Samuel is portrayed as a prophet who does not tolerate any opposition and demands Saul accept his authority.

SAMUEL AND DAVID

As noted before, Samuel was afraid to go and anoint David; he feared that Saul would kill him. True, no king would like to hear about the anointment of a successor. But Saul knew already that God rejected him from being a king and kingship would be given to a person who was worthier than him. Before, Samuel was not afraid to deliver this message to Saul; therefore, his fear here is puzzling. According to Abravanel, Samuel's fear of Saul was an excuse; he simply did not want to go. When Saul did not carry out the

18. Heschel, *Prophets*, 26.

order to destroy Amalek, he used the excuse of fear: "but I was afraid of the troops and I yielded to them" (1 Sam 17:24). Samuel did not accept Saul's explanation but he himself used the same excuse for not following God's order. Samuel failed in the same way that Saul failed.

Samuel passed over seven of Jesse's sons to find which one was the divine choice. He was waiting for God to tell him his choice. Since he did not receive an answer and God told him that one of Jesse's sons would be the king, he knew that there must be another son. Indeed, we are told that there was still a young one who was tending the sheep. David tending the sheep is a reminder of Joseph who was shepherding the flock with his brothers. For the first time, David is brought into direct contact with Samuel. The Bible describes his appearance as it did with Saul. David is red with beautiful eyes and handsome. The other person in the Bible who is described as red was Esau (Gen 25:25). Red was associated with the sinister and the dangerous. According to C. H. Gordon, the description of red shows "that they were born to be heroes."[19] The fact that David was handsome should be interpreted as a sign of divine favor (Exod 2:2). Robert P. Gordon pointed out that only Samuel knew the purpose of the anointing.[20] Radak in his commentary on verse 1 says that when God sent Samuel to anoint David, God spoke of "a king of myself," indicating that the new king, unlike Saul, would obey all of God's commandments. Throughout this entire time, there is no verbal exchange between Samuel and David. David is referred to as the youngest—but only after the spirit of the Lord gripped him is his name mentioned for the first time. The spirit gripped David like it gripped Saul to prepare David to carry out God's mission.

Following the anointment of David, the scene shifts. Saul and David are at center stage, where we read of David's arrival to the king's court, his victory against Goliath, and Saul's continued attempts to kill David. It is only in chapter 19 that Samuel is back, reunited with David. With the help of his wife Michal, David escaped from Saul's messengers who tried to capture him. He fled and escaped, then went to Samuel at Ramah. At their meeting, David told Samuel all that Saul had done to him. According to Kirkpatrick, David was "turning naturally for direction at this crisis to the prophet who had anointed him and hoping that Saul would at least reverence the age and authority of Samuel."[21] This is the first time that the

---

19. Gordon, *Before the Bible*, 231.
20. Gordon, *1 and 2 Samuel*, 151.
21. Kirkpatrick, *Samuel*, 173

Samuel

biblical narrator tells us that David spoke to Samuel, but Samuel's reaction is not recorded. It was natural for David to ask for advice and help from the old prophet Samuel. Later David would get help from other people, like Jonathan and Ahimelech, before he escaped to the wilderness. The fact that he received help to escape from the royal family and was able to get help from the prophet Samuel shows that YHWH was with David.

Samuel and David went together from Ramah to Naioth, which is located two or three miles north of Gibeah. Naioth was the place where the prophets, whom Samuel gathered in Ramah, were dwelling (2 Kgs 6:1). This place is only mentioned briefly here, probably a plural noun of *nāweh*, which means "shepherd's dwelling camp." The usage of the same or similar noun in our story suggests that "the prophetic fraternities of Israel [also] dwelt in such settlement."[22] This settlement of prophets is similar to Nob, which was a settlement of priests where later David escaped to. Since Naioth was a gathering site of prophets, Samuel and David went there, thinking that Saul would spare David's life out of respect for the prophets.

Discovering that David was at Naioth, Saul sent messengers to capture David. When the messengers arrived, they saw prophets prophesying and Samuel presiding over them. The spirit of God came upon the messengers and they also prophesied. Because the messengers failed to bring David, Saul sent messengers for a second and a third time, which is characteristic of epic.[23] Strangely, David is not mentioned at all when the prophets were prophesying with Samuel. It is possible that at this stage David already escaped. Since the messengers failed to capture David, Saul himself went to seize David. On his way to Naioth, the spirit of God came upon him.

When Saul reached Naioth, he showed ecstatic prophetic behavior and stripped off his garment. Radak and Ralbag understand the word *ʿārōm* ערום as "completely naked." Ralbag interpreted that Saul was naked all that day and all that night as to allow David to escape. Sperling points out that when the biblical writer wants to speak positively about the human anatomy, he usually refers to specific, beautiful parts of the body. On the other hand, the Hebrew word "naked" is found only in negative connotations such as with fear, humiliation, defeat, and negative sexual activity.[24] Fokkelman states that stripping anticipates Saul's death in the last battle

---

22. Malamat, "Mari," 146; McCarter, *I Samuel*, 328.

23. Three times groups of fifty were sent to arrest Elijah (2 Kgs 1:9–18); and three signs are mentioned in 1 Samuel 10:2–7. See Tsumura, *First Book of Samuel*, 497.

24. Sperling, *Original Torah*, 124–25.

at Mt. Gilboa against the Philistines: "and stripped him of his armor" (1 Sam 31:9).[25] *Tg. Jon.* also explains ʿārōm as "naked," but not stripped of his clothes but of his physical senses, to imply he was insane or mad. The removal of the clothes carried with it symbolism. Saul remained naked as if the kingdom was taken from him. His clothes, which symbolized his royalty and authority, were gone.

For the second time, we have an explanation for the origin of the saying, "Is Saul too among the prophets?" But this time it has a negative connotation, as Mettinger pointed out that 19:18 is a reversal of what 10:1–9 says of Saul's endowment with the Spirit. In both cases, the Spirit is a divine manifestation. In 10:1–9 it gives Saul strength to carry out his feat of bravery. In 19:18–23 it works in the reverse: "it makes Saul helpless and drives him to strip off his clothes . . . the clothes of a king."[26] Similarly, McCarter says that Saul appears in a less-than-favorable light. The spirit of YHWH now haunts him rather than helps him. In contrast to 10:10–12, he meets the prophetic group as an unwelcome intruder.[27] Not surprisingly it has been suggested that the two stories are very old pieces of propaganda from the time of David,[28] one story (19:18–24) being pro-Davidic and anti-Saulide, while the other (10:10–12) being pro-Saulide.

It is unlikely that this episode that describes David's escape and flight to Samuel was an original part of the tale about the rise of David to power. More than probable, as Wellhausen pointed out, it is a secondary insertion.[29] We must remember that the narrator in 15:35 said that Samuel would never see Saul again before he died. Here we find that Saul lies naked before Samuel. Therefore, it is doubtful that the same author wrote 15:35 and 19:18–24. Another difficulty is the second explanation to the saying, "Is Saul, too, among the prophets?" which again raises the question of whether the same writer would introduce a different explanation. This leads us to believe that 19:18–24 is a late edition that continues to describe Saul negatively. Saul, who is constantly in pursuit of David, has one purpose: to kill him. David on the other hand is mentioned only for the second time with Samuel. He

---

25. Fokkelman, *Narrative Art*, 2:285.
26. Mettinger, *King and Messiah*, 27.
27. McCarter, *I Samuel*, 329.
28. Mommer, "Ist auch Saul," 53–61; Nihan on the other hand sees the stories as late post-Dtr that reflect conflicting evaluations of charismatic groups in Persian period. See Nihan, "Saul among the Prophets," 88–118.
29. Wellhausen, *Prolegomena*, 267–68.

receives protection from the prophet Samuel to bolster his legitimation as the future king who would replace Saul. This late addition was done by a writer who was sympathetic to David. Probably it was written at David's court. It describes Saul in the most unfavorable terms. Saul is portrayed as a paranoid man who chased a demon, obsessed with the pursuit of David. In addition, he struggles constantly with his own family members as well as his circle of friends.

David, on the other hand, is described more favorably. He was a worthier man than Saul, a fact that is mentioned several times. He played the lyre to the king to keep away the evil spirit. He defeated Goliath and fought the king's war (18:27). Saul acknowledged that God turned away from him and was with David, a fact that is mentioned twice (18:12, 28). Not only was God with David, even all of Israel, as well as Judah, loved David (verse 16), as did Saul's courtiers (verse 5). More than that, Saul's own family loved David. His son Jonathan (verse 1) and his daughter Michal (verses 20, 28) loved him. The fact that God was with David and brought him success is repeated three times (18:5, 14–15). There is no rift between Samuel and David. Samuel anoints David and protects him from Saul.

In conclusion the clashes between Samuel and Saul were the first between a prophet and a king. It is the beginning of many between the Kings of Israel and the Prophets. The feuds between Samuel and Saul are between the old guard and the new order. The emergence of human kingship precipitated a decline of Samuel's influence. It was a direct threat to Samuel's authority and status. Examination of Samuel's criticism of Saul reveals that it was unjustified and self-motivated. By offering a sacrifice, Saul performed a cultic function that was permissible for him. More so, he waited for Samuel as he was instructed. If someone is in the wrong here, it is Samuel, who just arrived when Saul was finishing his sacrifice. Following the war against the Amalekites, King Saul is judged harshly for not completely destroying the Amalekites and their beasts. In doing so he wanted to give more honor to God and to show Agag as an example of what God does to his enemies. By sharing with the people, the spoils of war, Saul wanted to compensate his people for their services and to ensure their loyalty. This act was permissible according to the Book of Numbers (31:27). In contrast to a similar situation, David is "praised" for setting a statute which divides the spoils of war (1 Sam. 30:24).

While the break between Samuel and Saul appears at the beginning of Saul's reign (chapter 13), God on the other hand did not abandon Saul,

He aided his fight against the Philistines. The break between God and Saul took place only after the war against the Amalekites. On that instance Samuel used God's name in his personal battle against Saul, he added his own words to God's message of Saul's rejection. By doing so he undermines Saul and legitimized his authority and status. Saul as the first king of Israel tried to assert his independence, but his clashes with Samuel show that he remained dependent on Samuel and his support. This stems from the fact that the relationship between the kings' sacral and secular functions, vis-à-vis the prophet, were not clearly defined yet.

Strangely, when it came to David no criticism is to be found. The prophet anointed David and protected him. There is only one reference to a verbal exchange between Samuel and David, when David ran away from Saul. David's meeting with Samuel is an independent legend; it was linked to Saul prophesying in ecstasy to explain a proverb "Is Saul too among the prophets? This leads us to believe the stories about Samuel and David were a later interpolation which took place at David's court. The stories have one objective: to stress the legitimacy of David as a king. He is anointed by the prophet and received his protection. In the next chapter we examine the roles Samuel fulfills: priest, prophet, seer, man of God, and judge. We will see if Samuel indeed fulfills these functions.

8

Who was Samuel?

THROUGHOUT THE BOOK OF SAMUEL, there are several titles given which describe him, such as prophet, seer, judge, priest, and man of God. This can be interpreted as an indication of his influence, or it can be explained as the creation of different circles of tradition that existed side by side. These traditions were threaded together without an attempt at merging them. Wellhausen in his analysis on Samuel wrote: "But what sort of an idea can we form of the position of Samuel? As he appears in these chapters, we entirely fail to dispose of him in any of the characters applicable to the subject; he is not a judge, not a priest, not a prophet—if at least we use these words with their true historical meaning. He is a second Moses? Yes, but that does not tell us much. So much only is clear, that the theocracy is arranged on quite a different footing from the kingdoms of this world, and that it amounts to the failing away into heathenism when the Israelites place a king at their head like other nations."[1]

H. P. Smith, in his evaluation of Samuel, says that there are two different portraits of Samuel: "In one place Samuel appears as the theocratic ruler of the people, comparable to Moses and to Moses alone among the heroes of Israel. He administers the government as the representative of YHWH. The whole people gather at his call, and he rebukes and commands with more-than-kingly authority. In another place he is the seer of a small town, respected as one who blesses the sacrifice and presides at the local

---

1. Wellhausen, *Prolegomena*, 255.

festival, but known only as a clairvoyant whose information concerning lost or strayed property is reliable."[2]

According to a later tradition Samuel was a Levite (1 Chr 6:12–13), and he and David founded the system of assigning gatekeepers at the entrance of the Tent of Meeting (9:22). He served as intermediary between the people and God, like Moses (Jer 15:1). God spoke to Samuel as well as with Moses and Aaron in the cloud pillar (Ps 99:6). They called to the Lord and he answered them. Samuel is portrayed as a leader who guides the Israelites in a time of crisis, like Moses.[3] Because of the many roles attributed to Samuel, it is difficult to determine the historical validity of the Samuel tradition. In the current chapter the different titles that define Samuel will be examined to see if indeed they match Samuel's persona considering his deeds and description which appear in the book of Samuel. This ultimately will give us a better portrayal and understanding of who Samuel was.

PRIEST

The genealogy of 1 Chronicles 6:7–13 connects Samuel's lineage with Levi, while in 1 Samuel 1, he is related to the tribe of Ephraim. According to the Torah, only descendants of Aaron can serve as priests in the temple, and only members of the tribe of Levi can assist them. If Samuel was an Ephraimite, could he serve as a priest in Shiloh, which was controlled by a family of Levites? The service of Levites began at the age of twenty-five and ended at age fifty (Num 4:3; 8:24–28). Samuel was brought to the temple by his mother at the age of two, after he was weaned. He could not serve for twenty-five years, since the temple was destroyed before he died. If Samuel was a Levite, his mother did not need to make a vow to give her son to serve in the temple. He would already be obligated to serve in the temple. So, what kind of function could Samuel perform, since he did not belong to the priestly family and he was below the age of twenty–five?

Samuel's service in the temple of Shiloh is defined by the verb שרת *šērēt* (1 Sam 2:11, 18; 3:1). The verb is not always used to signify cultic services; it can describe the service of royal household servants (Gen 39:4; 40:4; 2 Sam 13:17; 1 Kgs 10:5; 2 Chr 9:4; Esth 2:2; 6:3), or Joshua's service to Moses (Exod 24:13; 33:11; Num 11:28; Josh 1:1) and services given to Elijah (1 Kgs

---

2 Smith, *Critical and Exegetical Commentary*, xvi.

3. Scammon and Sperling, "Samuel," 17:755.

19:21) and Elisha (2 Kgs 4:43; 6:15).[4] Samuel is said to have been serving before YHWH (1 Sam 2:18); and in 2:11 and 3:1 he was serving before Eli. In those three verses he is called נער *naʿar*, "boy," hence he probably was a priest's servant. The title *naʿar* was also known in the Phoenician world and described a subordinate temple servant.[5] More than likely, Hannah offered her son to YHWH's service as a servant under the supervision of the priest. She did not offer him as a priest where the Levitical family already existed.

Samuel wore a linen ephod while serving God in Shiloh (1 Sam 2:18). Later, when David brought the ark to the city of David, he also wore a linen ephod when he danced before YHWH (2 Sam 6:14). In ancient Israel and in the ancient world, when people entered a sacred area, they changed their clothes. They had to be purified in preparation for an experience with God (Gen 35:2–3; Exod 19:10; Josh 3:5). Samuel wore a linen ephod because he was in the presence of God. David changed his clothes because he was dancing before the ark. It was considered a sacred ritualistic activity because he was in the immediate presence of God.[6] Samuel and David wore a simple ephod of linen during sacred services and celebrations. This ephod was different from the precious ephod that was worn by the Israelite high priest.[7]

The fact that Samuel served in Shiloh, which was a place of worship and sacrificial center (1 Sam 2:11, 18; 3:1), has led to the understanding that he was a priest.[8] In some passages he performs sacrificial functions that were part of the priest's responsibilities. At Mizpah he took a suckling lamb and scarified it as a burnt offering to the Lord (7:9). He oversaw a sacred meal where he blessed the sacrifice (9:13, 22). Samuel told Saul to go down to Gilgal and to wait for him for seven days, where he would join him and offer burnt offerings (10:8). He invited the elders of Bethlehem to a sacrificial feast (16:1–5). He gathered the people for a fast day, prayed to God, and built an altar at Ramah to offer sacrifice (7:5–7, 17). It was these religious rituals, especially sacrifices, which led to the view that he was a priest.

However, examination of the cultic activities that were attributed to Samuel reveals that they were not entirely privileges of the priesthood.[9] The

---

4. Cody, *History of Old Testament*, 74.
5. Cody, *History of Old Testament*, 74.
6. Cody, *History of Old Testament*, 78.
7. Haran, "Ephod," 380–91.
8. Cody, *History of Old Testament*," 79.
9. Buber, *Darko šel Miqra*, 238–69; Uffenheimer, *Ancient Prophecy*, 264.

Who was Samuel?

building of altars is not a priestly entitlement; later we read of Elijah, who built an altar and also offered sacrifices (1 Kgs 18:30–38). Kings such as Saul, David, and Solomon are said to make sacrifices (1 Sam 13:9; 2 Sam 6:13, 18; 1 Kgs 8:5, 62–64). Blessing the sacrifice was not obligatory for the priest, nor was it his privilege. When Samuel blessed the sacrifice, he was not called a priest, but a seer, which was the earlier term for "prophet" (1 Sam 9:9). Praying for the people as well as serving as the intermediary between people and God was carried out by the prophets, kings, and the elders. The Urim and Thummin, procedures for the priest to inquire of God, and God to respond, are mentioned with both Samuel (1 Sam 10:20–22) and Joshua (Josh 7:14–18).

Samuel is never called a priest in the Hebrew Bible except for Psalm 99:6. Excluding his youth there is no link between Samuel and the priestly family. Samuel did not do anything to strengthen the priestly office after the humiliation at Apek. When the ark was returned it was left in obscurity at Kirjath-Jearim. Samuel did not join the priests that moved to Nob (1 Sam 22). He returned to his hometown, Ramah, and was not associated with Nob, which suggests that he was not one of Shiloh's priests.[10] During this time, people worshiped at places where Samuel administrated the affairs of the people, places like Ramah, Bethel, Gilgal, and Mizpah.

There is no suggestion in the text that Samuel took the place of Eli as the high priest. Despite calamity the house of Eli remained in office (1 Sam 14:3; 22:20). Samuel appointed his sons judges over Israel (8:1). On the other hand, the Bible says that the sons of Eli were priests who followed their father's tradition. If Samuel were a priest, we would expect to find a similar tradition concerning his sons. In contrast, the sons of Eli were unfit to follow their father's role as priest; young Samuel followed the path of Eli as one who serves the Lord. Eli was known for his ability to communicate with God and deliver his message (1 Sam 1:1–17), a mission that Samuel followed and fulfilled.

It was also thought that the prophecy of doom on the house of Eli, "I will raise Me up a faithful priest . . . I will build for him an enduring house" (1 Sam 2:35), might suggest that Samuel was a priest.[11] As pointed out previously, this is unlikely; the verse is polemic by the Zadokite priests under Solomon who justified the rejection of the priests of the house of Eli's

---

10. Steussy, *Samuel and His God*, 31.
11. Uppenheimer, *Ancient Prophecy*, 268

lineage.¹² The Zadokites are the ones who are referred to in this verse because they were the legitimate priests in Jerusalem at the time that the verse was composed. Buber, on the other hand, does not accept this explanation; according to him, it is unlikely that a dispute between the priestly families would be put into writing that "might reveal the disgrace of the priesthood itself."¹³ However, we should note that the text in 1 Samuel 3:20 says, "And all Israel... knew that Samuel was established to be a prophet of YHWH." In other words, the prophecy of "and I will build him an enduring house" (2:35) was never fulfilled. Samuel was known in Israel as an established faithful prophet and not a priest. The material which describes Samuel's service in the sanctuary does not come to depict Samuel as a priest. It describes Samuel as a person that received revelation from God, leading to his climax as a prophet.

JUDGE

First Samuel 7 portrays Samuel as a judge: "And Samuel acted as chieftain of the Israelites at Mizpah" (1 Sam 7:6). At the end of the chapter, the narrator stressed it three times: "Samuel *judged* Israel as long as he lived... and acted as *judge* over Israel at all these places... and there too he would *judge* Israel" (7:15–17). In modern terminology, a judge is a person who presides over legal matters and makes decisions as an adjudicator. By contrast, in the Hebrew Bible, the noun *šōpēṭ*, "judge," has several meanings, i.e., military, executive, or judicial activity.¹⁴ In the book of Judges some of the judges are described as military heroes. Jephthah led the Israelites into a victory against the Ammonites; he judged Israel for six years (Judg 12:6). There is no mention in the text of his judicial activities; not surprisingly, the JPS and NIV translate that he led Israel for six years. Similarly Samson judged Israel for twenty years, but the text describes his battles, not his administration of law. The Israelites asked Samuel to appoint "a king to govern *(špṭ)* us" (1 Sam 8:5). But the noun *šōpēṭ* is never used to describe Saul. So, what kind of judge was Samuel: a person who presides over legal matters, or was it a statement that came to summarize his life?

---

12. Cross, *Canaanite Myth*, 195–215; Mauchline, *1 and 2 Samuel*, 56; McCarter, *I Samuel*, 91.

13. Buber, *Darko šel Miqra*, 247

14. BDB, 1047–48.

Birch maintains that the formula in 1 Sam 7:6b, which states that Samuel judged Israel at Mizpah, does not belong to the material which precedes it or follows it.[15] The fact that Samuel judged Israel has little meaning. The ceremony described in verse 6 has nothing to do with the depiction of Samuel as judge. The military deliverance might suggest a type of judge which is found in the book of Judges. But examination of the text shows otherwise: Samuel is not portrayed as a military leader or warrior; he did not take part in the acts of war. The earlier judges fought against the enemies of Israel; Samuel only encouraged the people to fight the Philistines. In this aspect he is like Moses. Only Joshua and Saul were active warriors. The meaning of "judging Israel" in verse 6b refers to Samuel leading Israel into repentance and interceding on behalf of the people before God. In the following verses we read about the Philistine threat; hence, Samuel made an offering to God and cried unto the Lord for Israel. It was only then that God came to the aid of the Israelites and helped them to defeat the Philistines. In other words, God's aid came in response to Samuel's outcry. Samuel appears here as intercessor and prophetic announcer of victory. Samuel became the leader of Israel after the death of Eli and the destruction of Shiloh. There is no mention in 6b of Samuel presiding over legal matters, where cases were brought before him to make decisions. McCarter suggests that the statement "Samuel judged the sons of Israel at Mizpah" is an addition by the Deuteronomist to integrate the career of Samuel into the chain of Judges between Joshua and Saul.[16]

Samuel judging Israel is mentioned also in verses 15, 16, and 17. According to Birch, here Samuel is called a judge because of his judicial activities. Samuel is described as traveling and administering justice at different locales. According to him the usage of this formula in verse 6b is identical to verse 15 and it came to create a link between verses 5–11 and 16–17, since scholars maintain that verses 16–17 are originally independent tradition.[17]

Noth has suggested that the so called "minor judges" were legal officers of the amphictyony that were responsible for the supervision of the covenant. The phrase "and Samuel judged Israel" (verses 6, 15, 16, 17) is the exact phrase used to describe the list of minor judges in the book of Judges (10:1–5; 12:7–15). According to him these lists contain "the only exact and obviously authentic chronological information (not merely in

---

15. Birch, *Rise*, 13.
16. McCarter, *I Samuel*, 145.
17. Birch, *Rise*, 13

round figures) which the Old Testament contains for the period before the founding of the kingdom."[18] He therefore suggests that Samuel the judge is a Deuteronomistic fiction.[19] According to him "this formula, used four times in chapter 7 (verses 6, 15, 16, 17) makes sense only in light of Dtr's own picture of the judges period."[20]

The description of Samuel travelling each year at Bethel, Gilgal, and Mizpah administering justice is parallel to the area where Deborah the prophetess was active. Her place of activity was between Ramah and Bethel in the hill country of Ephraim, which points to the importance of this region (Judg 4:4-5). According to the LXX, Samuel judged not just *in all these places* but also in "holy places." His influence was not limited but reached to Bethlehem (1 Sam 16) and probably to Beer-Sheba, a place where his sons served as judges. The fact that Samuel was active outside his hometown was in sharp contrast to previous prophets.

Samuel traveling throughout the land should be compared to King Jehoshaphat of Judah who sent his officers with the priests and Levites to teach the people: "They offered instruction throughout Judah, having with them the Book of the Teaching of the Lord. They made the rounds of all the cities of Judah and instructed the people" (2 Chr 17:9). Thus, we believe that "judging" also meant instruction in the law. Instead of the priests and Levites, who were supposed to instruct and teach the law, it was Samuel who did it. It was part of his agenda to increase his power and influence. Samuel is also credited as a lawgiver: "Samuel expounded to the people the rules of the monarchy and recorded them in a document which he deposited before the Lord" (1 Sam 10:25).[21] Laws were written and witnessed and it was customary to place the document in the ark (Exod 25:16, 21; 40:20).[22] Depositing legal documents in a sacred place was common in the ancient Near East. It stressed the importance of the document and the fact that the deity witnessed it and guarded it.[23] Samuel also presided over legal matters. This can be inferred from the fact that he made his sons judges. Samuel nominated them as judges. They are described as not following their father's footsteps, as they took bribes and subverted justice (1

---

18. Noth, *History of Israel*, 101.
19. Noth, *Deuteronomistic History*, 48–49
20. Noth, *Deuteronomistic History*, 121n33.
21. Leuchter, *Samuel*, 66.
22. de Vaux, *Ancient Israel*, 301.
23. Sarna, *Exodus*, 160.

Sam 8:2). And as Josephus describes: "Now these men afford us an evident example and demonstration, how some children are not like dispositions with their parents."[24] They were the opposite from what God told Moses: to select "trustworthy men who spurn ill-gotten gain" (Exod 18:21). The transgression that was committed by Samuel's sons is similar to the behavior of the sons of Eli.

Samuel setting up an altar at Ramah his hometown is an older tradition, since Deuteronomy sees the altars outside of Jerusalem as illegitimate. The ark was not yet stationed in Jerusalem; therefore, Samuel's act was not condemned by the Deuteronomist. Samuel was a judge who gave his decision at the altar. Judging was considered a sacred activity (Exod 18:15; 22:7). People were seeking divine guidance in cases where human wisdom could not give an answer. Justice was an expression of the will of God, which was given through a human judge. Judgement was the concern of God; he gave the laws and the judge acted as God's representative. Individuals would get close to the altar where sacrifices were offered to obtain instruction from God (Num 9:8). In difficult cases when the law was not known, Moses would consult God (Lev 24:10–23; Num 9:1–14; 15:32–36; 27:1–11; 36:1–10). Similarly, Samuel in his capacity as God's voice would deliver the verdict. He built the altar in his hometown to receive the will of God in difficult cases.

What emerges from 1 Sam 7:6 and 16–17 is that Samuel served as intermediary between the people and God. In times of crisis, he turned to God to deliver his people. In more peaceful times he served as a judge and taught the law of YHWH in order to unify the bond of the convenant. The statement that Samuel judged Israel "all the days of his life" closes a period in Samuel's life as a leader and creates an analogy between him and the previous judges.

PROPHET

Albright viewed Samuel as a prophet. According to him, "[that] Samuel was the first great religious reformer after Moses, and he rejected—or diminished—the spiritual role of priests and Levites at the same time that he turned to ecstatic prophets and local sanctuaries to replace the Shilonite system is actually not hard to defend."[25] Rowley characterizes Samuel's

---

24. Josephus, *Ant.* 6.3.2.
25. Albright, *Samuel*, 18.

function at Gilgal and Ramah as that of a prophet. He is accessible for consultation at Ramah, where he led a sacred feast, and he told Saul to wait for him at the shrine of Gilgal. He is like other prophets such as Ahijah, Gad, Elisha, Nathan, and Elijah, who functioned also as individuals at different places, not always connected to a shrine.[26]

When Samuel served the Lord in Shiloh, he received a revelation from God. From that moment on his life changed, and he started to deliver the words of God to others. He served as mediator between God and the people. Samuel received a direct revelation from God, which was not the case with Eli, who was a priest but not a prophet. It was the revelation in Shiloh that made Samuel into a prophet. Samuel proclaimed the calamity that would befall the house of Eli and the people of Israel; at that time "the words of the Lord were rare" (3:1). But God continued to reveal himself to Samuel, his loyal servant: "All Israel, from Dan to Beer-Sheba, knew that Samuel was trustworthy as a prophet of the Lord" (3:20). By mentioning from "Dan to Beer-Sheba" the author stresses the wide recognition that Samuel gained. Rashi says that a new era had begun because of the faithfulness of Samuel. The word of God became more public; therefore others began to prophesy. The LXX has a longer version (verse 21), emphasizing Samuel as a renowned prophet, contrasting him with the house of Eli: "Eli was now very old, and his sons continued to live corruptly before the Lord." It appears that this addition is parallel to the description that is found in chapter 2:24, which describes the contrast between Samuel and Eli's sons. It is noteworthy that there are only two prophets in the Hebrew Bible who are referred to as trustworthy: Moses and Samuel (1 Sam 3:20; Num 12:7). These two prophets were leaders and prophets who led their people and also delivered the word of God. When the people wanted to know the will of God it was Samuel who announced it. It is a start for the new leadership that will emerge later with the rise of the prophetic office. The "loyal priest" that is mentioned (1 Sam 2:35) is fulfilled now by a "loyal prophet" (3:20).

The sin of the sons of Eli and the capture of the ark by the Philistine accelerated the decline of the priesthood. According to Budde, "It sounds like there is a description of allegorical myth of the death of the priesthood because of the difficult task it had to carry, and instead the rise of prophecy."[27] Buber does not accept the definition of allegorical myth; according to him the stories about the capture of the ark and the battle of

---

26. Rowley, *From Moses to Qumran*, 126–27.
27. Budde, *Die altisraelitische Religion*, 50.

Who was Samuel?

Eben-Ezer are not myth. These kinds of horrendous stories are not the fruit of the imagination but stories that were transmitted from generation to generation.[28] The stories are the description of the calamity that occurred to the Israelites. God punished the Israelites and its priests and delivered them into the hands of the Philistines.

The revelation to Samuel at Shiloh is a turning point, instead of the usage of Urim by the priests; God would appear to Samuel and deliver to him a direct message. At Mizpah God responded to Samuel's prayer and sacrifice without the aid of the ark or ephod (1 Sam 7:5-9) The ark was not returned to its place, and there is no need for the ark to receive a message from God. The decline of the ark as a center for God's worship appears already in the time of the judges. Instead of the ark it is the personal charisma of the savior-judge that comes to the aid of the people. The ark as the throne of the invisible God is reduced to the level of oracular device. For twenty years the ark was stationed in Kiriath-Jearim, which led to its degradation among the people; the people did not link it anymore to divine leadership in war.[29]

Samuel accentuated the process of decentralization of worship; he created a new emphasis of worship at the *bamot*, "high places." In addition, we read of the appearance of bands of prophets (10:5, 10-13; 19:18-24). They appeared on the "high place" during public worship and infected the people with their enthusiasm. Uffenheimer believes that the band of prophets encouraged the people with songs of war to fight against the Philistines. He suggests that the decentralization of the cult and the appearance of the bands of prophets is what prepared the ground for the charismatic savior-judge that was needed at that time.[30] The bands of prophets were disciples of the prophets; they appeared in groups and were attached to a shrine. Such a group appears when Saul encounters them near Gibeah (1 Sam 10:5, 10). He meets them and the spirit of God grips him, and he joins their prophetic frenzy. When David escaped from Saul, he met Samuel, who is described later as the leader of the band of prophets (1 Sam 19:20). The band of prophets are mentioned later in the middle of the ninth century in the Elijah and Elisha cycles.

The anointment of a king was one of the responsibilities that was carried by a prophet. Hence, Samuel anointed Saul as the king of Israel, and

---

28. Buber, *Darko šel Miqra*, 250.
29. Uffenheimer, *Ancient Prophecy*, 270.
30. Uffenheimer, *Ancient Prophecy*, 275.

later he anointed David. Likewise, Elisha ordered one of the disciples of the prophets to anoint Jehu (2 Kgs 9:6). As a prophet, Samuel knew about the arrival of Saul before he anointed him (1 Sam 9:15–16) because God revealed it to him. In Amos 3:7 we read, "Indeed My Lord God does nothing / Without having revealed His purpose / To His servants the prophets." Samuel asked Saul to dine with him, and in the morning he told him everything that was on his mind. Samuel appears here as the later prophets who know the future; he knows what will happen to Saul on his return journey and whom he will meet (1 Sam 10:5–6). Indeed, as Samuel predicted, the spirit of God gripped Saul, and he spoke in ecstasy and became a different man (10:9).

Like the classical prophets, Samuel played a prominent role in communal affairs. He was consulted for advice and delivered oracles from God. He told Eli the calamity that awaited his household. He delivered to Saul a prophecy about his future: "But now your dynasty will not endure" (1 Sam 13:14). Later, following Saul's failure to carry the ban against Amalek, "Yahweh has torn the kingdom of Israel from you today, and he has given it to your neighbor who is better than you" (15:28). On the eve of his last battle against the Philistines, when the witch of Endor raised Samuel from his grave, Samuel told Saul: "Further, the Lord will deliver the Israelites who are with you into the hands of the Philistines. Tomorrow your sons and you will be with me; and the Lord will also deliver the Israelite forces into the hands of the Philistines" (28:19).

Samuel also reprimanded Saul as the prophet Nathan rebuked King David for his conduct with Bathsheba, or Elijah who scolded Ahab for his involvement in the murder of Naboth. Samuel told Saul, "Does the Lord delight in burning offerings and sacrifices as much as in obedience to the Lord's command? Surely, obedience is better than sacrifice, compliance than the fat of rams" (1 Sam 15:22). It is a rhetorical question; obedience to God is preferable to sacrifice. Similar words would be uttered generations later by the prophet Hosea: "For I desire goodness, not sacrifice; obedience to God, rather than burnt offerings" (6:6).[31] Samuel pleaded with Israel to seek God and demanded faithfulness to the covenant (1 Sam 7:3). He called the Israelites to return to God (7:3), a theme that is prevalent among classical prophets. Like classical prophets he is described as an intercessor that pleaded on behalf of his people and prayed to God (1 Sam 7:5, 9; 12:19, 13; 15:11). These prayers by Samuel resonate with Moses imploring the Lord:

---

31. See also Amos 5:21–25; Isa 1:10; Jer 7:21–23; Ps 51:18–19.

"Let not Your anger, O Lord, blaze forth against your people . . . Turn from Your blazing anger, and renounce the plan to punish Your people" (Exod 32:11–12).

SEER

In the early stories about Saul, Samuel appears as a "seer," *rō' eh* ראה, and a *navi'*, "prophet": "for the prophet of today was formerly called a seer" (1 Sam 9:9). Accordingly, "seer" was the earlier name for "prophet." He is the "one who sees" into the future. He knows what is hidden from the eyes of ordinary man. The LXX has a different reading: "the people used to call a prophet seer." In other words, "seer" was a popular name for "prophet."[32] Scholars suggest that there were two stages in the development of Israelite's faith. At first the mantic man of God, the *ḥōzeh* and *rō' eh*, used mantic skills to guess God's will and used magic to impose his will on God.[33] At the second stage the prophet, *navi'*, is the ecstatic man of God, or the company of prophets, who wanted to be close to the deity and became absorbed in it. They attained their inspiration through a trance state where the ego was annulled. Orgiastic ecstatic practices were used, which probably were the result of Canaanite Phoenician influence. Divination and magic were part of the ancient desert tradition, while the ecstatic prophecy was a late development, as it appears in the reading of 1 Samuel 9, 10, and 19.[34] Hence, the *navi'* was ecstatic while the seer was not. Robinson suggested that during the period of the early monarchy the seer disappeared, and his characteristics and functions were assumed by the *navi'* or ecstatics.[35] But as Fenton pointed out, *navi'* "belongs to the most ancient stratum of Hebrew known to us."[36] This assertion was strengthened by Fleming, who pointed out the existence of *nb'* in Emar Akkadian of the second millennium BCE.[37]

There was probably a distinction between the characteristic and functions of a seer and a prophet. But examination of the Hebrew Bible reveals that the distinction between the earlier term and the later one is far from

---

32. Rowley, *Servant of the Lord*, 105.
33. Kuenen, *Prophets and Prophecy*, 552–58; Uffenheimer, *Ancient Prophecy*, 480.
34 Uffenheimer, *Ancient Prophecy*, 480.
35. Robinson, *Prophecy and Prophets*, 35.
36. Fenton, "Deuteronomistic Advocacy," 33.
37. Fleming, "Nābû and Munabbiātu," 175–83; Fleming, "Etymological Origins," 217–24.

clear. Both had common functions to proclaim the words of God and foretell the future. The seer possessed the ability to tell what was hidden from the ordinary mortal. He predicted the future for individual people about private problems and, in exchange, received gifts, like the case with Saul (1 Sam 9:6). Samuel, the seer, is affiliated with the shrine at Ramah, while Gad, David's seer, is attached to a court (2 Sam 24:11). Since Samuel's childhood and youth was linked to the Shilonite priesthood, Cohen suggested that Samuel was a seer-priest or diviner-priest.[38] But, as noted already, Samuel was never a priest, as a seer in Israel was not a priest.[39]

Wellhausen suggested that in 1 Samuel 9:1–10:16; 11:1–11 Samuel is portrayed as a country seer who people asked for advice.[40] This image of Samuel was changed in chapters 7; 8; 10:17–27; 12:1–25, where he appears as a prophet. It was the priestly author who lived in Babylon that transformed the image of Samuel. However, Abraham is already called a prophet and Moses' sister was known as a prophetess, but this also can be anachronistic (Gen 20:7; Exod 15:20). Probably there was some distinction between the terms "seer" and "prophet." However, from the time of Samuel, the seer's acts were incorporated within the sphere of the prophet's activity. The term "seer" was still in use during this era, but the term "prophet" became more popular. Samuel was known as a seer and a prophet alike. Following the Samuel era, the term "seer" became rare. The author of Chronicles refers to Samuel as a seer (1 Chr 9:22; 26:28; 29:29) and to an unknown Hanani of the time of Asa (2 Chr 16:7, 10). It is noteworthy that in 1 Chronicle 29:29 there is a different terminology which describes the prophets: "The acts of King David, early and late, are recorded in the history of Samuel the seer (rō' eh), the history of Nathan the prophet (navi'), and the history of Gad the seer (ḥōzeh)." The translation for this verse in the JPS shows the terms rō' eh and ḥōzeh, translated similarly as seer. Meanwhile, in Isaiah 30:10, the terms rō' eh and ḥōzeh, which appear parallel in the plural form, are translated in the JPS as "seer" and "prophets."[41] Gad is called both a prophet and a seer (ḥozeh) in the same verse (2 Sam 24:11), as is Amos (Amos 7:12, 14). We can see that demarcation between navi', rō' eh, and ḥōzeh is not clear and the translators struggled with it.

38. Cohen, "Role of the Shilonite," 66.
39. Plöger, "Priester und Prophet," 167.
40. Wellhausen, *Prolegomena*, 273–82.
41. Fuchs suggests that the ancient term for seer was ḥōzeh. See Fuchs, "רָאָה rā' ā," 239.

Uffenheimer maintains that there was a distinction between the word *ḥōzeh* and *rō' eh* in pre-biblical times, but the three terms *ḥōzeh, rō' eh,* and *navi''* appear in the Bible as comparable.[42] In some passages Samuel is called *rō' eh;* in others he is called *navi'*, or "prophet of the Lord." To bolster his claim, he points to the usage of the roots *r' h* and *ḥzh* in words which describe the prophetic experience, such as *ḥizzayon, maḥazeh, ḥazot, ḥazut, mar' eh, mar' ot,* and *mar' h*; all of which are translated as vision(s). Accordingly, there is no philological basis for the hypothesis that *ḥōzeh* or *rō' eh* signified a different type of prophecy than *navi'*.[43]

It is not clear when the transition of the usage of the term "seer" to "prophet" occurred. Based on this verse the biblical narrator assumed that it took place after the events happened (1 Sam 9:9). But, as mentioned before, the Torah speaks of Abraham, Aaron, and Moses as prophets, which suggests that both terms were known earlier. This leads us to believe that probably from the time of Samuel the term "prophet" became the more popular term.

Samuel was known as a seer, but at the same time a new phase started with him, a transition into the phenomenon of Israelite prophecy. He received the word of God and declared it; he instructed the people in the law and rebuked them for their disloyalty. Like the classical prophets who were involved with community affairs and had their feuds with the kings, so was Samuel. Although Samuel was a prophet, he is called "prophet" only a few times (1 Sam 3:20–21; 9:9), which is also the case with Moses (Num 11:29; 12:6–9; Duet 18:18; 34:10).

THE MAN OF GOD

Samuel is also called "the man of God" (1 Sam 9:6, 10). The term "(the) man of God," occurs seventy-five times in the Hebrew Bible. The only persons called "(the) man of God" are Moses, Samuel, David, Elijah, Elisha, Shemaiah, and Igdaliah. Elisha is called "a holy man of God" (2 Kgs 4:9). "The man of God" is synonymous with "prophet" (2 Kgs 1:9). In several passages, the identity of "the man of God" remains anonymous (1 Sam 2:27; 1 Kgs 13:1–31; 2 Kgs 23:16; 1 Kgs 20:28; 2 Chr 25:7, 9). The term "man of God" also refers to an angel. Manoah's wife went to her husband and told him: "A man of God came to me" (Judg 13:6). Only later when the

---

42. Uffenheimer, *Ancient Prophecy*, 481.
43. Uffenheimer, *Ancient Prophecy*, 484.

angel of God left, Manoah and his wife realized that it was an angel of God who appeared to them. "The man of God" appeared in the image of man. This is similar to other instances where angels appeared as humans (Gen 18–19; Judg 6:11–24). In 1 Samuel 2:27, it is "the man of God" who came to Eli and delivered to him a prophecy of doom. Following the theophany at Shiloh, Samuel became a trustworthy prophet of the Lord; therefore there is no need to send "the man of God," and it is Samuel who is "the man of God." Interestingly, the term "man of YHWH" never appears in the Hebrew Bible, while it uses "angel of YHWH" in addition to "angel of God." This is probably because *elohim* is a general designation for the deity and therefore better suited to describe an individual.

Hölscher compares the term "man of God" to the Arabic "possessor of an 'ilah, i.e., of a divine being or demon," who can also be a *kāhin*, "soothsayer."[44] In other words, *elohim* is not YHWH but "the demon," and the expression is comparable with a *ba' alath' obh*, "medium" (1 Sam 28:7), and *'ish haruach*, "man of the spirit" (Hos 9:7), and initially meant one possessed by God. Another interpretation is offered by Haldar, who points to Sum. *Lu-dingir-ra* and Akk. *Amēl ili*, "man of God," and explained this expression as "a man who is consecrated to the cultic service of a God."[45] Hence, priest or prophet could be referred to as "the man of god." They had something of the divine nature, so God can use them to deliver his message. However, in Israel, Elijah, Elisha, David, and the angel of Judges 13 are called "men of God" but did not belong to a temple staff.

In the Hebrew Bible, "the man of God" was possessed by powers which helped him to call upon the assistance of divine aid. Prophets like Elijah and Elisha, who are referred to as "men of God," were known to perform miracles such as reviving the dead (1 Kgs 17:17–24; 2 Kgs 4:18–37) and making plenty from small portions of food (1 Kgs 17:7–16; 2 Kgs 4:42–44). Another function that they were known for was their ability to prophesy. They had to be obedient to God and were sent from one place to another without knowing the reason for it. Elijah, for example, was sent to Bethel, Jericho, and then the Jordan River, most likely by the spirit of YHWH (2 Kgs 2). Later, the spirit of YHWH took him to heaven.

In the story of Saul and the lost asses of Kish, Saul and his servant turn to "the man of God" for help. They believed that his visionary powers would help them get information about their journey. "The man of God"

---

44. Hölscher, *Die Profeten*, 127n2.
45. Haldar, *Association of Cult Prophets*, 29–34;126.

predicted the future and performed miracles for people who needed help. Samuel is a man of God that receives guidance from God, which helps him to anoint Saul as a king. As Lindblom pointed out, "the man of God" is the bearer of God's message; therefore he has a close relationship to God and must go and do whatever God commands him to do.[46] It is noteworthy that the title "the man of God" appears without Samuel's name, which may point to a different and earlier source. This tradition described Samuel's activity as restricted to a local area with limited influence. This might explain why Saul did not know about the existence of "the man of God"; strangely it was the servant who knew about "the man of God." Samuel is portrayed as a local prophet that is known locally. In the other chapters, which were composed later, he is depicted as a leader and a prophet who is well-known all over Israel, and he is called Samuel.

In conclusion, the book of Samuel contains different literary units; therefore, not surprisingly, Samuel is described in different terms. At first, he is described as serving before YHWH at the temple in Shiloh. This led to the assumption that he was a priest. Our study shows otherwise; he was a priest-servant under the supervision of Eli. Building altars, the right to offer sacrifice and bless the sacrifice, serving as intermediary between the people and God; these acts which are attributed to Samuel were not restricted to priests. These acts were carried also by prophets and kings. Samuel is never called a priest in the Bible except for Psalms 99:6. Samuel is a servant at the service of the priests and God. In 1 Samuel 7:6 and 16–17, Samuel is called a judge.

The word šp̄ṭ has several meanings; thus in 7:6b, at a time of crisis, it refers to Samuel leading Israel into repentance and interceding on behalf of the people of Israel before God. In more peaceful times he served as a judge and instructed the law of YHWH to unify the bond of the covenant with YHWH. It was the revelation in Shiloh that made Samuel into a prophet. Just as the classical prophets played a prominent role in communal affairs, Samuel was consulted for advice and delivered oracles from God. He proclaimed the calamity that would befall the house of Eli, the people of Israel, and the end of Saul's kingship. When the people wanted to know the will of God, it was Samuel who revealed it. He anointed Saul and later David as king, which was the task of the prophet. Samuel is described as "a trustworthy prophet of the Lord," an expression that also designates Moses. Moses and Samuel were leaders and prophets who led their people

46. Lindblom, *Prophecy*, 62.

but also delivered the words of God. Samuel is also called a "seer," which was believed to be the earlier name for "prophet." But as noted the term "prophet" was also known from the most ancient stratum of Hebrew literature. It appears that the term "prophet" became more popular during Samuel's period and it signals the start of a new phase of Israelite prophecy. "The man of God" is another term that refers to Samuel. In the Hebrew Bible "the man of God" was possessed by powers which helped him to call for the assistance of divine aid. Samuel, "the man of God," was a prophet and judge who interceded on behalf of the people of Israel, instructed the law of YHWH, and delivered his words. As we can see Samuel was an exceptional person even after his death. Twice the text mentions that he died, and more notably, that he returned from the land of dead. This will be the subject of our last chapter.

9

Returning from the Dead

SAMUEL WAS A UNIQUE PERSON, both during his life and after his death. Twice we are told that Samuel died (1 Sam 25:1; 28:3). A public mourning was held, and the entire nation came to lament and honor him. Although Samuel had been dead for some time by the eve of Saul's battle against the Philistines, he was raised from his grave by the medium at Endor (28:3–25). Nowhere else in the Hebrew Bible is there a description of a person who descends to the netherworld and then returns from it. Samuel was raised from the grave—he then met Saul and delivered a message of doom to him.

What rituals did the medium employ to raise Samuel? Was it Samuel himself that she raised, or was it his shade, his spirit, the divine component of the human being? Why was Samuel so angry with Saul? According to the Hebrew Bible, when a person dies, he descends to Sheol, a place that has gates and bolts; there is no return from it. This underworld is a void; the dead cannot praise the Lord and do not know anything about the living. Samuel, on the other hand, returned from the dead and knew the future that awaited Saul and his sons: "Tomorrow your sons and you will be with me; and the Lord will also deliver the Israelites forces into the hand of the Philistines" (28:19). How can we explain this? Did the belief in the resurrection of the dead already exist in the Hebrew Bible? Did the witch of Endor not have special powers, and was it God who allowed Samuel to rise from his grave?

THE DEATH OF SAMUEL

According to 1 Samuel 25:1, "Samuel died, and all of Israel gathered and made lament for him; and they buried him in Ramah, his home." The public mourning which was held for Samuel indicates that the Israelites respected and honored him. This gathering is reminiscent of a previous gathering, when the people of Israel demanded Samuel appoint a king. Just as Samuel traveled through the land to serve the people, now the people assembled from all around to take part in his funeral. This gathering is also mentioned in reference to Aaron: "All the house of Israel bewailed Aaron for thirty days" (Num 20:29) and to Moses: "And the Israelites bewailed Moses in the steps of Moab for thirty days" (Deut 34:8). This kind of public gathering with shows of emotion could not have been done without the consent of King Saul.

In his writings, Josephus described, at length, the death of Samuel and summarized his life:

> About this time Samuel the prophet died. He was a man whom the Hebrews honored in extraordinary degree; for that lamentation which the people made for him and this during a long time, which manifested his virtue and affection which the people bore for him; as also did the solemnity and concern that appeared about his funeral, and about the complete observation of all funeral rites. They buried him in his own city Ramah; and wept for him a very great number of days, not looking on it as a sorrow for the death of another man, but as that in which they were every one themselves concerned. He was a righteous man, and gentle in his nature; and on that account he was very dear to God. Now he governed and presided over the people alone, after the death of Eli the high priest, twelve years, and eighteen years together with Saul the king.[1]

The Israelites lamented for Samuel before they buried him. Many biblical passages, in fact, placed the *misped* lament before internment (Gen 23:2; 50:10, 13; 1 Sam 25:1; 28:3; Jer 22:18; 25:33). The act of lamentation consists of beating the breast (Isa 32:12)[2] and chanting a dirge or lament, saying, "'Ah my brother!' or 'Ah sister!'; they shall not lament for him, saying, 'Ah lord! or 'Ah his majesty!'"(Jer 22:18; cf. Jer 34:5; 1 Kgs 13:30). The

---

1. Josephus, *Ant.* 6.13.5.

2. The sense is also found in the Akkadian verb *sapādu*, "beat the breast." *CAD*: S 150–51, *Sapādu*.

misped may also have originally been a bitter cry, i.e., "for this I will lament (*'espedah*) and wail ... I will make lamentation (*misped*) like the jackals" (Mic 1:8; cf. Jer 4:8; 49:3; Joel 1:13). This also appears in association with fasting (2 Sam 1:12; Joel 2:12; Zech 7:5), with wearing sackcloth and rending one's garment (2 Sam 3:31; Esth 4:1), and with cutting oneself (Jer 16:6).

Samuel was buried in his house, which is also what we read about Joab and Manasseh (1 Kgs 2:34; 2 Chr 33:20). According to the Bible, tombs are impure, and therefore burial in one's own house is unlikely. Burial beneath the floor of a house, especially before the Iron Age, is now known through archeological excavation,[3] while the kings of Ugarit were buried in niches inside their palace.[4] In the three biblical cases, however, it is possible that the word "house" means the family mausoleum, since according to Chronicles, Manasseh was "buried ... in his house" (2 Chr 33:20), whereas the parallel account in Kings reports that he "was buried in the garden of his house" (2 Kgs 21:18). We should point out that archeological data shows that the Israelites buried their dead outside the community.[5] It is stated that Samuel was buried in Ramah, his hometown, compared to some of the judges, where only a general location is specified.[6]

The reference to Samuel's death in chapter 25:1 has no link to the previous chapter, nor to the new story which is narrated in chapter 25. Samuel is last mentioned in 1 Samuel 19:22. According to McCarter, it is probably the prophetic hand that formed the earlier stories of Samuel and Saul that added this note here.[7] It anticipates the story of Saul at Endor, where Samuel's death is also cited (28:3). It is possible that it is mentioned at this juncture because of chronological necessities. In other words, Samuel died, and it took place after the meeting between Saul and David at Engedi and before the encounter between David and Nabal. Another explanation links the death of Samuel to David's escape to the wilderness of Paran. Since Samuel could prevent the fights between Saul and David, Samuel's death was a major setback—as David had lost an important supporter. Now there was no force that could stop Saul from chasing after David—so

---

3. Johnston, *Shades of Sheol*, 52n13.
4. Gray, *I & II Kings*, 101.
5. Pitard, "Tombs and Offering," 149.
6. Tola at Shamir in Epharaim (Judg 10:2); Jair at Kamon in Gilead (10:4); Jephthah in one of the towns of Gilead (12:7); Ibzan in Bethlehem (12:10); Elon the Zebulunite in Aijalon in the territory of Zebulun (12:12); Abdon son of Hillel the Pirathonite in Pirathon in the territory of Ephraim (12:15).
7. McCarter, *I Samuel*, 388.

SAMUEL

David escaped to the wilderness of Paran. In the Hebrew Bible, the death of an important person is not always recorded at the actual time death, but rather when he completes his task. Abraham's death is mentioned after he arranged the marriage of his son Isaac, although he lived for another thirty-eight years. According to Radak, Samuel's death is mentioned after Saul acknowledged that David would become the king (24:1); in other words after he completed his commission.

POSTHUMOUS MEETING OF SAMUEL WITH SAUL

In chapter 28, Samuel's death is mentioned a second time, but this time it is a flashback that reminds us of his death. In addition, there is reference to Saul's removal of the ghost and familiar spirit. The death note is repeated because it is necessary for understanding the following story, the posthumous meeting of Samuel with Saul. According to Malbim, the verse sets the stage for the upcoming episode. If Samuel were alive, Saul would have gone to him for advice and the events of this chapter would not have taken place.

It is ironic that Saul, who had exterminated the 'ovot and yidde 'onim, found himself needing the services of a medium. The very fact that he makes this request reflects his sincere belief that the dead know what will happen in the world of the living.[8]

When the medium sees Samuel rising from the grave she cries out and then rebukes Saul for deceiving her. Readers have long wondered why she did not recognize Saul before Samuel appeared. According to the Talmudic sages and traditional commentators, including Rashi and Radak, the dead rise feet first. Samuel, however, arose in the normal upright posture, out of respect for the king. Seeing this, the woman realized the identity of her visitor.[9] Verse 14 in the Septuagint, evidently based on this midrash, has her telling Saul that she sees ἄνδρα ὄρθιον, "a man upright" (reflecting a Vorlage of זקוף instead of the MT זקן). According to Josephus, it was Samuel himself who revealed Saul's identity,[10] and Budde believed that Samuel made a gesture toward Saul, spoiling the latter's incognito.[11]

It is unclear which rites the medium employed in order to raise Samuel. The midrash reports laconically that "she did what she did, and she

---

8. On the other hand, according to Ecclesiastes 9:5, the dead know nothing.
9. Lev. R. 26:7; Tanh. Lev. 21:1; Sanh. 65b.
10. Josephus, Ant. 14.2.333.
11. Budde, Die Bücher Samuel, 180.

said what she said, and raised him."[12] Of course, it is possible that she was a fraud, that the Lord worked a miracle and Samuel really did rise from his grave. When Samuel appears, the woman is taken aback and cries out. Some explain that she knew she had done nothing and was consequently astonished to see a spirit rise up.[13] Several manuscripts of the Septuagint have "the woman saw (i.e., recognized) Saul and cried out," instead of the MT "Samuel"; some scholars adopt this reading. However, the emendation seems to be ruled out by Saul's question, "What do you see?" and the woman's response, which describes Samuel's appearance (verses 13–14).

According to Kaufmann, this passage deals with a method of gaining foreknowledge of the future by getting dead souls to declare what they know.[14] The spirits of the dead are referred to as *elohim*; as the woman tells Saul, "I see *elohim* coming up from the earth" (verse 13; cf. Isa 8:19). They have a mantic power to know and reveal what is concealed in the future, a revelation they express in human language, just as prophets do. The spirit of the dead recounts what it sees or knows through its mantic power. This is a special form of prophecy, that of the Rephaim.[15] Kaufmann maintains that enchanters worked themselves into an ecstatic state and became mediums. That is, the medium's mind merged with or was taken over by that of the dead person. During the encounter, the medium was in a prophetic trance and had supernatural knowledge. When the woman raised Samuel's spirit, she was imbued with supernatural knowledge that enabled her to recognize Saul.

The problem with Kaufmann's reading is that if the woman were in a trance, how could she suspend it to accuse Saul of deceiving her? Furthermore, according to the biblical narrative, the woman served only as an instrument to make the initial connection between Saul and Samuel, who speak directly to each other. She is not a party to the conversation. The implication of verse 21, "the woman came into Saul," i.e., *wa-tavo'* (went up to) is that she was not present during the dialogue of king and prophet but returned from another room and saw Saul's panicked reaction to the encounter. Kaufmann, however, believes that the entire conversation was conducted by and through the medium.

---

12. *Lev R.* 26:7.
13. Lewis, *Cults of the Dead*, 115.
14. Kaufmann, "On the Story," 210.
15. Kaufmann, "On the Story," 210.

Samuel

Another possibility is that it is not the dead himself who is being raised, but only his shade, which ascends from under the earth and speaks in a chirping voice (Isa 29:4; 8:19). According to this scenario, the medium and the inquirer sat in separate rooms. The medium saw the spirit of the dead in smoke or as a silhouette rising from the earth and translated its chirps into human language. At Endor, however, Samuel appeared in his full form, not as a silhouette or smoke. The woman was startled and then realized that it was only because of Saul that she had been able to raise Samuel. After the two verify that it is indeed Samuel who was brought up by her enchantments, Saul and Samuel converse directly. The woman goes away and returns only at the end of their dialogue.

We have already noted that the woman describes Samuel as *elohim*,[16] meaning a shade or superhuman being, as in Isaiah 8:19. Some scholars, such as Spronk and Lewis, cite various extrabiblical texts as evidence for the use of *elohim* to refer to the dead.[17] One possibility is that the spirit is called *elohim* because it is the divine part of a human being. Here, Targum Jonathan renders the word as "angel" when it cannot refer to God: "I saw an angel of the Lord rising up." This meaning is supported by "all *elohim* bow down to Him" (Ps 97:7). Radak explains that here *elohim* means "a great man" (cf. Exod 22:8, 27). This reading is plausible; when Moses hesitates to accept his mission to Egypt and the Lord promises to send his brother Aaron with him, he tells him, "He shall speak for you to the people; and he shall be a mouth for you, and you shall be to him as ʾ *elohim*" (Exod 4:16; cf. Exod 7:1).

As for the plural participle *'olim* (coming up), it agrees in number with ʾ *elohim*, which is a plural form; compare "He is a holy God (ʾ *elohim qedošim huʾ*)" (Josh 24:19) and "living God (*ḥayyim*)" (Deut 5:26; 1 Sam 17:26, 36; Jer 10:10; 23:36). In the next verse, however, the medium describes what she sees in the singular; perhaps the woman saw more than one spirit, but Saul asked to speak only with Samuel. Such an interpretation is found in the Talmud: *'olim* implies two, one was Samuel, but [who was] the other Samuel went and brought Moses with him, saying to him: "Perhaps, heaven forfend, I am summoned to judgment: arise with me, for

---

16. Other instances of *elohim* with a plural adjective are Josh 24:19; Deut 5:23; 1 Sam 17:26, 36.

17. Spronk, *Beatific Afterlife*, 163; Lewis, *Cults of the Dead*, 49–51, 115. See also Arnold, who says that *elohim* "denotes the ancestral dead and not simply ghost or spirit of the dead." Arnold, "Necromancy and Cleromancy," 203.

there is nothing that you wrote in the Torah that I did not fulfil."[18] The Tosafists explain that "although Moses was not of [Samuel's] generation, he said, 'This is how I interpreted the text and what I practiced. Come and bear witness for me, for you, too, have learned.'"

Hutter offers the interesting suggestion that the location of the ritual and the ritual itself are evidence of Hittite influence. According to him, "gods rising" echoes an ancient Hittite incantation formula for conjuring up underworld gods, which was used by the pre-Israelite residents of Endor.[19] Inquiring of the dead is very similar to consulting with pagan deities, which is why it was banned in Israel. Later, when the denizens of the underworld were no longer considered to be gods, Samuel could be included in the category of ʾelohim without being identified as a god. As Johnston noted, however, a link between Endor and the Hittites is far from certain, and taking the term ʾelohim as denoting both forbidden pagan gods and licit nondivine beings seems to be contradictory.[20] The best interpretation, then, is that mentioned above: the ghost of the dead is the spirit, the divine component of the human being.

When the medium raises Samuel, Saul asks her to describe what she sees; the implication is that Saul himself sees nothing. According to *Midr. Tanḥ*, Emor (quoted in *Yalkut Shimoni* 1:28), the medium does not hear what the dead person says but sees him; whereas the inquirer does not see the shade, but hears its voice. Saul may be in the corner of the room or in the next room and does not see what is happening; this is why he must ask the woman whether it is indeed Samuel who has risen. The woman described Samuel as "an old man wrapped in a cloak"; apparently this robe was symbolic of Samuel's prophetic or judicial status.[21] It may be the robe that Hannah made each year to bring to Samuel when she made her pilgrimage to Shiloh (1 Sam 2:19) or the cloak (it was Samuel's) that was torn in two to symbolize the rift between the Lord and Saul (1 Sam 15:27). The reference to the cloak indicates that the dead, while in the underworld, have the same appearance as they did in the world of the living.[22] In any case,

---

18. Ḥag. 4b; Tanḥ Lev. Emor 2.
19. Hutter, "Religionsgeschichtliche Erwägungen," 32–36.
20. Johnston, *Shades of Sheol*, 146.
21. Similarly, King Ahaziah identified the man who met his messengers as Elijah from the leather girdle he wore (2 Kgs 1:8).
22. 22. Isa 14:9; Ezek 32:27; *Sanh.* 90b.

when he hears the woman's description Saul knows that it is indeed Samuel who has risen and consequently bows low out of respect for the prophet.

Saul is committing a grievous sin by inquiring of the dead—a practice that is abhorrent to the Lord (Deut 18:12)—instead of inquiring of the Lord. Raising up a prophet of the Lord by magical means as a way to force the Lord to respond is a detestable action. Samuel's reaction is to rebuke Saul: "Why have you disturbed me (*hirgaztani*) and brought me up?" (1 Sam 28:15). There is a bitter irony here, given that the next day Saul and his sons would join Samuel in the world of the dead.

We will understand Samuel's complaint more clearly if we compare it to Phoenician royal tomb inscriptions: that of Tabnit of Sidon—"Don't, don't open it, and don't disturb (*trgzn*) me, for such a thing would be an abomination to Astarte! But if you do open it and if you do disturb me, may [you] not have any seed among the living under the sun or resting place together with the shades!"[23] A similar description is found on the great sarcophagus of Eshmun'azar, discovered near Sidon: "Whoever you are, ruler and (ordinary) man, may he not open this resting place, and may he not search in it for anything, for nothing whatever has been placed into it! May he not take the casket in which I am resting, and may he not carry me away from this resting-place to another resting place!" There is also a curse against any ruler or a man who opens the tomb or steals the casket: "May they not have a resting place with the shades, may they not be buried in a grave, and may they not have a son and seed to take their place!"[24]

A comparison with these inscriptions suggests that Samuel sees Saul's act as desecrating his grave and disturbing his rest, a transgression that is severely punished by heaven.[25] In fact, Saul has sinned twice, both by inquiring of the dead rather than of God and by disturbing the dead. The Gemara, by contrast, sees Samuel's reaction as fear of judgment day: "Samuel said to Saul, 'Why have you disturbed me and brought me up?' Now if Samuel, the righteous, was afraid of the judgment, how much more so should we be fearful!"[26] The Jerusalem Talmud is even clearer about Samuel's trepidation, with Samuel telling Saul: "What is more, I thought that it was the Day of

23. Rosenthal, "Tabnit of Sidon," 662.

24. Rosenthal, "Eshmun'azar of Sidon," 662.

25. The grave should be a place where a person could rest in peace; see Job 3:13–19. Several passages in the Bible insist that the dead cannot be awakened from their sleep (2 Kgs 4:31; Jer 51:39; Job 14:12). For the subject of disturbing the rest of the dead see Hallo, "Disturbing the Dead," 183–92.

26. b. Ḥag. 4b.

Judgment and I was afraid."²⁷ On judgment day Samuel will be like every other human being. According to the Midrash Rabba, Samuel explains his candor to Saul as follows: "When I was with you, I was in a false world and you might have heard untrue words from me, for I was afraid of you lest you should kill me, but now that I am in a world of truth you will only hear from me words of truth."²⁸

Samuel acts as a prophet even after his death. He delivered a prophecy of doom to Saul. He reminds Saul that God departed from him and YHWH is now with David. This fulfills what Samuel already told Saul in chapter 15; that YHWH was tearing the kingdom from him (verses 27–28) and giving it to David. He repeats his previous rebuke of Saul who did not destroy Amalek (chapter 15). The fate of Saul and his sons are sealed: they will join him.

According to the biblical account, when Saul learns that he will fall in battle on the morrow, he falls powerless to the ground.²⁹ Saul collapses both because of the terror inspired by the prophet's words and because he has eaten nothing for a whole day and night. Here the biblical narrator turns the spotlight on the woman, whose merciful and kind nature is revealed when she slaughters her fatted calf to feed Saul.³⁰ Josephus, too, took note of her positive qualities, despite the fact that biblical law condemned her to death:

> Now it is but just to recommend the generosity of this woman ... she still did not remember to [Saul's] disadvantage that he had condemned her sort of learning, and did not refuse him as a stranger, and one that she had had no acquaintance with; but she had compassion upon him, and comforted him, and exhorted him to do what he was greatly averse to, and offered him the only creature she had, as a poor woman ... It would be well therefore to imitate the [woman's] example and to do kindnesses to all such as are in want and to think that nothing is better, nor more becoming mankind, than such a general beneficence, nor what will sooner render God favorable, and ready to bestow good things upon us.³¹

---

27. J. Ḥag. 2a.
28. Lev. R . 26:7.
29. The verb *npl* occurs four times in chapter 31 (vv. 1, 4, 5, and 8).
30. On the character of the medium, see Simon, *Reading Prophetic Narratives*, 73–92.
31. Josephus, *Ant.* 6.14. 4.

Samuel

LIFE AFTER DEATH

According to the Biblical belief, when a person dies, he descends to Sheol. It has gates and bolts, so there is no return from it. The underworld is a void; the dead cannot praise the Lord and do not know anything about the living. Sheol is a place of total disconnection between the living and the powerless dead.

In the Sumerian and Akkadian myths of the descent of the goddess of fertility (Inanna and Ishtar, respectively) to the underworld, that place is referred to as the "land of the dead," the "land of no return," and "the house which none leave who have entered it . . . the road from which there is no way back."[32] The concept of the netherworld as a place from which there is no return developed against the background of the fear that the shades of the dead, which must be fed, might try to come back from the underworld, usurping the place of the living and harming them. In the Akkadian version of the myth, Ishtar threatens the guardian of the underworld: "If thou openest not the gate so that I cannot enter, I will smash the door, I will shatter the bolt, I will smash the doorpost, I will move the doors, I will raise up the dead, eating the living, so that the dead will outnumber the living."[33]

In the Hebrew Bible, too, we find the idea, evidently derived from Mesopotamian mythology, that there is no return from the underworld. Job, for example, avers that none who descend to the underworld return: "As a cloud fades away, so whoever goes down to Sheol does not come up; he returns no more to his home; his place does not know him" (Job 7:9–10). The idea of no return is repeated: "Before I depart—never to return—for the land of deepest gloom" (10:21). No man returns from the underworld; we find the idea that a person remains there forever, as implied by "so man lies down never to rise" (14:12). Ezekiel, too, says that those who dwell in the netherworld remain there forever (Ezek 26:20–21).

These images of the netherworld and of the powerlessness of the dead first emerged from Josiah's reform in the seventh century BCE, of which we read in the book of Kings: "Josiah also did away with the ghosts and familiar spirits, the idols and the fetishes—all the detestable things that were to be seen in the land of Judah and Jerusalem" (2 Kgs 23:24). Job, written in the fifth century BCE, continues in this vein: the dead know nothing about the living. Hence, it is not surprising that Job offers graphic descriptions

---

32. Speiser, "Descent of Ishtar," 107, lines 5–6.
33. Speiser, "Descent of Ishtar," 107, lines 16–20.

of the netherworld as a dark and repulsive place. Lang holds that Josiah's reform led to the decline in the importance of the netherworld and dead ancestors.[34] From his time the focus was on this world and the reward that human beings merit. Consequently, it is in his lifetime, and not in the hereafter, that God gives Job double what he had had before, providing him with health, family, and wealth (Job 12:10).

The Hebrew Bible mentions two mortals who may have ascended to heaven: Enoch and Elijah. Enoch is said to have been taken by God (Gen 5:24). Elijah ascended in a whirlwind to the sky (2 Kgs 2:11). If these two accounts do refer to an ascent to heaven, they are intended to bolster the belief that the future existence after death is not in the underworld but with God. Nowhere except for the unique case of Samuel being brought up from his grave by the medium (1 Sam 28:3–24) is a return from the netherworld mentioned in the Hebrew Bible. Unlike those references to the netherworld as a place from which there is no return, the book of Samuel propounds the opposite view: "The Lord deals death and gives life, casts down into Sheol and raises up" (1 Sam 2:6). This expresses the hope that the Lord who casts the living down to the underworld will also bring them back. Deuteronomy entertains a similar idea: "I deal death and give life; I wounded and I will heal: None can deliver from My hand" (Deut 32:39), as well as in Psalms: "O Lord, You brought up my soul from Sheol, restored me to life from among those gone down to the Pit" (Ps 30:4 RSV). The Talmudic sages cited these verses as evidence for the resurrection of the dead, as did medieval commentators such as Radak and Gersonides.[35]

In the Talmudic era resurrection became one of the key tenets of Judaism. According to *tractate Sanhedrin*, all of Israel have a portion in the world to come, for it is written, "Thy people are all righteous; they shall inherit the land for ever, the branch of my planting, the work of my hands, that I may be glorified" (Isa 60:21). Rejecting the views of heretics and sectarians, the Talmudic sages underscored the doctrine of resurrection and assigned it its own blessing in the daily *amidah*. Another question that preoccupied the sages was what people would look like after resurrection. The consensus seems to have assumed some sort of biological continuity, with the reborn looking just as they had when alive. Otherwise, the tenet of reward and punishment for the righteous is problematic. Rabbi Meir was asked whether the dead would arise clothed or naked; another question

---

34. Lang, "Afterlife," 19.
35. *Pesaḥ* 68a.

referred to the resurrection of the physically handicapped.[36] The dead will rise wearing the same clothes they had on when they died (see our story of the witch of Endor and Samuel). The disabled, too, will rise with their handicaps; the lame will be lame and the blind, blind,[37] to make it possible to identify them. Only then will the Lord heal them (Deut 32:39).[38]

According to the Talmud, when a man dies, the soul leaves the body, but for the first twelve months, it still has a link to the body, coming and going until the body has disintegrated. Therefore, it was believed that the prophet Samuel was raised from the dead within the first year of his death. After a year the righteous go to paradise. The fact the Saul went and asked the witch to divine by a ghost shows that he believed in the afterlife; more, that he believed that the dead have knowledge about the future. Indeed, according to this Biblical story Samuel knows what will happen to Saul: "Tomorrow your sons and you will be with me; and the Lord will also deliver the Israelite forces into the hands of the Philistines" (1 Sam 28:19).

In conclusion, Samuel's death is mentioned twice. At first in chapter 25:1, where it has no link to the previous chapter nor to the new story which is narrated in chapter 25. It is mentioned at this juncture because Samuel ended his task and Saul acknowledged that David would become the king (24:1). In 1 Samuel 28, the death note is repeated because it is necessary for understanding the following story, the posthumous meeting of Samuel with Saul. The public mourning which was held for Samuel indicated how much the Israelites respected and honored him. The lamentation for Samuel was before he was buried. He was buried in his hometown of Ramah. Since God did not answer him, Saul the king of Israel went to the witch of Endor, there he asked her to raise Samuel from his grave. It is unclear what rites the medium employed to raise Samuel; more than likely, the Lord worked a miracle and Samuel rose from his grave. When she raised Samuel, she said, "I see *elohim* coming up from the earth." The woman described him as "an old man wrapped in a cloak." The description of Samuel as *elohim* refers to his spirit, the divine component of the human being. Samuel was angry with Saul because he inquired of the dead rather than of God; in addition, it was a sin to disturb the dead from their sleep. Unlike the references to the netherworld as a place from which there is no return and the dead do not know the living, Samuel is back and delivers a message of doom to

---

36. *Sanh.* 90–91
37. *Eccl. Rab.* 1:4.
38. *Gen. R.* 95:1.

Saul: "Tomorrow your sons and you will be with me." This return of Samuel coincides with "The Lord deals death and gives life, casts down into Sheol and raises up" (1 Sam 2:6), which the Talmudic sages cited as evidence for the resurrection of the dead.

Conclusion

THE PROPHET SAMUEL WAS UNIQUE, during life as well as after death. Therefore, it is no wonder that he is compared to Moses and Aaron. He led Israel through one of the most tumultuous times of its history: the transition into the monarchical period. His arrival opened a new chapter in Israelite history; it signified the decline of the Elides priesthood and Samuel's rise to prominence as a trustworthy prophet of the Lord. In his first public appearance at the gathering in Mizpah Samuel displayed his abilities as a leader when he interceded on behalf of the people, and God responded. Samuel is depicted as a well-known prophet that the people listened to and obeyed. He is described at the height of his powers as both prophet and judge.

In two major speeches known as "the rights of the King" (1 Sam 8:1-22) and his farewell speech to the people of Israel (1 Sam 12), Samuel rejected the idea of kingship. Evidently, Samuel had his own personal agenda. He tried to establish his own prophetic dynasty; human kingship meant the decline of his power and status; it posed a threat to his authority. Although he rejected the idea of human kingship, his role was pivotal to the introduction of a monarchy in Israel. Samuel anointed Saul and later David as kings. There are many similarities between the anointment of Saul and David; this resemblance in the stories is not accidental, its purpose is to stress that David is the chosen king instead of Saul.

Since Samuel rejected the idea of human kingship from the start, we witness a power struggle between Samuel and Saul which is the first between a prophet and a king. It is the beginning of many future clashes between the kings of Israel and the prophets. This stems from the fact that relationships between the kings' sacral and secular functions, vis-à-vis the prophet, were not clearly defined yet. Examination of the feuds between Samuel and Saul

CONCLUSION

reveals that on several occasions Saul did what was permissible to him. Saul acted as a king, to do whatever he saw fit since God was with him (1 Sam 10:7). Samuel did not like that Saul acted independently; an independent king was a threat to his authority and status. Samuel's criticism was personal, most tellingly after the battle against the Amalekites when he used God's name in his personal battle against Saul, adding his words to God's message of Saul's rejection. By doing so he undermined Saul and legitimized his authority and status. Strangely, when it came to David no such criticism is to be found. The prophet anointed David and protected him. This leads us to believe that the stories about Samuel and David were a later interpolation which took place in David's court and were written by a sympathetic author.

The fact that Samuel served in Shiloh and on several occasions performed cultic activities led to the assumption that he was a priest. Samuel was from the tribe of Ephraim, he was not a Levite, and he was a priest servant in Shiloh. In Shiloh, Samuel received a revelation where he became a trustworthy prophet of the Lord; from the moment he delivered the words of God. In the early stories he is remembered as "the man of God." In the Hebrew Bible the man of God was possessed by powers which helped him to call for the assistance of divine aid. Samuel is also called a seer which was believed to be the earlier name for prophet. In several instances Samuel is referred to as judging Israel (1Sam 7:6 and 16-17). During a time of crisis, it denotes Samuel leading Israel into repentance and interceding on behalf of the people of Israel before God (1Sam.7:6b). In more peaceful times it signifies his judicial activities as an arbiter of disputes: "Each year he made the rounds of Bethel, Gilgal, and Mizpah, and acted as judge over Israel at all those places" (7:16). As the last "judge" of Israel he went out from his home at Ramah and made the rounds, he judged the people and instructed the Law of Yahweh to unify the bond of covenant with Yahweh (7:16-17). But above all Samuel was a prophet, a person who delivered the words of God. Like the classical prophets Samuel played a prominent role in communal affairs. He was consulted for advice and delivered oracles from God. He told Eli the calamity that awaited his household and delivered a prophecy to Saul about his future.

According to the Hebrew Bible the dead descend to Sheol, a place of no return. Samuel, however, was raised from the dead by the witch of Endor. Even after his death he had an impact on the life of Israel and he continued to fulfill his role as a prophet and delivered a message of doom to

Samuel

Saul "Tomorrow your sons and you will be with me; and the Lord will also deliver the Israelite forces into the hands of the Philistines" (1 Sam 28:19). Samuel was the religious leader of his time; he was God's spokesman in guiding Israel, the forerunner of the classical prophets of the eight century BCE.

Bibliography

Ackroyd, Peter. *The First Book of Samuel*. CBC. Cambridge: Cambridge University Press, 1971.
Albright, William Foxwell. "A Catalogue of Early Hebrew Lyric Poems (Psalm LXVIII)." *HUCA* 23 (1950–51) 1–39.
———. "The Oracles of Balaam." *JBL* 63 (1944) 207–33.
———. "The Psalm of Habakkuk." In *Studies in Old Testament Prophecy Presented to T. H. Robinson*, edited by H. H. Rowley, 1–18. Edinburgh: T. & T. Clark, 1946.
———. *Samuel and the Beginning of the Prophetic Movement*. Cincinnati: Hebrew Union College, 1961.
———. "Some Remarks on the Song of Moses in Deuteronomy XXXII." *VT* 9 (1959) 339–46.
———. "The Song of Deborah in Light of Archeology." *BASOR* 62 (1936) 26–31.
Alt, Albrecht. "The Formation of the Israelite State in Palestine." In *Essays on Old Testament History and Religion*, translated by R. A. Wilson, 173–237. Oxford: Basil Blackwell, 1966.
———. *Kleine Schriften zur Geschichte des Volkes Israel*. 3 vols. Munich: Beck, 1953–59.
Alter, Robert. *The Art of Biblical Narrative*. New York: Basic, 1981.
Amit, Yaira. "He Is Lent to God." *BethM* 27 (1982) 238–43.
———. "The Story of Samuel's Consecration to Prophecy in the Light of Prophetic Thought." In *Moshe Goldstein Volume*, edited by B. Z. Luria, 29–36. Jerusalem: Society for Bible Research, 1987.
Arden-Close, C. F. "The Rainfall of Palestine." *PEQ* 73 (1941) 122–28.
Arnold, Bill T. "Necromancy and Cleromancy in 1 and 2 Samuel." *CBQ* 66 (2004) 199–213.
Bach, R. *Die Aufforderungen zur Flucht und zum Kampf im alttestamentlichen Prophetenspruch*. Neukirchen, Germany: Neukirchener Verlag, 1962.
Balentine, Samuel E. "The Prophet as Intercessor: A Reassessment." *JBL* 103 (1984) 161–73.
Bar, Shaul. *A Letter That Has Not Been Read: Dreams in the Hebrew Bible*. Cincinnati: Hebrew Union College Press, 2001.
Bar-Efrat, Shimon. *I Samuel*. Tel Aviv: Am Ovad, 1996.
Barr, James. *Comparative Philology and the Text of the Old Testament*. Oxford: Clarendon, 1968.
Batten, Loring W. "The Sanctuary at Shiloh and Samuel's Sleeping Therein." *JBL* 19 (1900) 29–33.

Bibliography

Birch, Bruce C. "The Development of the Tradition of the Anointing of Saul in I Sam 9:1–10:16." *JBL* 90 (1971) 55–68.

———. *The Rise of Israelite Monarchy: The Growth and Development of 1 Samuel 7–15*. SBLDS 27. Missoula, MT: Scholars, 1976.

Bourke, Joseph. "Samuel and the Ark." *Dominican Studies* 7 (1954) 73–103.

Brettler, Marc. "The Composition of 1 Samuel 1–2." *JBL* 116 (1997) 601–12.

Bright, John. *A History of Israel*. 3rd ed. Philadelphia: Westminster, 1982.

Brinker, R. *The Influence of Sanctuaries in Early Israel*. Manchester, UK: Manchester University Press, 1946.

Brockington, Leonard H. "Audition in the OT." *JTS* 49 (1948) 1–8.

Brooks, Simcha S. *Saul and the Monarchy: A New Look*. Burlington, VT: Ashgate, 2005.

Buber, Martin. *Darko šel Miqra '*. Jerusalem: Bialik Institute, 1964.

———. "Die Erzählung von Sauls Königswahl." *VTSup* 6 (1956) 113–73.

Budde, Karl. *Die altisraelitische Religion*. 3rd ed. Giessen: Töpelmann, 1912.

———. *Die Bücher Samuel*. Kurzer Hand Commentar zum Alten Testament 8. Tübingen: Mohr/Siebeck, 1902.

Cassuto, Umberto. "Biblical Literature and Canaanite Literature." *Tarbiz* 14 (1942) 1–10.

Coats, George W. "The Song of the Sea." *CBQ* 31 (1969) 1–17.

Cody, Aelred. *A History of Old Testament Priesthood*. AnBib 35. Rome: Pontifical Biblical Institute, 1969.

Cohen, Harold R. *Biblical hapax legomena in Light of Akkadian and Ugaritic*. SBLDS 37. Missoula, MT: Scholars, 1978.

Cohen, Martin A. "The Role of the Shilonite Priesthood in the United Monarchy of Ancient Israel." *HUCA* 36 (1965) 59–98.

Cooper, Jerrold S., and W. Heimpel. "The Sumerian Sargon Legend." *JAOS* 103 (1983) 67–82.

Cross, Frank Moore. *Canaanite Myth and Hebrew Epic: Essays in the History of the Religion of Israel*. Cambridge, MA: Harvard University Press, 1973.

———. "Notes on a Canaanite Psalm in the Old Testament." *BASOR* 117 (1950) 19–21.

Cross, Frank Moore, and David Noel Freedman. "A Royal Song of Thanksgiving." *JBL* 72 (1953) 15–34.

———. "The Song of Miriam." *JNES* 14 (1954) 237–50.

Daube, D. *The New Testament and Rabbinic Judaism*. London: Athlone Press, 1956.

Donner, H. "Basic Elements of the Old Testament Historiography Illustrated by the Saul Traditions." *OTWSA* 24 (1981) 40–54.

Drazin, Israel. *Who Was the Biblical Prophet Samuel?* Jerusalem: Gefen, 2017.

Driver, Samuel Rolles. *Notes on the Hebrew Text and the Topography of the Books of Samuel*. 2nd ed. Oxford: Clarendon, 1984.

Edelman, Diana. "Saul." *ABD* 5:989–99.

———. "Saul's Rescue of Jabesh-Gilead (I Samuel 11:1–11): Sorting Story from History." *ZAW* 96 (1984) 195–209.

Ehrlich, Arnold B. *Mikrâ ki Pheschutô*. 3 vols. New York: Ktav, 1969.

Ehrlich, Ernst L. *Der Traum im Alten Testament*. BZAW 73. Berlin: Topelman, 1953.

Eichrodt, Walther. *Theology of the Old Testament*. 2 volumes. Translated by James A. Baker. Philadelphia: Westminster, 1961.

Eissfeldt, Otto. *Die Komposition der Samuelisbücher*. Leipzig: J. C. Hinrich, 1931.

Elat, Moshe. *Samuel and the Foundation of Kingship in Ancient Israel*. Jerusalem: Magnes, 1998.

BIBLIOGRAPHY

Eslinger, Lyle M. *Kingship of God in Crisis: A Close Reading of 1 Samuel 1-12*. Sheffield, UK: Almond, 1985.
Faust, Avarham. "Settlement Patterns and State Formation in Southern Samaria and the Archeology of (a) Saul." In *Saul in Story and Tradition*, edited by C. S. Ehrlich and M. C. White, 14-38. FAT 47. Tübingen: Mohr/Siebeck, 2006.
Fenton, Terry L. "Deuteronomistic Advocacy of nābî: 1 Samuel ix 9 and Questions of Israelite Prophecy." *VT* 47 (1997) 23-42.
Fleming, Daniel E. "The Etymological Origins of the Hebrew nābî': The One Who Invokes God." *CBQ* 55 (1993) 217-24.
―――. "Nābû and Munabbiātu: Two New Syrian Religious Personnel." *JAOS* 113 (1993) 175-83.
Finkelstein, Israel. "The Emergence of the Monarchy in Israel: Environmental and Socio-Political Aspects." *Cathedra* 50 (1988) 3-26.
―――. "The Emergence of the Monarchy in Israel: The Environmental and Socioeconomic Aspects." *JSOT* 44 (1989) 43-74.
Fohrer, Georg. "Die Sage in der Bibel." In *Sagen und ihre Deutung*, 59-80. Evangelisches Forum 5. Göttingen: Vandenhoeck & Ruprecht, 1965.
Fokkelman, J. P. *Narrative Art and Poetry in the Books of Samuel: The Crossing Fates (1 Sam. 13-31 and II Sam. 1)*. SSN 23. 4 vols. Assen, The Netherlands: Van Gorcum, 1986.
Fowler, M. D. "The Meaning of lipne YHWH in the Old Testament." *ZAW* 99 (1987) 384-90.
Freedman, David Noel, ed. *The Anchor Bible*. 6 vols. New York: Doubleday, 1992.
―――. Archaic Forms in Early Hebrew Poetry." *ZAW* 72 (1960) 101-07.
―――. "Psalm 113 and the Song of Hannah." *ErIsr* 14 (1978) 56-69.
Frick, Frank S. *Formation of the State in Ancient Israel: A Survey of Models and Theories*. Social World of Biblical Antiquity Series 4. Decatur, GA: Almond, 1985.
Frisch, Amos "'For I feared the people, and I yielded to them' (I Sam 15, 24)—Is Saul's Guilt Attenuated or Intensified?" *ZAW* 108 (1996) 98-104.
Fuchs, H. F. "רָאָה rā' â; רֹאֶה rō' eh I and II; רְאִי re' î; רְאוּת re' ut; מַרְאֶה mar' eh; מַרְאָה mar' â." In *TDOT* XIII (1990-92) 208-242.
Garsiel, Moshe. "The Dispute between Samuel and the People on the Question of Appointing King in Israel." *BethM* 87 (1981) 325-43.
―――. *The First Book of Samuel: A Literary Study of Comparative Structures, Analogies, and Parallel*. Ramat-Gan, Israel: Revivim, 1985.
Gaster, Theodor H. "Dreams: in the Bible." In *EncJud* 6:208-09. Jerusalem: Keter, 1971.
―――. *Thespis, Ritual, Myth, and Drama in the Ancient Near East*. New York: Schumann, 1950.
Gerleman, Gillis. "The Song of Deborah in Light of Stylistics." *VT* 1 (1951) 168-80.
Givati, M. "משפט המלך ומשפט המלוכה" *BethM* 98 (1984) 220-27.
Gnuse, Robert Karl. *The Dream Theophany of Samuel*. Lanham, MD: University Press of America, 1984.
―――. "A Reconsideration of the Form-critical Structure of I Samuel 3: An Ancient Near Eastern Theophany." *ZAW* 94 (1982) 379-90.
Goetze, Albrecht. "Hittite šipant." *JCS* 23 (1970-71) 77-94.
Goldman, S. *Samuel*. London: Soncino, 1987.
Gordon, Cyrus H. *Before the Bible: The Common Background of Greek and Hebrew Civilizations*. London: Collins, 1962.

Bibliography

———. "Eblaitica." In *Eblaitica: Essays on Ebla Archives and Eblaite Language*, edited by Cyrus H. Gordon, Gary A. Rendsburg, and Nathan H. Winter, 1:19–28. Winona Lake, IN: Eisenbrauns, 1987.

Gordon, Robert P. *1 & 2 Samuel*. Exeter, NH: Paternoster, 1986.

Gottwald, Norman K. "Samuel." In *EncJud* 17:758–763. Jerusalem: Keter, 1971.

———. *Tribes of Yahweh: A Sociology of Liberated Israel, 1250–1050*. Maryknoll, NY: Orbis, 1979.

Gray, John. *I & II Kings*. Philadelphia: Westminster, 1963.

Greenspahn, Frederick E. "Egyptian Parallel to Judg 17:6 and 21:25." *JBL* 101 (1982) 129–30.

Habel, Norman. "The Form and Significance of the Call Narrative." *ZAW* 77 (1965) 297–323.

Haldar, Alfred. *Association of Cult Prophets among the Ancient Semites*. Uppsala: Almqvist & Wiksells Boktryckeri, 1945.

Hallo, William W. "Disturbing the Dead." In *Minhah le-Nahum: Biblical and Other Studies Presented to Nahum Sarna in Honour of His 70th Birthday*, edited by Marc Brettler and Michael Fishbane, 183–92. JSOTSup 154. Sheffield, UK: JSOT, 1993.

Halpern, Baruch. *The Constitution of the Monarchy in Israel*. HSM 25. Chico, CA: Scholars, 1981.

Haran, Menachem. "The Ephod according to Biblical Sources." *Tarbiz* 24 (1954–55) 380–91.

———. *Temples and Temple-Service in Ancient Israel: An Inquiry into Biblical Cult Phenomena and the Historical Setting of the Priestly School*. Winona Lake, IN: Eisenbraus, 1985.

Hertzberg, Hans Wilhelm. *I & II Samuel*. Translated by J. S. Bowden. Philadelphia: Westminster, 1976.

Heschel, Abraham J. *The Prophets: An Introduction*. New York: Harper & Row, 1962.

Hoffner, Harry A. "Crossing of the Taurus (1.73)." *CS* 1:184–85.

Hölscher, Gustav. *Die Profeten: Untersuchungen zur Religionsgeschichte Israels*. Leipzig: Hinrichs, 1914.

Hurowitz, Victor. "The 'Sun Disk' Tablet of Nabû-apla-iddina (2.135)." *CS* 2:364–68.

Hutter, Manfred. "Religionsgeschichtliche Erwägungen zu ' elohim in 1 Sam 28, 13." *BN* 21 (1983) 32–36.

Ishida, Tommo. *History and Historical Writings in Ancient Israel: Studies in Historiography*. SHCANE 16. Leiden: Brill, 1999.

Japhet, Sarah. *I & II Chronicles*. Louisville, KY: Westminster John Knox, 1993.

Jirku, Anton. "Ein Fall von Inkubation im AT (Ex 38:8)." *ZAW* 33 (1919), 151–53.

Jobling, David. *1 Samuel*. Berit Olam: Studies in Hebrew Narrative & Poetry. Collegeville, MN: Liturgical Press, 2000.

Johnston, Philip S. *Shades of Sheol*. Downers Grove, IL: Inter Varsity, 2002.

Josephus, Flavius. *Jewish Antiquities*. Translated by Henry St. John Thackeray. Cambridge, MA: Harvard University Press, 1930.

Kalimi, Isaac. *The Book of Chronicles Historical Writing and Literary Devices*. Jerusalem: Mosad Bialik, 2000.

Kaufmann, Y. "On the Story of the Medium." In *Mi-kivshonah shel ha-yetsirah ha-mikrai' t: kovets ma' amarim*, 208–15. Tel Aviv: Dvir, 1966.

———. *Toledot ha-' emunah ha-yisre' elit*. 8 vols. Tel Aviv: Bialik Institute & Dvir, 1937–57.

BIBLIOGRAPHY

Kempinski, A. I. F. "Shiloh." *NEAHL* 4:1364–70.
Kennedy, Archibald Robert Stirling. *Samuel.* London: Thomas Nelson and Sons, 1904.
Kirkpatrick, Alexander Francis. *The First Book of Samuel.* Cambridge: Cambridge University Press, 1886.
Klein, Ralph W. *1 Samuel.* WBC 10. Nashville: Thomas Nelson, 1983.
Knierim, Rolf P. "The Messianic Concept in the First Book of Samuel." In *Jesus and the Historian,* edited by F. Thomas Trotter, 20–51. Philadelphia: Westminster, 1968.
Knutson, Brent B. "Literary Genre in PRU IV." *RSP* 2:153–214.
Kraus, Hans Joachim. *Worship in Israel: A Cultic History of the Old Testament.* Translated by Geoffrey Buswell. Richmond: John Knox, 1965.
Kuenen, Abraham. *The Prophets and Prophecy in Israel.* Translated by Adam Milroy. London: Longmans, Green, 1877.
Lambert, Wilfred G. *Babylonian Wisdom Literature.* Oxford: Clarendon, 1960.
Lang, Bernhard "Afterlife: Ancient Israel's Changing Vision of the World Beyond." *BibRev* 4 (1988) 12–23.
Langdon, Stephen. *Die neubabylonischen Königsinschriften.* VAB 4.
Leuchter, Mark. *Samuel and the Shaping of the Tradition.* Oxford: Oxford University Press, 2013.
———. "Something Old Something Older: Reconsidering 1 Sam 2:27–36." *Journal of Hebrew Scriptures* 4.6 (2003). https://doi.org/10.5508/jhs.2002.v4.a6.
Levine, Baruch A. *The JPS Torah Commentary: Leviticus.* Philadelphia: Jewish Publication Society, 1989.
Lewis, T. J. *Cults of the Dead in Ancient Israel and Ugarit.* Atlanta: Scholars, 1989.
———. "The Textual History of the Song of Hannah: 1 Sam 2:1–10." *VT* 44 (1994) 18–46.
Lindblom, Johannes. *Prophecy in Ancient Israel.* Oxford: Basil Blackwell, 1962.
Lipiński, E. "Peninna, Iti'el et L'Athlète." *VT* 17 (1967) 68–75.
Lods, Adlophe. *Israel—From Its Beginning to the Middle of the Eight Century.* London: K. Paul Trench, Trubner, & Co, 1932.
Long, Burke. "Prophetic Call Tradition and Reports of Visions." *ZAW* 84 (1972) 494–500.
Longman, Tremper, III. "1 Sam 12:16–19: Divine Omnipotence or Covenant Curse?" *WTJ* 45 (1983) 168–71.
Luckenbill, Daniel David. *Ancient Records of Assyria and Babylonia.* 2 vols. Chicago: University of Chicago Press, 1926.
Malamat, Abraham. *Mari and the Bible: A Collection of Studies.* 2nd ed. Jerusalem: Hebrew University, 1984.
———. "Mari and the Bible: Some Patterns of Tribal Organizations and Institutions." *JAOS* 82 (1962) 143–50.
McAlpine, Thomas H. *Sleep, Divine and Human, in the OT.* JSOTSup 38. Sheffield, UK: JSOT, 1987.
McCarter, P. Kyle, Jr. *I Samuel.* Garden City, New York: Doubleday, 1980.
McCarthy, Dennis J. "II Samuel and the Structure of the Deuteronomist History." *JBL* 84 (1965) 131–38.
McCown, Chester Charlton, et al. *Tell En-Nasbeh Excavated under the Direction of the Late William Frederic Badè.* Berkeley, CA:Palestine Institute of Pacific School of Religion and The American Schools of Oriental Research, 1947.
McKenzie, Steven L. *King David: A Biography.* Oxford: Oxford University Press, 2000.
Mauchline, John. *1 and 2 Samuel.* New Century Bible. London: Oliphants, 1971.

Bibliography

Mendelsohn, I. "Samuel's Denunciation of Kingship in Light of Akkadian Documents from Ugarit." *BASOR* 143 (1956) 17–22.

Mettinger, Tryggve N. D. *King and Messiah: The Civil and Sacral Legitimation of the Israelite Kings*. Coniectanea Biblical: Old Testament Series 8. Lund: Gleerup, 1976.

The Midrash on Psalms. Translated by William G. Braude. Yale Judaica Series xiii. 2 vols. New Haven: Yale University Press, 1959.

Midrash Samuel. Edited by Solomon Buber. Krakow: Joseph Fischer, 1893.

Milgrom, Jacob. "The Alleged Wave Offering in Israel and the Ancient Near East." *IEJ* 22 (1972) 33–8.

Miller, Maxwell J. "Saul's Rise to Power: Some Observations Concerning 1 Sam 9:1–10:16, 10:26–11:15, and 13:2–14:46." *CBQ* 36 (1974) 157–74.

Miller, Patrick D., Jr., and J. J. M. Roberts. *The Hand of the Lord: A Reassessment of the Ark Narrative of 1 Samuel*. Baltimore: The Johns Hopkins University Press, 1977.

Miqra'oth Gedoloth: The Rabinnic Bible: Commentaries of Rashi, Abraham ibn Ezra, David Kimhi, & Mesudoth. New York: Pardes, 1961.

Miscall, Peter D. *I Samuel: A Literary Reading*. Bloomington, IN: Indiana University Press, 1986.

Mommer, Peter. "Ist auch Saul unter den Propheten? Ein Beitrag zu 1 Sam 19, 18–24." *BN* 38–39 (1987) 53–61.

Muilenburg, James. "Chapters III and IV in Tell en-Naṣbeh." edited by C. C. McCown, 23–49. New Haven: American Schools of Oriental Research, 1947.

———. "Mizpah of Benjamin." *ST* 8 (1955) 25–42.

Ne'eman, P. "המלכת שאול." *BethM* 30 (1967) 94–110.

Newman, Murray. "The Prophetic Call of Samuel." In I*srael's Prophetic Heritage Fs J. Muilenburg*, edited by B. W. Anderson and W. Harrelson, 86–97. New York: Harper, 1962.

Nihan, Christophe. "Saul among the Prophets (1 Sam 10:10-12 and 19:18-24): The Reworking of Saul Figure in the Context of the Debate on 'Charismatic Prophecy' in the Persian Era." In *Saul in Story and Tradition*, edited by C. S. Ehrlich and M. C. White, 88–118. FAT 47. Tübingen: Mohr/Siebek, 2006.

Noth, Martin. *The Deuteronomistic History*. JSOTSup 15. Translated by Jane Doull et al. Sheffield: JSOT, 1981.

———. *Geschichte Israels*. Göttingen: Vandenhoeck & Ruprecht, 1956.

———. *The History of Israel*. Translated by Stanley Godman. 2nd ed. New York: Harper & Row, 1960.

———. "Samuel und Silo." *VT* 13 (1963) 390–400.

———. *Überlieferungegeschichtliche Studein*. 2nd ed. Tübingen: Max Niemeyer, 1957.

Oppenheim, A. Leo. *The Interpretation of Dreams in the Ancient Near East: With a Translation of Assyrian Dream Book*. Transaction of the American Philosophical Society, New Series, vol. 46. Philadelphia, American Philosophical Society, 1956.

———, trans. "The Mother of Nabonisus." *ANET* 560–62.

Pardee, Dennis. "The Ba'lu Myth (1.86)." *CS* 1:241–74.

Paul, Shalom M. "I Samuel 9:7: An Interview Fee." *Bib* 59 (1978) 542–44.

Peden, A. J. *Egyptian Historical Inscription of the Twentieth Dynasty*. Documenta Mundi Aegyptiaca 3. Jonsered, Sweden: Åströms, 1994.

Pfeiffer, Robert H. trans. "Akkadian Oracles and Prophecies." *ANET* 449–50.

Bibliography

Pitard, Wayne T. "Tombs and Offerings: Archeological Data and Comparative Methodology in the Study of Death in Israel." In *Sacred Times, Sacred Place*, edited by Barry M. Gittlen, 145-67. Winona Lake, IN: Eisenbraus, 2002.
Plöger, Otto. "Priester und Prophet." *ZAW* 63 (1951) 157-92.
Polzin, Robert. *Samuel and the Deuteronomist*. San Francisco: Harper & Row, 1989.
Press, Richard. "Der Prophet Samuel." *ZAW* 56 (1938) 177-225.
Rendsburg, Gary A. "Some False Leads in Identification of Late Biblical Texts: The Case of Genesis 24 and 1 Samuel 2:27-36." *JBL* 121 (2002) 23-46.
Resch, Andreas. *Der Traum im Heilsplan Gottes: Deutung und Bedeutung des Traums im Alten Testament*. Freiburg: Herder, 1964.
Richter, Wolfgang. *Die sogenannten vorprophetischen Berufungsberichte*. FRLANT 101. Göttingen: Vandenhoeck & Ruprechts, 1970.
Robinson, Theodore H. *Prophecy and Prophets*. London: Gerald Duckworth, 1953.
Rofé, Alexander. *The Prophetical Stories*. Jerusalem: Magnes, 1982.
Rosenthal, Franz., trans. "Eshmun'azar of Sidon." *ANET* 523-25.
———, "Tabnit of Sidon." *ANET* 662.
Rowley, H. H. *From Moses to Qumran*. New York: Association, 1963.
———. *The Servant of the Lord*. 2nd ed. Oxford: Basil Blackwell, 1965.
Sarna, Nahum M. *The JPS Torah Commentary: Exodus*. Philadelphia: Jewish Publication Society, 1991.
———. *The JPS Torah Commentary: Genesis*. Philadelphia: Jewish Publication Society, 1989.
Scammon, John H., and David Sperling. "Samuel." *EncJud* 17:754-757.
Schmidt, Ludwig. *Menschlicher Erfolg und Jahwes Initiative: Studien zu Tradition, Interpretation und Historie in Überlieferungen von Gideon, Saul und David*. WMANT 38. Neukirchen-Vluyn, Germany: Neukirchener Verlag, 1970.
Schultz, Alfons. *Die Bücher Samuel*. Exegetisches Handbuch zum AT VIII/1. Münster: Aschendorff, 1919.
Schunck, K. D. *Benjamin: Untersuchungen zur Entstehung und Geschichte eines israelitischen Stammes*. BZAW 86. Berlin: Alferd Töpelmann, 1963.
Segal, Moshe Z. *The Books of Samuel*. Tel Aviv: Dvir, 1948.
Simon, Uriel. *Reading Prophetic Narratives*. Translated by Lenn J. Schramm. Bloomington, IN: Indiana University Press, 1997.
Smith, Henry Preserved. *A Critical and Exegetical Commentary on the Books of Samuel*. ICC. Edinburgh: T. & T. Clark, 1899.
Speiser, E. A., trans. "Descent of Ishtar to the Nether World." *ANET* 106-09.
Sperling, David. *Original Torah: The Political Intent of the Bible's Writers*. New York: New York University Press, 1988.
Spronk, Klass. *Beatific Afterlife in Ancient Israel and in the Ancient Near East*. Kevelar: Butzon & Bercker: Neukirchen-Vluyn, Germany: Neukirchener Verlag, 1986.
Stager, Lawrence E. "The Archaeology of the Family in Ancient Israel." *BASOR* 260 (1985) 1-35.
Steussy, Marti J. *Samuel and His God*. Columbia, SC: University of South Carolina Press, 2010.
Stoebe, Hans Joachim. *Das erste Buch Samuelis*. Kommentar zum Alten Testament 8/1. Gütersloh: Mohn, 1973.
Thornton, T. C. G. "Studies in Samuel." *CQR* 169 (1967) 413-23.

BIBLIOGRAPHY

Tigay, Jeffery H. *The JPS Torah Commentary: Deuteronomy*. Philadelphia: Jewish Publication Society, 1996.
Tidwell, N. L. "The Linen Ephod." *VT* 24 (1974) 505-07.
Tsevat, Matitiahu. "Emergence of the Israelite Monarchy: Eli, Samuel, and Saul." In *The Age of the Monarchies: Political History*, edited by A. Malamat and I. Eph'al, 61-75. WHJP 4:1. Jerusalem: Masada, 1979.
———. "Studies in the Book of Samuel." *HUCA* 32 (1961) 191-216.
Tsumura, David Toshio. "'The Deluge' (mabbûl) in Psalms 29:10." *UF* 20 (1988) 351-55.
———. *The First Book of Samuel*. Grand Rapids, MI: Eerdmans, 2007.
———. "The So-called 'Chaos Tradition' behind Psalms 46." *Evangelical Theology* 11 (1980) 95-96.
Vannoy, J. R. *Covenant Renewal at Gilgal: A Study of 1 Samuel 11.14-12.25*." Cherry Hill, NJ: Mack, 1978.
de Vaux, Roland. *Ancient Israel: Its Life and Institutions*. Translated by John McHugh. London: Darton, Longman, & Todd, 1961.
de Ward, E. F. "Eli's Rhetorical Question: 1 Samuel 2:25." *JJS* 27 (1976) 117-37.
Weinfeld, Moshe. *Deuteronomy and the Deuteronomic School*. Oxford: Clarendon, 1972.
Weiser, Artur. *The Old Testament: Its Formation and Development*. Translated by Dorothea M. Barton. New York: Association, 1961.
———. *Samuel: Seine geschichtliche Aufgabe und religiose Bedeutung Traditions geschichtliche Untersuchungen zu 1 Samuel 7-12*. FRLANT 81. Göttingen: Vandenhoeck & Ruprecht, 1962.
Wellhausen, Julius. *Der Text der Bücher Samuelis*. Göttingen: Vandenhoeck & Ruprecht, 1871.
———. *Die Composition des Hexateuchs und der Historischen Bücher des Alten Testament*. Berlin: de Gruyter, 1963.
———. *Israelitische und Jüdische Geschichte*. Berlin: de Gruyter, 1958.
———. *Prolegomena to The History of Israel*. Translated by J. S. Black and A. Menzies. Edinburgh: A. & C. Black, 1885.
Westermann, Claus. *Basic Forms of Prophetic Speech*. Translated by Hugh Clayton White. Philadelphia: Westminster, 1966.
Whithelam, Keith W. "King and Kingship." *ABD* 4:40-48.
Wildberger, Hans. "Sage and Legende." *BHH* 3:1641-45.
Willis, John T. "An Anti-Elide Narrative Tradition." *JBL* 90 (1971) 288-308.
———. "Cultic Elements in the Story of Samuel's Birth and Dedication." *ST* 26 (1972) 33-61.
———. "Samuel Versus Eli." *TZ* 35 (1979) 201-12.
———. "The Song of Hannah and Psalm 113." *CBQ* 34 (1973) 139-54.
Wilson, John A., trans. "The Divine Nomination of Thut Mose III." *ANET* 446-47.
———, "A Divine Oracle through a Dream." *ANET* 449.
———, "The Instruction of the Vizier Ptah Hotep." *ANET* 412-13.
Wright, G. E. "The Lawsuit of God: A Form-critical Study of Deuteronomy 32." In *Israel's Prophetic Heritage Fs J. Muilenburg*, edited by B. W. Anderson and W. Harrelson, 26-67. New York: Harper, 1962.
Uffenheimer, Benjamin. *Ancient Prophecy in Israel*. Translated by David Louvish. Jerusalem: Magnes, 1999.
Yonick, Stephen S. "The Rejection of Saul: A Study of Sources." *AJBA* 4 (1971) 29-50.

Zakovitch, Yair. "A Study of Precise and Partial Derivations in Biblical Etymology." *JSOT* 15 (1980) 31–50.

———. "יפתח=בדן." *VT* 22 (1972) 123–25.

Zalevski, S. "Hannah's Vow." *BethM* 78 (1978) 304–26.

Index

HEBREW BIBLE

Genesis

1:2	88
5:24	137
6:6	104
18–19	124
18:23–24	89
19:15	89
19:17	89
20:3	28
20:7	87, 122
21:1	20
22:11	27
23:2	128
25:25	105
27	53
27:1	25
28:11	37
28:13	27, 37
28:18	47
28:20–22	13
28:22	47
31:11	27, 37
31:24	28
31:31	87
35:2	43
35:2–3	112
35:5	43
38:12	96
39:4	111
39:6	65
40:4	96, 111
41:32	25
46:2	27, 37
46:3	83
50:10	128
50:13	128

Exodus

2:2	65, 105
2:10	20
3	24n3
3:6	87
3:7	65n7
3:9	65n7
3:10	65n7
3:11	65n7, 67
3:12	65n7
3:15	65n7
4:1	65n7
4:10	65n7
4:12	65n7
4:16	132
7:1	132
10:16–17	100
13:10	11
14:31	87
15:1–18	17, 17n46
15:2	17
15:6–7	17
15:9	17
15:17	17n46
15:18	52
15:20	122

INDEX

(Exodus continued)

15:26	89
18:13	5
18:15	117
18:21	117
19:3–6	83
19:10	112
19:19	28n22
20:17	88
22:7	117
22:8	132
22:27	132
23:6	53
23:8	53
23:18	19n51
24:1	67
24:13	111
25:16	116
25:21	116
27:11	26n9
27:20	26n9
29:13	19n51
32:11–12	121
33:11	111
34:5	27n20, 28
34:30	87
39:9	31
40:20	116

Leviticus

3:3–5	19, 19n51
3:5	19n51
7:28–36	19n51
7:30	19
8:32	68
9:23	86
16:29–31	44
20:2	26n9
23:27–32	44
24:10–23	117

Numbers

	101
1:50–51	10
3:5–9	10
4:3	111
6:22–27	14
8:24	13
8:24–28	111
9:1–14	117
9:8	117
11:16	67
11:24	67
11:28	111
11:29	123
12:3	71
12:6–9	123
12:7	118
15:32–36	117
16:15	61n30, 82
16:28	82
18:2–4	10
18:22–23	10
20:29	128
22:22	28
23:7–10	17, 17n46
23:18–24	17
23:21	52
24: 3–9	17
24:15–19	17
24:20–24	17
27:1–11	117
27:19	68
29:7	44
30:6–15	13
31:27	101, 108
36:1–10	117

Deuteronomy

	2, 19n51, 42, 53, 86, 87, 90, 117
5:23	132n16
5:26	132
6:18	89
7:7–8	88
10:8	14
10:17	53
11:14	86
12–26	85
12:28	89
16:19	53
17:19	90
18:3	19, 19n51
18:5	26

18:12	134	4:15	47
18:15	87	4:23	48
18:18	123	5	17, 17n46
21:19	75	5:2–31	17
27:25	53	5:20	46, 47
28:11	85	5:24–27	18n48
31:1—34:12	80	6–8	84
31:4–8	83	6:11–17	24n3
31:12	80	6:11–24	124
32:1–43	17	6:14–15	65n7
32:15	92	6:15	65n7, 67, 71
32:39	137, 138	6:16	65n7
34:7	25	6:22	87
34:8	128	6:34	65n7
34:10	123	6:37	103
		7:7	103

Joshua

		7:22	47
		8:22–23	58, 103
	2	8:23	52
1:1	111	8:28	48
3:5	112	9:8–15	58
4:14	87	9:27	13
7:1	70	9:50	26n12
7:9	92	10:1–5	115
7:14–18	113	10:2	129n6
10:11	47	10:4	67n18, 129n6
10:14	46	10:6	42
21:20	10	10:10	84
23	73, 80	10:12	103
23:4–5	83	10:16	42
24	91	11:27	83
24:2–4	83n13	11:29–34	55
24:2–13	83	11:30–31	13
24:7	46, 47	11:33b	48
24:14	85, 89	11:40	11
24:19	132, 132n16	12:1–7	55
24:23	42	12:3–4	14
24:27	47	12:6	114
24:29–30	80	12:7	14, 129n6
		12:7–15	115

Judges

		12:9	67n18
	1, 2, 9, 41, 48, 115	12:10	129n6
1:7	101	12:12	129n6
2:6—3:6	80	12:15	129n6
2:11–23	42	13	16, 124
2:18	103	13:2	9, 14
3:30	48	13:5	14
4:4–5	5, 116	13:6	123

Index

(Judges continued)

13:7	14
13:25	14
14:6	70n29
14:11–13	67n18
14:19	67n18, 70n29
15:14	70n29
16:20	77
17–21	56
20:1	43, 45
20:3	43
20:23	98
20:26	44
20:27	98
20:31	67n18
20:39	67n18
21:1	43
21:5	43
21:8	43
21:19	11
21:21–23	13

1 Samuel

	1, 2, 9, 13, 16, 20, 24, 111
1–2	33n37
1–3	4, 7, 8, 20, 34, 35
1–4	49, 50
1–24	1
1:1	10
1:1–3a	7
1:1–17	113
1:1–28	7, 8
1:2	20
1:3	11, 20
1:4–28	7
1:5	11, 20
1:6	11, 20
1:6–7	18
1:7	11, 26
1:11	11, 14
1:14	13
1:15	14
1:16	14
1:17	14, 16, 20
1:18	19
1:19	9, 20, 46
1:20	14, 20
1:21	11, 20
1:24	11
1:24–28	14
1:27–28	14
1:27	16, 20
1:28	15
1:51	10, 24, 35, 38
2–4	29
2:1	17
2:1–10	7, 8, 16, 21
2:2	18
2:4–5	18
2:5	11
2:6	137, 139
2:10	18, 46
2:11	7, 8, 9, 19, 20, 21, 23, 25, 111, 112
2:11b	18, 19
2:11–19	19
2:12	14, 19, 27n19
2:12–17	7, 8, 18, 19, 21, 53
2:13	19
2:13–18	20
2:17	19
2:18	19, 21, 23, 25, 111, 112
2:18–21	7, 8, 19, 20, 21
2:19	11, 20, 133
2:20	14, 20
2:21	11, 20, 21
2:22	13, 32, 53
2:22–24	21, 29
2:22–25	8
2:22–26	7
2:22–36	7
2:23–25	21, 34
2:24	118
2:25	20, 21
2:26	2, 8, 19, 21
2:27	31, 123, 124
2:27–28	31
2:27–34	8
2:27–36	2, 7, 8, 24, 28n24, 31, 34, 35
2:29	19, 31, 32
2:30	31, 32, 34
2:30–36	31
2:31	21, 32

Index

2:32	32	7	4, 40, 41, 46, 49, 50, 92, 116, 122
2:35	113, 114, 118	7–12	90
2:35–36	8, 21, 22, 23, 24, 26, 35, 38	7–15	41
3–4	48	7:2–17	40
3:1	10, 21, 23, 24, 25, 39, 111, 112, 118	7:3	40, 40n1, 84, 88, 92, 120
3:1–10	8	7:3–4	42
3:1–20	8	7:3–13	47
3:1–21	7	7:5	120
3:2	13, 25, 30, 53	7:5–7	112
3:3	26, 36	7:5–9	119
3:5	36	7:5–11	115
3:9	28, 36	7:5–14	50
3:10	23, 27	7:6	114, 115, 116, 117, 125, 141
3:11	29, 31		
3:11–14	2, 8, 24, 28	7:6b	115, 125, 141
3:11–18	35	7:8	88, 103
3:12	34	7:9	45, 86, 98, 112, 120
3:13	29n26, 53	7:9–10	87
3:13–14	34	7:10	47, 89, 92
3:14	19	7:11–12	43
3:15	26, 26n11, 36	7:11–14	55
3:15–21	8	7:13	2-3, 18, 48
3:17	30	7:15	115, 116
3:18	30, 34	7:15–17	5, 114
3:19	2, 22	7:16	43, 115, 116, 141
3:19–20	5	7:16–17	115, 117, 125, 141
3:20	33, 34, 41, 114, 118	7:17	54, 112, 115, 116
3:20–21	39, 123	8	4, 41, 59, 60, 74, 85, 122
3:21	23, 24, 118		
4	22, 29, 32, 47, 49–50	8:1	113
4:1	40, 40n1, 47	8:1–5	81
4:1b–7	40	8:1–22	53, 62, 140
4–6	27, 34, 47	8:2	91, 116-17
4:2	30	8:4	9
4:3	45, 103	8:5	53, 56, 114
4:11	31	8:6	43, 53
4:13	29	8:7	52, 91, 103
4:14	29	8:7–8	58n21
4:15	13, 21	8:10	15
4:18	21, 32	8:10–17	91
4:19	29	8:11–17	54, 82, 92
4:21–22	32	8:11–18	58n21, 60
5–12	48	8:12	25
5:5	2	8:18	60
6:6	120	8:19	54
		8:20	54, 56, 60

Index

(1 Samuel continued)

8:22	82	10:18	31
9	5, 121	10:19	52, 54, 91, 103
9:1	9	10:20–22	113
9:1f	72	10:20–24	2
9:1–4	16	10:22	65, 71
9:1–10:16	122	10:22–23	76
9:2	65	10:24	68n23
9:6	122, 123	10:25	116
9:9	2, 113, 121, 123	10:27	72
9:10	123	11	72, 81, 85
9–10	4	11:1–11	122
9:13	112	11:6	70n29, 90
9:15	64n7, 74	11:12	72, 74
9:15–16	67, 120	11:12–14	4
9:16	55, 65n7, 75, 90	11:14	72, 74
9:16–17	64n7	11:14—12:25	91
9:18	16	11:14–15	85
9:20	67	11:15	2
9:21	64n7, 65n7, 67, 71, 77, 99	12	4, 53, 60, 62, 79, 80, 81, 86, 90, 91, 92, 93, 140
9:22	112	12:1	81
9:23	12, 78	12:1–5	81, 91
10	85, 121	12:2	5, 81, 90
10:1	2, 64n7, 65n7	12:1–25	122
10:1–9	107	12:2–6	91
10:1b	64n7	12:3–5	5
10:2	68	12:6–15	91
10:2–7	106n23	12:7	89, 91
10:3–4	68	12:10b	93
10:4	68	12:12	52, 54, 55, 85, 90, 94, 103
10:5–6	68, 120	12:13	15, 71, 90, 120
10:5	119	12:14	89, 90, 91, 93
10:5–7a	64n7	12:14–15	85, 93, 101
10:6	65n7, 70	12:15	92
10:7	98, 141	12:16	89
10:7b	64n7, 65n7	12:17	15, 89
10:8	96, 112	12:18	92
10:9	70n29, 120	12:19	15, 43, 89, 91, 120
10:10	90	12:20	87, 89, 93
10:10–11	68	12:20b–22	86, 93
10:10–12	107	12:21	88, 92, 93
10:10–13	119	12:22	92, 93
10:12	58n21	12:23	43, 91, 92, 93
10:16	71	12:24	89, 90, 91, 92, 93
10:17	43, 71	12:24a	93
10:17–19	58n21	12:24–25	81
10:17–27	122	13	96, 98, 100, 108

13–14	48, 63, 96	15:28	100, 120
13:1	4	15:30	102
13:2	61	15:35	95, 107
13:4–12	45	16	116
13:7–15	95	16:1–5	112
13:7b–15a	96, 97	16:1–13	4
13:8	96	16:4b	75–76
13:8–9	96	16:5a	75–76
13:8–15	4	16:7	65, 71
13:9	113	16:11	77
13:9–14	96	16:11–12	77
13:10	56	16:12	65
13:11	94	16:13	74, 76
13:13–14	3	16:18	77
13:13	103	16:20	78
13:14	63, 97, 100, 120	16:23	3
14:3	113	17	3
14:8–10	98	17:3–5	68
14:15	47	17:12–31	76
14:20	47	17:13	68
14:23	103	17:24	105
14:24	44	17:26	132, 132n16
14:27	72	17:28–29	76
14:24–29	70	17:36	132, 132n16
14:33–35	56	17:52	55
14:37	98	17:55	3
14:44	30n29	18:1	108
14:52	72	18:5	108
15	95, 96, 101, 135	18:11	3
15–17	48	18:12	108
15:1	99, 105	18:14–15	108
15:1–34	97	18:16	2, 108
15:2	31	18:20	108
15:3	94	18:23	71
15:11	104, 120	18:27	108
15:12	100	18:28	108
15:13–30	99	19	3, 121
15:14	99	19:5	73n42
15:17	71	19:10	3
15:20	99	19:18	107
15:22	99, 120	19:18–23	107
15:22–23	100	19:18–24	5, 107, 119
15:23	100, 101	19:20	119
15:25	100, 102	19:21	67n18
15:26	3	19:22	129
15:26–27	63	20	3
15:27	20, 102, 133	20:13	30n29
15:27–28	135	21:1–9	11

INDEX

(1 Samuel continued)

21:7	69n28	4:5	36n46
21:11–16	3	4:7	36n46
21:27	3	5:3	74
22	113	5:19	98
22:11–23	32	5:23	98
22:20	113	6:13	56, 98, 113
23:2	98	6:14	112
23:4	98	6:17	56
24	3	6:17–18	98
24:1	130, 138	6:18	113
24:15	83	7:5	31
24:21	102	7:8	31
25	129, 138	7:18–21	71
25:1	5, 9, 127, 128, 129, 138	11:9	36n46
		11:13	36n46
25:22	30n29	12:1–15	56
26	3	12:7	31
26:5	36n46	12:16	44
26:7	36n46	12:16–23	44
28	5, 130, 138	13:17	111
28:3	9, 127, 128, 129	14:1–24	56
28:3–20	5	14:25	65
28:3–24	137	15:1–6	56
28:3–25	127	15:8	13
28:6	98	15:26	30—31n30
28:7	124	16:18	71
28:9	100	19	105
28:13	131	19:14	30n29
28:13–14	131	21:19	3
28:14	20, 130	22	17, 17n46
28:15	134	22:14	46
28:17	102	22:15	46
28:19	120, 127, 138, 142	23:13	67
28:21	131	23:18	67
29:1	26n12	24:11	122
30:7–8	98	24:12	31
30:24	101, 108	24:25	56, 98
31:9	107		

2 Samuel

1 Kings

		1–2	74–75
		1:6	53
	1	1:25	71
1:12	129	1:32–39	68
2:4	74	1:34	71
3:5	30n29	1:39	68n23, 71
3:9	30n29	2:4	29n25
3:31	129	2:23	30n29

160

2:26–27	35	1:9–18	106n23
2:27	12, 32	2	124
2:34	129	2:8	20
3	56	2:11	137
3:4	37n52, 56, 98	2:12–14	20
3:7	71	3:1	93n46
3:15	56, 98	3:4	72n35
4:22–28	59	3:15	70n29
5:1	72n35	3:19	68n22
8:5	113	3:25	68n22
8:62	56	4:9	123
8:62–64	113	4:18–37	124
9:15–22	59	4:31	134n25
9:25	56	4:42	66
10:5	111	4:42–44	124
11:4	53	4:43	112
11:26	59	6:1	106
11:29–31	20	6:15	112
11:29	68	6:23	48
11:29–31	102	6:31	30n29
11:38	89	8:17	93n46
12:32	56	8:26	93n46
13:1	56	9:5–10	24n3
13:1–31	123	9:6	120
13:30	128	9:10	68
14:3	66	9:13	68n23
14:21	93n46	9:29	93n46
15:1–2	93n46	11:12	68, 68n23, 71
15:9–10	93n46	11:14	68
15:25	93n46	17:3–4	72n35
17:7–16	124	17:7–23	80
17:17–24	124	20:19	31n30
18:30–38	113	21:12	29
18:33–35	44n13	21:18	129
18:38	46	23:16	123
18:45–46	68n22	23:24	136
19:2	30n29		
19:21	111–12	Isaiah	
20:10	30n29	1:10	120n31
20:28	123	6	24n3
21:1–20	56	8:19	131, 132
21:12	29n25	14:9	133n22
21:27	44	28:7	13
		29:4	132
2 Kings		30:10	122
1:8	133n21	32:12	128
1:9	123	39:8	31n30

Index

(Isaiah continued)

44:9	88
58:3	44
58:10	44
60:21	137

Jeremiah

1:4–10	24n3
1:5–6	69
4:8	129
4:23–27	88
7:12	11
7:14	11
7:21–23	100, 120n31
10:10	132
15:1	4, 43, 111
16:6	129
19:3	29, 29n25
22:18	128
23:36	132
25:33	128
26:6	11
26:9	11
34:5	128
49:3	129
51:39	134n25

Ezekiel

1–3	24n3
26:20–21	136
32:27	133n22

Hosea

3:4–5	58
3:5	58
8:4	58, 73–74
8:10	58
9:7	124
13:10–11	58

Joel

1:13	129
2:12	129

Amos

3:7	75, 120
5:21–25	120n31
7:7	28n22
7:12	66, 122
7:14	122
9:1	28n22

Micah

1:8	129
2:4	42
3:5	66
3:6	25
17:1	9

Habakkuk

3	17, 17n46

Zechariah

7:5	129

Psalms

	75
18	17, 17n46
29	17, 17n46
30:4	137
35:13	44
51:18–19	120n31
68	17, 17n46
74:9	25
78:60	11
94:14	88
97:7	132
99:6	4, 43, 86, 111, 113, 125

Job

3:13–19	134n25
7:9–10	136
7:14	78
10:21	136
12:10	137
14:12	134n25, 136

INDEX

Ruth

	1, 30
1:17	30n29

Lamentations

2:9	25
2:19	44

Ecclesiastes

9:5	130n8

Esther

2:2	111
2:7	65
4:1	129
6:3	111

Ezra

32:18	42

Nehemiah

9	83

1 Chronicles

	75
6:7–13	111
6:11	9
6:12	9
6:12–13	111
6:19	9
7:17	84n14
9:22	111, 122
26:28	122
29:22	73n41
29:29	1, 122

2 Chronicles

9:4	111
16:7	122
16:10	122
17:9	116
19:4–11	56
24:5	73
24:12	73
25:7	123
25:9	123
33:20	129

DEUTEROCANONICAL BOOKS

1 Maccabees

3:46–48	43

2 Maccabees

7:27	16

Psalm 151

	77

ANCIENT JEWISH WRITERS

Josephus

Against Apion

1.106–27	4, 4n10

Jewish Antiquities

4.46–50	82n9
5.10.1	21n57
5.10.4	25, 25n6
6.2.2	45, 45n16, 45n17
6.3.2	54n1, 117, 117n24
6.4.1	67, 67n19

(Jewish Antiquities continued)

6.13.5	128, 128n1
6.14.4	135, 135n31
14.2.333	130, 130n10

RABBINIC WORKS

Talmud

Berakot

12b	89n31
31a	13n28
48b	67n16

Pesaḥim

68a	137n35

Yoma

8:1	44

Roš Haššanah

25a	34n39, 84, 84n14

Taʿanit

1:7	86n23
19b	86n22
27a	4n8

Megillah

14a	9n9, 17n44

Ḥagigah

2a	135n27
4b	133n18

Sanhedrin

65b	130n9
90b	133n22
90–91	138n36

Ketubbot

60a	16n41

Nedarim

38a	4n8, 82n9

Baba Bathra

14b	1n1
15a	1n2

Makkot

10b	90n33

Midrash

Genesis Rabbah

95:1	138n38

Tanḥumah Leviticus

Emor 2	133n18
21:1	130n9

Leviticus Rabbah

26:7	130n9, 131n12, 135n28
35:12	86n22

Ecclesiastes Rabbah

1:4	138n37

Midrash Samuel

2	45n19
3.3	4n9
11:1	64n2
13	45n19

Midrash Psalms

	45n19
	45n1

Index

32	64n2

Exodus Rabbah

16:4   4n8

Yalkut Shimoni

1:28   133

Numbers Rabbah

18:8   4n8

MEDIEVAL COMMENTATORS

Rashi (Rabbi Solomon ben Isaac), 28, 29n26, 44, 130

Ibn Ezra (Abraham ben Meir Ibn Ezra), 44

Gersonides (Ralbag or (Levi ben Gershon), 4, 33, 106, 137

Rabbi David ben Joseph Kimḥl (Radak), 15, 28, 29, 30n28, 32, 44, 48, 75, 89, 106, 130, 137

Malbim (Mein Loeb ben Yehiel Michael), 75, 76

Abravanel (Rabbi Don Isaac ben Judah Abravanel), 75, 104

NEW TESTAMENT

Matthew

27:57   9n8

John

19:38   9n8

INDEX

GRECO-ROMAN LITERATURE

Illiad

10:84   65n12

Odyssey

8:98   68
11:185   68

www.ingramcontent.com/pod-product-compliance
Lightning Source LLC
Chambersburg PA
CBHW050812160426
43192CB00010B/1728